The View from Officers' Row

The View from Officers' Row

ARMY PERCEPTIONS OF WESTERN INDIANS

Sherry L. Smith

THE UNIVERSITY OF ARIZONA PRESS / TUCSON

Third printing 1995

The University of Arizona Press
Copyright © 1990
The Arizona Board of Regents
All Rights Reserved

This book was set in Linotype CRT Trump.
Manufactured in the United States of America
♾ This book is printed on acid-free, archival-quality paper.

LIBRARY OF CONGRESS CATALOGING-IN-PUBLICATION DATA

Smith, Sherry Lynn.
    The view from officers' row : army perceptions of western Indians
/ Sherry L. Smith.
        p.   cm.
    Includes bibliographical references.
    Cloth ISBN 0-8165-1018-0 (acid-free paper)
    Paper ISBN 0-8165-1245-0 (acid-free paper)
    1. Indians of North America — West (U.S.) — History — 19th century —
Sources.   2. United States. Army — Military life — History — 19th
century — Sources.   3. Indians of North America — West (U.S.) —
Government relations.   4. Indians of North America — West (U.S.) —
Removal.   I. Title.
E78.W5S67   1990   89-5216
978'.00497 — dc20   CIP
British Cataloguing-in-Publication Data
A catalogue record for this book is available from the British Library.

For my parents,
Atwood Earl Smith and Adeline Behnke Smith

Contents

List of Illustrations ix

Acknowledgments xi

Introduction xiii

1 / Officers as Observers 1

2 / Indian Character 15

3 / Tribes and Chiefs 28

4 / Indian Women 55

5 / Thoughts on Indian Policy 92

6 / Explanations of the Indian Wars 113

7 / Indian Warfare 139

8 / The Indian Scout as Ally 163

Conclusion 182

Notes 187

Bibliography 231

Index 253

Illustrations

Map of the western forts and major tribes   xx–xxi

The Shoshone leader Washakie   49

Toos-clay-zay, wife of Cochise and mother of Natchez   70

Captain S.B.M. Young and family   74

A wounded Chiricahua Apache captive   81

Chief Joseph and General John Gibbon   156

A Yuma-Apache army scout   167

Acknowledgments

In preparing this book, I relied on the invaluable help and expertise of a number of people. At the University of Washington, Lewis O. Saum provided inspiration, encouragement, guidance, and careful criticism during the dissertation stage. Robert Burke, the late Carl Solberg, Paul Hutton, and the University of Arizona Press's anonymous readers also offered valuable suggestions for improvement.

A Newberry Library Fellowship allowed me to use that facility's excellent holdings on western and Indian history. An American Historical Association Albert J. Beveridge Award provided funds to conduct research at the National Archives, and a University of Washington Arthur A. Denny Fellowship made it possible to work at the Huntington Library and the United States Army Military History Institute. Dr. Richard Sommers's knowledge of the latter's extensive holdings and John Aubrey's help at the Newberry Library greatly enhanced my productivity at both places.

Portions of this book appeared in an earlier form as "Beyond Princess and Squaw: Army Officers' Perceptions of Indian Women," in Susan Armitage and Elizabeth Jameson, eds., *The Women's West* (Norman: University of Oklahoma Press, 1987); "Officers' Wives, Indians and the Indian Wars," *Order of the Indian Wars Journal* 1 (Winter 1980): 35–46; "Private Conscience versus Public Duty: Army Officers' Reflections on the Indian Wars," in David Tebaldi, ed., *Reflecting on Values: The Unity and Diversity of the Humanities* (Laramie, Wyoming: Wyoming Council for the Humanities, 1983); and "A Window on Themselves: Perceptions of Indians by Military Officers and Their Wives," *New Mexico Historical Review* 64 (October 1989).

The map of the western tribes and forts is based on maps in Edward M. Coffman, *The Old Army: A Portrait of the American Army in Peacetime, 1784–1898* (New York: Oxford University Press, 1986), 213, 214; and Robert M. Utley, *The Indian Frontier of the American West, 1846–1890* (Albuquerque: University of New Mexico Press, 1984), 5.

Finally, I wish to extend the deepest gratitude and affection to my husband, Dr. Robert W. Righter, who gave much-needed editorial advice, constant support, and love; to Roy E. Hawkinson, who long ago inspired me with his tales of the West and its people; and to my parents, Atwood and Adeline Smith. Among their many gifts to all their children was an appreciation for the past and the dignity of all people.

Introduction

This is a book about ideas. It examines nineteenth-century army officers' and their wives' thoughts on Indians and the Indian wars. It presents military men in contemplation rather than combat. This is a rather unusual pose, for these men do not typically inspire images of figures bent over desks or scribbling into field journals by campfire light. Nor do they usually appear in history books as people who pondered issues of politics or morality. The men of the frontier army take on significance more for their actions than their ideas. They bring to mind flashing sabers, blaring trumpets, and thunderous hoofbeats as the cavalry rides to the rescue of a beleaguered wagon train or bears down upon an unsuspecting Indian village. For many years, historians have presented army officers as pursuing their purposes uncomplicated by sentiment, doubt, or moral qualm. But army officers were not unreflective. How they viewed Indians and the Indian wars is its own story, and one worth telling.[1]

From another perspective, it is surprising that officers' thoughts about Indians have remained relatively unexamined. The frontier army—certainly the cavalry, if not the infantry—has played a central role in the American mythology of westward expansion. Between the close of the Indian wars and the middle of the twentieth century, the frontier soldiers, particularly the officers, represented to many an heroic aspect of America's westering experience as they rode off in dusty columns to avenge supposed Indian depredations and extend the American way of life to the far reaches of the continent. While that image of the Indian-fighting army officer has waned recently, for many years it was an enduring and powerful one.[2]

Further, the U.S. Army was the largest national organization in substantial contact with Indians in the trans-Mississippi West between 1848 and 1890. Military men were critical to the execution, if not the formation, of Indian policy during the latter half of the nineteenth century. And army officers were among the most educated, articulate, and informed people in the West, writing about Indians and Indian affairs in their letters, diaries, and reminiscences as well as in their official correspondence and reports. Some were voracious readers; others were prodigious writers. Ethan Allen Hitchcock, for instance, not only read widely but wrote seven books on philosophical and literary topics. Twenty-four percent of the men who graduated from West Point between 1870 and 1879 published articles or books.[3] Nevertheless, these individuals' attitudes toward Indians have not received much attention.

This book addresses the following questions: How did army officers and their wives perceive Indians, and what did they think about the army's role, and their own role, in the dispossession of Indian lands? Did they support the concept of acculturation? Did their attitudes change over time with respect to Indian issues? Did such new ideas as social Darwinism or notions of professionalism, organization, and efficiency alter officers' attitudes? Did the Civil War or the final military acquiescence of the Indians beget noteworthy changes in the ways army people viewed Indians?

In addition, this book explores whether the relationship between army officers and Indians was different from that between any other distinguishable group on the frontier and Indians. Were officers more sympathetic to Indian points of view than settlers, who often coveted Indian property? Or were officers more prone to support a policy of physical suppression than either westerners or eastern humanitarians? Were they, for that matter, in accord with one another on any of these issues? Was there, in other words, a monolithic military mind?

Finally, military people offer an opportunity to examine the relationship between gender and ideas about Indians. Although only a few military wives chose to join their husbands at frontier outposts, many who did venture west wrote about their experiences, and Indians were often the subject of their attention. Sharing their husbands' social status, and often better educated than many contemporary American women, officers' wives provide us with an opportunity to investigate how a rather special population of nineteenth-century women viewed Indian people. They also provide an opportunity to compare men's and women's attitudes, an approach not always followed by scholars who have argued that women differed markedly from men in their perceptions of western experiences.[4]

This book investigates what military men and women, as individuals, thought about these matters. It looks at the comments the officers made in the context of their work as soldiers rather than as explorers, scientists, agents, or other roles they sometimes took on. Clearly, the fact that the men served as military officers colored their experiences and presumably their perceptions, attitudes, and responses. The uniform and the officers' military role provided a common frame of reference. But did the physical uniform translate into uniform values and beliefs about Indians? While the officers certainly identified with their institution, and while they ultimately represented their country, officers were also individuals. They were not mere mouthpieces of the military hierarchy. One historian has even argued that not even West Point's attempts to enforce rigid conformity or its "mechanistic approach to knowledge and human behavior" could subdue "the unconquerable individuality of the stout-hearted youths who wore cadet grey."[5] And, of course, not all officers attended West Point.

Moreover, while professional considerations certainly colored their depictions of Indians, officers did not limit their accounts to military matters. Sheer curiosity, as well as the sense that an understanding of Indians could serve their work, motivated military men to investigate them. Observing and writing about natives helped pass the time at frontier posts, where boredom was not unknown, and it helped fill the pages of letters home. Indians were a natural, even exotic, subject.

Officers and their wives, then, certainly saw themselves as individuals, and they wrote as individuals. Because its intent is to focus on personal attitudes, this study rests primarily on personal documents, including diaries and letters as well as memoirs published in retirement or essays and books written for public consumption. This does not mean that official correspondence and reports have been ignored, but personal papers were given more weight than official documents, for a number of reasons. Investigators have already combed through many official papers and, based on their readings of these documents, have come to some general conclusions about the most prominent officers' attitudes toward, and relations with, Indians.

Such individuals as Generals John Pope, George Crook, William T. Sherman, and Philip Sheridan expressed their opinions about Indian affairs quite freely in official correspondence. Officers of lesser prominence and rank, however, were disinclined to express personal opinions in their official reports of engagements with Indians. Yet these lesser-ranking officers did openly express opinions about Indians and Indian fighting in their letters to wives and families and in their retirement reminiscences. This book presents evidence from a representative sample of the officer corps at all levels of power, status, and influence. Prominent individuals such as Sheridan, Sherman, and Crook receive attention, but this study is equally interested in the more obscure, less influential middle-level and junior officers.[6]

In an attempt to understand the professional military men's point of view, this work focuses solely on army regulars, bypassing officers of the volunteer militia. It also omits noncommissioned officers, enlisted men, and their wives from consideration. This choice reflects, in part, the availability of documents. Some enlisted men's accounts are available, but not many. The same holds true for noncommissioned officers. Commissioned officers and wives, by contrast, wrote prolifically, leaving abundant documentation of their attitudes.

Further, the army officer has long symbolized the profession of arms. Since these men chose the military as their life's work, it is perhaps plausible that officers were more inclined to view Indians and Indian affairs in a more professionally defined military manner than were enlisted men. Officers, through their social, political, and professional status, also maintained considerable power in their relationships with Indians, which underscores the value of examining the officers' perceptions. Enlisted men and noncommissioned officers, on the other hand, were expected to take orders but not to give them when it came to Indian affairs. This is not to suggest that the opinions of enlisted men and noncommissioned officers are insignificant and unworthy of scholarly attention but rather that evidence on their opinions is relatively scarce. In time, more of their documents may become available, providing greater opportunity for an analysis of their attitudes.

Indian points of view are also not included. Focusing on officer attitudes risks perpetuating notions of Indians as faceless, passive victims, mere foils for the "important" actors in the history of the American West. An occasional officer or officer's wife relayed an impression of an Apache's or a Cheyenne's attitude toward the army or individual men, but their reliability on such matters is suspect. So the investigator of Indian ideas, attitudes, and reflections on the United States military must look elsewhere for data and take into consideration tribal and cultural diversity. Officer accounts of interactions with individual Indian men and women do suggest some things about certain Indian attitudes toward military people, and those are offered below. For the most part, however, the task of evaluating Indian points of view remains for another work.

The present study is confined to the period 1848 to 1890, starting with the acquisition of the Mexican Cession and ending with the Battle of Wounded Knee—often used as the symbolic end of Indian military resistance to American invasion, although that event clearly did not mark the end of either Indian resistance to the dominant culture in other forms or traditional Indian ways of life. Yet, during this relatively short period, Indians of the West were militarily conquered and then concentrated on reservations, where Anglo-Americans began their acculturation efforts. Officers actively implemented both phases of Indian policy throughout this critical period.

Finally, this work deals with the entire trans-Mississippi West, because individual officers served throughout that vast region, being transferred from one department to another and encountering many different tribes, cultures, and situations along the way. As a result, they noted tribal distinctions but also assumed that one could generalize about Indian character and about what was often referred to as the Indian Problem. To limit the study to a particular section of the trans-Mississippi West—say, the Pacific Northwest or the Southwest—would be to impose cultural restrictions and boundaries that were not particularly significant to military men. They felt completely comfortable generalizing about Indians, Indian fighting, and Indian policy, often with little concern for tribal or regional distinctions. In so doing, army people reflected a centuries-old tradition of thinking and writing about the Indian in general. From Columbus's time to the present, according to Robert Berkhofer, white people have demonstrated "the tendency to speak of one tribe as exemplary of all Indians and conversely to comprehend a specific tribe according to the characteristics ascribed to all Indians."[7]

The purpose here, then, is twofold. First, the study is intended partly to meet historian Paul Prucha's challenge to place the frontier army "in the social and intellectual milieu of the times." Urging historians to push beyond the traditional research issues and questions about the frontier army, Prucha asked, "Were frontier officers and men, fundamentally, much different in their outlook from the Christian humanitarians who clashed with them so bitterly over the *means* of reforming Indian policy? Were the army men one with the westerners who supported them—or were they outsiders who could take an independent stand on vital questions?"[8] Officers clearly operated within their culture's social and intellectual context. This work attempts to define more precisely the officers' position within that context.

The second purpose is to expand the discussion of white attitudes toward Indians by examining a largely ignored yet crucial group on the frontier. Perhaps no other individuals played so critical a role in the implementation of federal Indian policy in the West. Presumably, these officers and their wives can provide additional insight into the larger problem of Anglo-American civilization's intellectual approach to Indians in the course of military conquest.

It is important to remember that the officers' and their wives' comments about Indians indicate reactions, points of view, and subjective responses rather than necessarily an accurate portrait of nineteenth-century Indians, in all of their diversity. Yet images and ideas can be of great consequence. Other investigators of Anglo-Americans' attitudes toward Indians have concluded that their observations reveal much more about their own values and worldviews than they do about the Indians'. Likewise, military peoples' comments on Indians reveal much more about Anglo-American ideas on culture, civilization, savagery, and race than they do about the realities of Indian lives and cultures. Nineteenth-century Americans, according to Roy Harvey Pearce, tended to define civilization in terms of savagery. This process "forced Americans to consider and reconsider what it was to be civilized and what it took to build a civilization. Studying the savage, . . . in the end they had only studied themselves."[9]

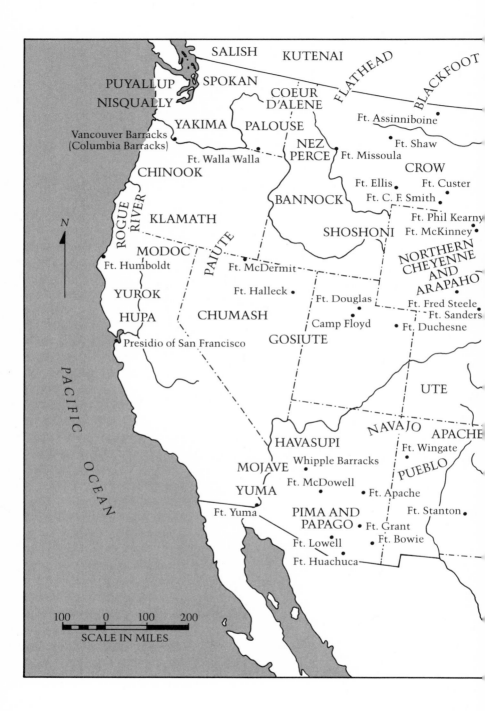

SALISH KUTENAI

PUYALLUP SPOKAN FLATHEAD BLACKFOOT

NISQUALLY COEUR D'ALENE

Ft. Assinniboine

Vancouver Barracks YAKIMA PALOUSE Ft. Shaw
(Columbia Barracks) NEZ PERCE Ft. Missoula
Ft. Walla Walla

CHINOOK CROW

Ft. Ellis Ft. Custer
Ft. C. F. Smith

ROGUE RIVER BANNOCK Ft. Phil Kearny

KLAMATH SHOSHONI Ft. McKinney

N PAIUTE NORTHERN CHEYENNE AND ARAPAHO

MODOC Ft. McDermit

Ft. Humboldt Ft. Halleck Ft. Douglas Ft. Fred Steele
Ft. Sanders

YUROK CHUMASH Camp Floyd Ft. Duchesne

HUPA GOSIUTE

Presidio of San Francisco

PACIFIC UTE

OCEAN NAVAJO APACHE

HAVASUPI Ft. Wingate

MOJAVE Whipple Barracks PUEBLO

YUMA Ft. McDowell Ft. Apache

Ft. Yuma Ft. Stanton

PIMA AND PAPAGO Ft. Grant

Ft. Lowell Ft. Bowie

Ft. Huachuca

100 0 100 200
SCALE IN MILES

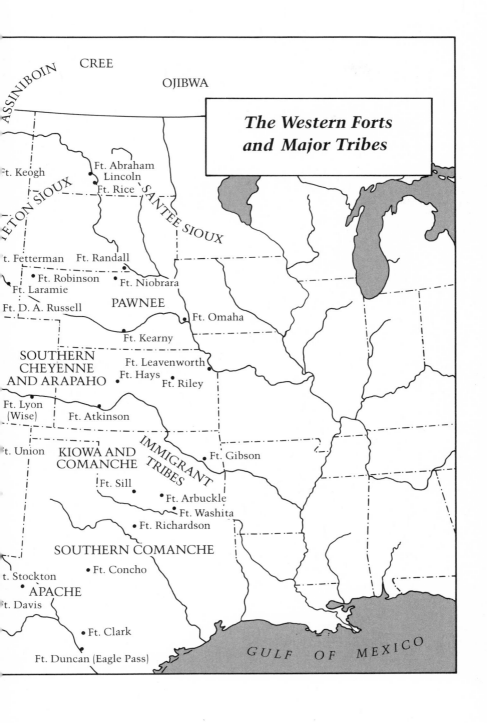

CREE

ASSINIBOIN

OJIBWA

**The Western Forts
and Major Tribes**

Ft. Keogh

Ft. Abraham
Lincoln

TETON SIOUX

Ft. Rice

SANTEE SIOUX

t. Fetterman   Ft. Randall

• Ft. Robinson   • Ft. Niobrara
Ft. Laramie

Ft. D. A. Russell   PAWNEE

• Ft. Omaha

Ft. Kearny

SOUTHERN
CHEYENNE   Ft. Leavenworth
AND ARAPAHO   • Ft. Hays
    • Ft. Riley

Ft. Lyon
(Wise)   • Ft. Atkinson

t. Union   KIOWA AND   IMMIGRANT   • Ft. Gibson
    COMANCHE   TRIBES

    Ft. Sill •

    • Ft. Arbuckle
    • Ft. Washita
    • Ft. Richardson

SOUTHERN COMANCHE

t. Stockton   • Ft. Concho

APACHE
t. Davis

• Ft. Clark

Ft. Duncan (Eagle Pass)   GULF OF MEXICO

The View from Officers' Row

1 / Officers as Observers

If . . . the story of a single participant is accepted, the real
truth will be swamped under the errors of the personal
equation which exists more or less in all men.
                              —LIEUTENANT W. H. CARTER

In the autumn of 1867, Louis Laurent Simonin, a French mining
expert and inveterate traveler, arrived in Cheyenne, Dakota Territory, after a torturous stagecoach trip from Denver. Not even
that twenty-four-hour ride sandwiched between a corpulent
minister and a German engineer of similarly formidable propor-
tions, however, could diminish his enchantment with the
mountain scenery. Among Simonin's stops in Cheyenne was
one of the army's newest posts, Fort D. A. Russell. He found
assembled there a variety of types. Some, he wrote in a letter to
a Parisian friend, had studied at West Point, "the Saint-Cyr of
the United States." Others were "soldiers of fortune who took
up the musket in the War of Secession, and who have preferred
to remain soldiers rather than become lawyers or merchants
like so many others." All of them, he noted, displayed "the most
polished and civilized manners." The officers' wives, Simonin
gallantly added, were "courageous women [who] have said fare-
well to New York or Boston, and have come without a word of
complaint to settle at the end of the desert with their husbands
and children."

As if to buttress his argument for their "civilized manners,"
the Gallic observer noted that this army post included a library,
though he admitted that, in truth, most officers preferred bil-
liards, hunting, or drinking as pastimes—particularly the last.
Not that Simonin meant to criticize, for, he wrote, "what can
one do in the desert if he doesn't drink?" In fact, he rather admired the officers' style and taste:

> Each officer is the owner of a little chest with compartments
> which he carries with him in his travels. You might take it for a

chest of books, the library of the amateur tourist. In it glasses and flasks are skillfully arranged. "Will you take a drink?" is the first word uttered, as soon as you enter the tent. You say yes and the "old Bourbon whiskey" is forthwith poured in your honor. The glasses go the rounds. . . . What a bouquet, my friend, and what a treacherous liquor is this "old Kentuck"! Our old cognac is nothing in comparison.[1]

In this brief vignette, Simonin presented a familiar though ambiguous portrait of the frontier army officer. He was, in fact, only one of many nineteenth-century observers who attempted to categorize this group but found the effort elusive. Were officers mannerly gentlemen or more nearly mercenaries who preferred muskets to merchants' ledger books? Were they scholars or sops? Were they courageous men who sacrificed the comforts of home to civilize the West and its Indians, or ne'er-do-wells who drained whiskey bottles and the national treasury at the same time, performing little in the way of useful service?

General William T. Sherman thought he knew how most Americans would answer such questions. He believed that officers never received fair treatment in contemporary accounts of the frontier army. But then, Sherman himself could be charged with relying upon stereotypes. "There are two classes of people," he once wrote, "one demanding the utter extinction of the Indians and the other full of love for their conversion to civilization and Christianity. Unfortunately the army stands between and gets the cuffs from both sides."[2] Many nineteenth-century army officers agreed. These men served in what amounted to a frontier constabulary charged with mediating among various foes. They envisioned themselves, therefore, as occupants of an unhappy middle ground—separating rapacious westerners, who demanded that the army sweep away the Indians, from eastern humanitarians, who demanded that the army get out of Indian affairs altogether and allow civilians to resolve the Indian Problem.

Twentieth-century observers of the frontier army have rarely been any more evenhanded, choosing either to glorify or despise frontier officers. Contrasting Captain Charles King's romantic, heroic images of frontier soldiers with more recent bumper stickers that proclaim "Custer died for your sins," historian Robert Utley noted that "What we choose to remember and the way we choose to remember it may unduly flatter or unfairly condemn our military forebears, may indeed be more legend than history. . . . The US Army's frontier heritage . . . has furnished a galaxy of heroes and villains."[3] To understand officers' perceptions of Indians, however, one must move beyond legends, heroes, and villains. Who *were* the men and women of the army blue who occupied the posts of the trans-Mississippi West? How did they see themselves? Did their training and background prepare them for their duties among American Indians? What kinds of observers of Indians did they make?

To begin with, their backgrounds were more diverse and their attitudes more complex and ambiguous than legends indicate, partly because the varied regional and social makeup of the officer corps worked against consensus. In the antebellum period, the cadets at West Point, who comprised 73 percent of the officer corps by the mid 1850s, well represented the geographic distribution and concomitant regional sentiments of the American people. While the Academy somewhat successfully engendered a spirit of nationalism in the cadets, army officers were not a like-minded group of professionals. Instead, they argued along North-South, cavalry-infantry, line-staff, West Point–non-West Point divisions. They also quarreled about rank (both brevet and substantive), promotions, leaves of absence, rules and regulations, desirable quarters, and the authority to command. Living together in close quarters, yet often isolated from the rest of society, tensions percolated. On top of that, "a keenly honed sense of honor and inherent self-importance could trigger a demand for a duel on the basis of a suspected slight."[4]

Relations were not any more harmonious after the Civil War, when the frontier officer corps was composed of former regulars who had held a high rank in a volunteer militia unit during the war, and former volunteers who sought regular-army appointments after 1865. The officers, then, were a mixture of West Point graduates and Civil War veterans from the Northeast, Midwest, and West. In 1866–67, 8.8 percent of the officers were appointed from civilian life (presumably on the basis of their wartime volunteer experience), 7 percent from West Point, and the rest from the regular ranks. In addition, an 1867 law required that one-fourth of all second lieutenants be from the enlisted ranks. Most of these officers, often veterans of the Indian wars of the 1850s who had received their commissions during the Civil War, were Irish or German immigrants. By 1874, 30 percent of the line officers had been commissioned from the ranks, and about half of these were foreign-born. Although few of them were ever promoted beyond a captaincy, they added a distinctive element to the frontier army, and they further demonstrate the regional and ethnic diversity within the officer corps.

Through the rest of the century, West Pointers reasserted their dominance. By 1897 they composed 60 percent of the officer corps, while civilian appointees and "rankers" made up 30 and 10 percent respectively. Moreover, West Pointers claimed a disproportionate share of general and field-grade officers in the Division of the Missouri. That rankled non–West Pointers and encouraged grumbling about a West Point clique.

Garrison life continued to breed animosity and to underscore differences among army officers. The problems of boredom and monotony were compounded by the demoralizing absence of opportunities for advancement. More than 42 percent of the officers who served between the Civil War and the Spanish-American War received their commissions in the first two years after Appomattox. This meant that a large number of officers of approximately the same age saw little hope of advancement. A generation of men found themselves stymied by an army that did not increase in size and so did not make many promotions.[5] The army women who joined their husbands in the West approximated their spouses in social status and economic background. Some could claim relatively privileged upbringings as daughters of merchants, lawyers, ministers, and even army officers. But others revealed more modest backgrounds, and a few served as laundresses before their enlisted-man husbands received their commissions.[6]

It is true that most officers and wives shared a largely middle-class background, and several historians have pointed out their affinity with the values of middle-class businessmen and community leaders. Generals such as Philip Sheridan associated with leading figures of the business world, including railroad tycoons, and officers of lesser rank sometimes enjoyed similar associations. As a group, army officers did not sympathize with labor or associate with union organizers, and during the railroad strikes of 1877 they supported the managers.[7]

A shared middle-class upbringing, however, still left much room for disagreement and diversity. For example, army men presented a range of assessments in private correspondence about the very people who made up the officer corps. On the positive side, Lieutenant James Parker counseled his brother in 1876, "if you want to strike a lot of good fellows, gentlemen to the backbone with none of the nonsense of society, you may have to come to a frontier post." A recent graduate of West Point, Parker could not conceal his delight in Fort Sill—not only with the surrounding countryside, the bountiful game, and the glorious prairie sky, but also with the officers who greeted him there. "With everything so strange . . . they will make you perfectly at home in a day," he wrote.[8] DeWitt Clinton Peters, an assistant surgeon stationed at Fort Massachusetts in New Mexico Territory in the 1850s, offered a different view. While some gentlemen might be found among officers, he wrote, others were more accurately identified as rascals and fools. Scandal rocked the corps, he claimed. Moreover, "officers are jealous of rank and in their hearts, I believe one half the army wishes the other dead." Peters' circumstances no doubt partially inspired these remarks. He was one of only three officers at the fort, and the other two did not speak to each other. But his evaluation endured the passage of time. A year and a half later, Assistant Surgeon Peters cautioned his sister, "I should be sorry to see you married to an officer," for such a union would subject a woman "not only to privations but to a life with confirmed drunkards and blackguards." "I have seen enough," he concluded, "to give me a poor opinion of them as a body of men."[9]

In truth, both Peters and Parker were simultaneously right and wrong. The men who served between 1848 and 1890 defied such easy categorization. Some were ambitious, aggressive, and energetic. Some were merely competent. Some were lethargic, dissipated, and alcoholic. Some were excellent soldiers who commanded respect from their peers and enlisted men alike. Some were martinets who commanded only contempt and even hatred.

Publicly, officers offered a more positive and consistent appraisal of their colleagues. It was perhaps easier to speak favorably of officers in general than of the many flawed individuals who inspired Peters' judgments. If army regulars tended to present the ideal as the real in public statements, the wealth of negative views of military men that circulated among the citizenry makes their interpretations understandable. An overzealous defense was a necessary corrective. In public accounts, officers presented themselves as gentlemen, as patrician leaders, and occasionally as an educated elite—but perhaps above all else, as men of honor. The officers' code of honor, as defined by the *Army and Navy Journal*, included "patience, fortitude, courage, temperance, chastity, probity and that large charity of self-forgetfulness which would sacrifice life for the protection of the weak and the helpless."[10] This heightened sense of duty, morality, and good character was reinforced through repeated acknowledgment of the ideal and through self-policing. Individuals did not always live up to such standards, but the ideal remained a crucial element of officers' self-image.

These men also considered themselves military professionals. This aspect of the image, however, developed only gradually, slowly eclipsing the patrician-gentleman model. Not until the end of the nineteenth century did the officer finally succumb to what Robert C. Kemble has called "a combination of contrary forces including military professionalism, social Darwinism, and philosophical naturalism." Professionalism in the military, of course, was part of a much broader nineteenth-century cultural movement that transformed law, medicine, politics, education, and scholarship. It involved creating a sense of being part of a community distinct from society at large; organizing, disciplining, and increasing communication among members of the profession; and enhancing the profession's credibility among the public. Defining themselves in large part by rejecting amateur practices (in the case of the army, this meant rejecting volunteer militias), the emerging professionals endeavored to establish standards and confer authority upon men who met these standards. Over time, then, officers defined themselves as professionals in terms of calling rather than class, aspiring to be, in Kemble's words, "proficient members of an efficient machine, meticulous students of the enemy, and accomplished manipulators of thoroughly trained units and carefully calculated supplies." Slowly they embraced the professional stance of remaining aloof from political controversies and being the "tools of, not part of, the government."[11]

This changing image sometimes produced an ambivalence about the officers' proper role. Should they publicly express personal opinions on political issues, including frontier and Indian affairs? Officers seemed uncertain. One introduced his sketches of the frontier army by claiming, "Officers of the army are not greatly given to the platform and the monthly magazine, and what they know and might so easily relate they seem purposely to be silent about. Yet they have had most to do with the development of Western civilization, [and] have mingled with all the characters of the border."[12] Military men's experience on the frontier in dealing with all manner of men meant they could speak authoritatively about frontier issues. Yet they understood that professionalism required reticence. Presumably reluctant to express their opinions on political matters, when they did so, they saw themselves as objective observers with broad, cosmopolitan views, unsullied by self-interest, partisan politics, or devotion to special interests. As self-proclaimed gentlemen and military professionals, then, officers both observed and wrote prolifically about controversial issues involving Indians, and they believed that their experience on the border rendered them worthy commentators.

They also believed that their frontier lives, far from the routine lives of their countrymen, rendered them both physically and psychologically isolated. In 1885 one eastern woman exclaimed upon meeting a colonel, "What, a colonel of the Army? Why, I supposed the Army was all disbanded at the close of the [Civil] war!"[13] Her ignorance of the frontier army and its purposes was not uncommon. The consequent sense of isolation, another important element of officers' self-image, undoubtedly influenced their relationships with and attitudes toward Indians.

Physical isolation stemmed, of course, from the army's responsibilities during much of the nineteenth century. With the close of the Mexican War in 1848, the United States acquired vast territories in the West. Plains, valleys, mountains, and even deserts beckoned settlers. But the Indian occupants seldom welcomed them, so the military established small, widely scattered posts as a defense system to protect overland routes and settlements. But it had an additional responsibility: the army was also expected to protect the Indians and the public lands from abusive frontiersmen and to play a role in the management of Indian peoples. Management authority, however, became problematic and controversial after 1849, when Congress transferred the control of Indian affairs from the War Department to the Interior Department.

For the rest of the century, then, the army served as a frontier constabulary. It came with a mission to provide for the settlement of Indian lands and the acculturation of dispossessed Indians. Many officers, reflecting their government's policy, hoped to introduce Indians to what they saw as the blessings of civilization. This would be accomplished on reservations, where the Indians would learn the principles of farming (if they did not already know them), Christianity, and Anglo-American forms of government. Thus, officers viewed themselves as both conquerors and protectors. They met Indians as foes on battlefields, but they also encountered them as people on reservations, in camps near army posts, and even in their own camps when Indians served as scouts or auxiliaries. All this took place, of course, far from their countrymen's eyes and even consciousness.

The officers' sense of psychological isolation was thus related to their physical isolation, but it was also born out of Americans' traditional suspicion of militarism. Antipathy toward a standing army in particular colored many nineteenth-century Americans' attitudes about the frontier army. In fact, Edward

M. Coffman recently noted that the central commonality that bound officers together was the experience of being soldiers in a country that disliked the military. Suspicion of the military certainly preceded the twentieth century and Vietnam. In fact, from the earliest days of the republic through the Civil War years, Americans regarded the regular army as "a doubtful necessity," the enlisted men "as drunkards and 'mercenaries,'" and the officers as "haughty 'aristocrats.'"[14] This antipathy toward a standing army, Captain Parmenus Turnley explained,

> was of course, the fruit of seeds planted by our ancestors, a century previously in their enmity to British troops, and . . . such dislike has been fostered by every demagogue and stump speaker in the land. . . . In fact to caution the dear people against the military was the chief stock in trade of nine-tenths of the political mountebanks, whose fields of action were far removed from the large cities, and among constituencies not accustomed to see or mingle with the military of our frontiers.[15]

Some argued that a standing army posed a threat to the republic. Others found the social divisions between officer and enlisted man not only distasteful but inappropriate in a democracy.

The antimilitary ethos strengthened after Appomattox and the mustering out of volunteer regiments. Once again critics renewed the charge that officers were ne'er-do-wells, hired killers, and even potential dictators. Post–Civil War involvements in such partisan political conflicts as Reconstruction and labor unrest only inflamed these sentiments. In addition, eastern "friends of the Indians" increasingly charged the military with inflicting misery on Indians and exacerbating rather than solving the Indian Problem. Congressional hostility was partly linked to the inevitable concerns of economy: a standing army was costly. For all these reasons, congressional funding of the Indian-fighting army was exceedingly spare both before and after the Civil War.

If army men considered themselves at odds with their countrymen, especially those living east of the Mississippi, relations in the West were not much better. Westerners tended to support the army, demanding more troops and military posts to protect them and to bolster their local economy. But they also severely criticized the army when it was unable to stem Indian raiding or to contain Indians on the reservations. They resented actions designed to protect Indians from Anglo-American aggression or to enforce treaties or public-land laws, and they sometimes argued that volunteer militias would be more effective than the regular army because the citizenry knew the terrain and the local Indians better than did the regulars. Officers, for their part, socialized with local townspeople and moved quite freely in civilian circles, yet some accused western civilians of inciting Indian wars by their greed and unwillingness to respect Indian treaty rights.[16]

In reflecting on the nation's assessment of them, military people felt unappreciated, not to mention unheralded. With a good deal of sense, Lieutenant W. H. Carter observed that "soldiers are but average exponents of the good and evil of their own communities." But their countrymen rarely saw it that way, and rarely had they, Carter complained, "taken to heart the services of the regular army on the frontier; in fact, it was not until [Frederic] Remington and his confreres pictured the life in all its character-making incidents and rough manhood that general interest was awakened." Officers, he explained with an edge of self-pity, simply "went about their work of carving the path of empire without expectation of other reward than a consciousness of duty right nobly performed."[17]

For their role as carvers of the path of empire, and—what is more important for this study—as observers of Indians, most army officers were not formally prepared. They received little training in frontier warfare or Indian fighting and, of course, absolutely no formal education in Indian cultures, whether they rose up through the ranks, attended West Point, or received a commission after dutiful service in a Civil War volunteer regiment.[18]

Occasionally, however, military tactics professors at West Point gave tidbits of advice. Professor Dennis Hart Mahan offered suggestions for the "westering" officers in one of his courses. They should take advantage of their superior firepower in Indian warfare, he urged. They should also exploit intertribal tensions, encouraging tribes to fight one another and thus spare the soldiers. After the Custer disaster on the Little Big Horn, General John Schofield suggested the wisdom of expanded instruction in cavalry tactics and rifle training. But for the most part, the art of warfare taught at West Point was, as army surgeon Rodney Glisan observed, "badly adapted for carrying on a war with a savage foe."[19] More irreverently, enlisted man H. H. McConnell believed that West Pointers joined their regiments "fresh from the perusal of the 'Leather Stocking Tales' or the more recent dime literature of the period," and thus they foundered around in frontier service. McConnell went on:

> It was for years an interesting and unanswered question in my mind as to what the cadets of this period *were* taught at West Point. I had *heard* of the "premium fellows"—those who graduated at the head of their class and for whom very brilliant careers were predicted—but I never saw any of them. I think all that we got were from the other end—left over, as it were. As a matter of fact, I never saw one that could drill a squad, ride a horse, knew how to wear a sabre without getting it tangled up with his legs, mount a guard, make out a ration return, or inspect a carbine.[20]

Perhaps McConnell was given to hyperbole, but it is clear that training in warfare centered on the European experience. Nor were non–West Pointers better off. Those who served as volunteers during the Civil War discovered that their experience in "civilized" fighting did not prepare them adequately for the Indian wars. They found themselves up against foes with totally different military structures, techniques, and goals of warfare.[21]

Officers might lack formal training in fighting or understanding Indians, but military men and women were well acquainted with the perceptions of Indians circulating in their own culture. They were, then, observers with well-defined preconceptions about Indians, and they clearly operated within the context of nineteenth-century attitudes about civilization, savagery, and race. Several basic notions about Indians prevailed. Anglo-Americans, for instance, assumed that it was possible to delineate general Indian characteristics without reference to tribal or cultural distinctions. In other words, they believed one could write about "The American Indian." Further, the prevailing image of Indians was ambivalent, stressing both good and bad, noble and ignoble qualities. Good Indians were brave, proud, dignified, handsome, and friendly to whites; bad Indians were warlike, fiendish, lascivious, filthy, indolent, and brutal. In addition, according to Robert Berkhofer, white observers described Indians "in terms of their deficiencies according to White ideals rather than in terms of their own various cultures," and they combined "moral evaluation with ethnographic detail," allowing "moral judgments all too frequently [to pass] for science." Added to these ideas was the conviction, gathering strength as the century wore on, that Indians represented a vanishing people. As Brian W. Dippie recently defined this powerful and widely accepted belief, they "have been wasting away since the day the white man arrived, diminishing in vitality and numbers until, in some not too distant future, no red men will be left on the face of the earth."[22]

Consequently, as objective observers of Indian cultures, behaviors, worldviews, values, and manners, army observers have limited value. To a certain degree, the West Pointers (and some others) demonstrated a general dedication to detail, concrete reality, and an objectivist framework. Although unversed in anthropology, they were rigorously trained to observe details and to sketch the realities they encountered. Although not intellectuals, they were educated, articulate, and inclined to write. As a result, their accounts can reveal some useful information about Indian material culture, apparent behavior, and points of view as conveyed through a recorded speech or conversation.

The officers certainly perceived themselves as qualified to speak with authority on Indian behavior and policy because they had more contact, whether friendly or otherwise, with Indians than any other group on the frontier. They saw themselves as realists in an almost technical, even epistemological way, in contrast to eastern romantics, who, officers believed, were unduly swayed by James Fenimore Cooper's heroic Indians or, later in the century, Helen Hunt Jackson's images. And they certainly saw themselves as more objective participants in the frontier conflicts than frontiersmen who coveted Indian lands.

On the other hand, military men and women rarely questioned their fundamental assumptions about their own civility or the Indians' supposed savagery. They operated on surface appearances and seldom explored intellectual or philosophical issues. They did not acknowledge the unfathomable in all human life, including that of the Indians. They reacted to, rather than deeply pondered, Indians and Indian affairs. A small number of officers became pioneer ethnologists, and their works remain useful sources for ethnographic detail. The overwhelming majority, however, never truly understood any Indian culture or society—or demonstrated a desire to do so.

In the final analysis, one looks to officers' accounts less to learn about the realities of Indian lives than to examine officers' perceptions of those realities. And since they varied so in background, sophistication, temperament, and personality, their subjective responses present a wide array of images and impressions. Some were fascinated with Indians; others had nothing to say about them. Some were sympathetic; others indifferent. Some contemplated the morality of the Indian wars; others never doubted it. Some were quite introspective; others not at all. Most never doubted their capacity to understand Indians on the basis of superficial observation. Nor were they bothered by a concern for intellectual consistency. An officer might present an Indian group as fiendish in his campaign diary and write much more sympathetically about the same Indians in a later memoir. A wife might rail against the Indian enemy while her husband's life was endangered and then express sincere concern for the enemy's well-being when the danger had passed.

In these ways, military men and women were strikingly uninstitutional in their writings about Indians. There is a tendency among historians and the general public to think of military people as a monolithic group who lauded themselves while despising their Indian enemies. Such a view represents myth more than reality. Their personal letters and diaries convey little hesitance about speaking frankly about fellow officers, government policy, warfare, or Indians. They usually refrained from criticizing one another and the army itself in published works, but otherwise they freely expressed themselves on matters of policy. Officers were career military men who took pride in their profession and their affiliation with the United States Army, but they were also individuals and expressed themselves as such. The women who joined their husbands at "the end of the desert," as Simonin put it, may have shared a degree of courage and pluck that set them apart as a group. But they, too, spoke up as individuals. The result was a chorus of voices rarely in unison.

2 / Indian Character

Barbarism torments the body; civilization torments the soul. The savage remorselessly takes your scalp, your civilized friend as remorselessly swindles you out of your property. —COLONEL RICHARD IRVING DODGE

During the frosty winter of 1874, the soldiers of the Seventh Cavalry waited for the spring thaw. In Dakota Territory the men scattered at Forts Totten, Rice, and Lincoln performed the usual garrison duties and otherwise passed the time until warmer weather would bring renewed activity and even an exploring expedition to the Black Hills. The regiment's Lieutenant Colonel George Armstrong Custer spent those winter days putting the final touches on the closing chapter of his autobiography. It had appeared serially in *Galaxy* magazine since May 1872 and would be published in book form later that year as *My Life on the Plains*. The flamboyant Custer became better known for his battlefield exploits and his bloody end at the Little Big Horn than for his prose, but write and publish he did. Indians, of course, were a favorite topic.

Most Anglo-Americans who ventured west of the Mississippi after 1848, including army officers and wives, assumed that one could describe a monolithic Indian character with little regard for individual, cultural, or regional distinctions. Custer, however, understood something about tribal differences. In fact, in the beginning of his book he emphasized that "between the tribes which inhabited the Eastern States and those originally found on the Plains a marked difference is seen to exist . . . while a difference equally marked is discovered between the Indians of the Plains and those of the mountain regions." To have this knowledge is one thing; to use it consistently is another. "In studying the Indian character," Custer also wrote, "while shocked and disgusted by many of his traits and customs, I find much to be admired and still more of a deep and unvarying interest." Custer generalized about Indian character, but he was indecisive about it. He explained that, among other things, the Indian displayed "remarkable taciturnity . . . deep dissimulation . . . wonderful power and subtlety of his senses . . . lack of curiosity" and "stoical courage."[1]

Custer and other officers recognized the rich variety of native peoples, yet they could not resist the temptation to lapse into easy stereotypes and outrageous generalizations. In the twentieth century, observers have rejected the idea of a monolithic Indian character. But nineteenth-century military observers accepted it and trusted their own experiences and impressions in defining it. Far from being analytical in their approach to Indian character, however, they attempted to describe rather than to explain it. The result was an ambiguous image that conveys more information about these Anglo-Americans than it does about the Indians. In some cases, it also reveals something about what they expected to find among the native people of the West.

Some, inspired by the works of James Fenimore Cooper, expected to find noble savages. But when military people wrote about the Indians they actually encountered, they universally rejected this model. In fact, for many Cooper's name became a shorthand symbol of all romanticized, and hence unrealistic, Indians. "It is to be regretted," Custer typically charged, "that the character of the Indian as described in Cooper's interesting novels is not the true one." To Custer and many others, Cooper's stories were fanciful and his Indians purely products of the imagination. Officers, by contrast, viewed themselves as realists, contending that their perceptions of Indians and Indian character, forged in personal experience with actual Indians, were indisputably more authentic. The result was predictable: "Stripped of the beautiful romance with which we have been so long willing to envelope him," Custer declared, "transferred from the inviting pages of the novelist to the localities where we are compelled to meet with him, in his native village, on the war path, and when raiding upon our frontier settlements and lines of travel, the Indian forfeits his claim to the appellation of the '*noble* red man.'"[2]

To a certain extent, the vigor with which seasoned veterans, and some wives, rejected Cooper's images of Indians reflected embarrassment over their own naivete in accepting the writer's view of Indians as realistic, only to find something quite different on the frontier. As neophytes inspired by Cooper and a complex of ideas including noble savagery and primitivism, they had anticipated heroic Indians. Actual contact, however, diminished their enthusiasm, for Indians, humans after all, inevitably revealed feet of clay. Reality could not possibly equal expectation.

Others expected to find savages devoid of any nobility or humanity. Here again, fiction-inspired expectations did not match reality. Army women, for example, believed that Indians posed special dangers to white females on the frontier. As a result, initial statements of terror typified their writings. In this respect, they diverged from the men, who only occasionally admitted trepidation, usually in the context of combat. On her way to Fort Riley, Jennie Barnitz wrote her mother: "Oh! you can have no idea how I felt coming across those plains—expecting every moment to see any number of Indians . . . but we got through all safe and I can hardly tell you or describe to you the relief I felt, when this fort came in view." Martha Summerhayes remembered that upon leaving for Fort Apache, she believed, that "we were facing unknown dangers in a far country . . . infested with roving bands of the most cruel tribe ever known, who tortured before they killed. We could not even pretend to be gay."[3]

Interestingly, fear often preceded actual contact and then tapered off after the individual met some Indian people. This suggests that many army wives went west with preconceptions about the terrors Indians posed and women's appropriate response. Recalling an Indian alarm at Fort Wingate, Alice Baldwin expressed surprise at her composure since she had "read and heard that women had hysteria and swooned and were bathed in tears in times of danger." Instead, she concluded "that I was not at all romantic, because in the midst of my solitude, I bethought me of eating a piece of pie—which I did!" It was only when her husband returned unharmed that she broke into sobs and hysterics, "while the men folks praised and complimented my pluck."[4]

The white woman as victim dominated the culture's popular image of American females in the West. Further, many books about frontier women presented them as reluctant to leave their eastern homes, repulsed by wilderness landscapes, and hateful toward the West's inhabitants. Such literature prescribed behavior for women, and officers' wives uncritically accepted its dictates—at least until they encountered actual Indians or, in the case of Baldwin, had an audience who expected "romantic" reactions.

Captivity narratives, a popular genre during the eighteenth and nineteenth centuries, also clearly colored the wives' expectations of frontier life and Indians, and continued to inform the women's writings after they arrived in the West. In these narratives, according to Roy Harvey Pearce, "the Indian . . . was the consummate villain, the beast who hatcheted fathers, smashed the skulls of infants, and carried off mothers to make them into squaws." Although no officer's wife was captured by Indians, many of them wrote about the terrors of captivity, and one or more of the genre's basic elements appeared in their accounts of it. Thus Lydia Lane wrote,

> Woe to the hapless party that fell into the devilish hands of a band of Indians! Men were generally put to death by slow torture, but they were allowed to live long enough to witness the atrocities practiced on their wives and children, things as only fiends could devise. Babies had their brains dashed out before the eyes of father and mother, powerless to help them. Lucky would the latter have been, had they treated her in the same way; but what she was to endure would have wrung tears from anything but an Indian.

Elizabeth Custer, who seemed particularly fascinated by the topic, informed an aunt that women captives suffered unspeakable degradation, and she assured her relative that "death would be merciful in comparison." And when Camp Cooke in Montana Territory was under Indian attack, Sarah Canfield wrote in her diary that the women "held a 'council of war,' and decided if the Ft. could not be held that we preferred to be shot by our own officers rather than to be taken captive."[5] Their dread of captivity, of course, far exceeded its likelihood.

Once on the frontier, many army people cast aside images that did not match their experience. Apprehension gave way to curiosity. They visited camps, invited Indians into their homes for social engagements, and expressed a genuine interest in learning about Indian cultures. In addition, the Indians' reactions to them, particularly gestures of friendship and reciprocal curiosity, eroded mutual fears and underscored their common humanity.

When military men and women wrote about Indian character, then, they found fiction-inspired expectations insufficient. They offered, instead, generalizations rooted in a blend of cultural stereotype and personal experience. And, as already mentioned, they did not concern themselves much with consistency. Custer might scoff at "the beautiful romance" of Cooper's Indians, yet he revealed a romantic bent of his own in his depictions of Plains warriors. Nelson Miles combined the ideas and images of pre–Civil War romantics with those of post–Civil War evolutionists. Officers, who were not particularly systematic thinkers when it came to questions about Indians, borrowed the language and ideas of ethnologists such as Henry Schoolcraft or Lewis Henry Morgan. But they did not study them carefully or strive for a scientific or even especially coherent analysis of Indian people. In this regard, for all their experience with actual Indians, military men and women stood firmly in the mainstream of American thinking about them. A general inconsistency about Indians had always pervaded American thought.[6] Consequently, they reached no consensus on the matter of Indian character other than demonstrating an ambivalence about it. For some, this ambivalence about savagery spilled over to an ambivalence about civilization as well.

What any of these officers or their wives actually meant by savagery or civilization, of course, is difficult to determine, as they rarely bothered to define their terms. This absence of precision only enhanced the sense of equivocation, hesitation, and vacillation. Military training provided no definitions or carefully constructed frames of reference. Not particularly concerned with linguistics in any systematic way, officers used words such as "savages," "primitives," and "wild Indians" interchangeably. Several, however—apparently influenced by theories of progress and evolution—provided at least some informal definitions. Civil War veteran Captain J. Lee Humfreville, typically claimed that his point of view represented an accurate account of Indians "as I knew them in their natural state." He defined the savage as a "wild man [who] lived in a state of nature and followed his natural impulses. He neither dwelt on the past nor anticipated the future. He lived solely in the present and his life and actions were controlled by the primeval laws of necessity."[7] The savage, then, was man at his most basic, primitive level—though not necessarily man at his most base.

To Richard Irving Dodge, the Indian as savage "has the ordinary good and bad qualities of the mere animal, modified to some extent by reason." What distinguished primitive man from other animals, according to Dodge, was "the greater development of the reasoning faculties." In fact, he believed that the "condition of the races of mankind is simply the greater or less progression of each from the starting point. The Indian, so far behind in this race of progress as to be still a savage, is yet far ahead of many tribes and people." Yet Indians did not know or care about political or economic issues, "or the thousand questions of social or other science, that disturb and perplex the minds of civilized people." "And," he added, "with reasoning faculties little superior to instinct, there is among Indians no such thing as conversation as we understand it. . . . The ordinary mental activity of the Indian may be estimated at zero."[8]

Just as it was difficult to define savagery, so was it difficult to identify its origins. Was savagery an inherited state, or did physical environment explain it? General Hugh Scott saw environment in a very literal sense as the crucial factor that molded Indian character. Indians of the gloomy eastern forests, he explained, "partook of the nature of those forests" and were "vindictive and cruel beyond limit," while the "nature of the Plains Indian reflected upon the open sunny character of his habitat, and his rages were soon over."[9]

Colonel Philippe Regis de Trobriand, a French-born journalist and country gentleman who emigrated to the United States in the 1850s and joined the army during the Civil War, disagreed with this analysis. American Indians, who had fulfilled their "fleeting mission in the march of humanity," resisted assimilation with whites because of "a seed of destruction which the race carries in itself." As a result, Indians were doomed to extinction—dying out, as had others before them, in the "chain of eternal progress." In Trobriand's deterministic view of things, Indians had no choice. When they failed to assimilate with whites, they merely obeyed an inborn impulse to remain a lower link on the chain of human progress and thus to fade away gradually so that a superior race could carry on. Trobriand did not see the Indians' state of savagery as rooted in their environment; it was the product of something deeper and more meaningful. Indian people had their mission, and as the nineteenth century drew to a close, they were fulfilling it, serving their historical purpose in that evolutionary chain of events wherein "some other race will rise in a future time, as superior to the caucasian of today as that race was to the American which is now dying out." Indians' savagery and inevitable inferiority, according to this officer, were simply part of a natural plan; extinction was their destiny.[10]

An officer's view of the Indians' capacity for change, and even survival, would affect his assessment of the reservation and assimilation policies, as well as of the amorphous Indian character, and it would shape his view of his role in the West. Moreover, an officer's reflections on the meaning and origin of savagery affected his view of "civilization," that is, of his own way of life. It was not at all uncommon for military men to end a discussion of Indians by discussing themselves, or more accurately, their civilized countrymen. Army officers merely repeated a timeworn European tradition of using Indians as a springboard for comments on whites. The idea of the Indian became a device to examine facets of American culture, or in some cases to reproach American culture. Ironically, in such cases even army officers slipped into the convention of noble savagery as a useful mechanism for social criticism. Assaults on Cooper's veracity aside, they fell back on the noble-savage idea to air their griev- ances against their own society or to warn about the pitfalls of overcivilization.

As a result, the majority of military people viewed "Indian character" with uncertainty and even perplexity. They did not regard savagery as necessarily either more or less moral than civilization. They strove to avoid creating images of total nobil- ity or venality in their accounts of Indians. They attempted to form a balanced view. While not cultural relativists or modern observers, neither were army officers and wives absolutists. They moralized, but not in predictable ways. They had learned on the frontier that even civilized men were capable of savage behavior. The Indian, for his part, had not exhibited civilization's virtues before contact, but neither had he exhibited its vices. Only after encounters with white traders and other disreputable sorts did the Indian acquire much of civilization's corruption and little of its righteousness. "The first thing he learned from his civilized brother," Humfreville explained, "was his vices; these he acquired and retained with wonderful proficiency and tenacity, and instead of improving, degenerated."[11]

Richard Irving Dodge came to similar conclusions, asserting that while important distinctions separated the savage from the civilized man, "an Indian is, to my mind, an evidence of the unity of the races. Wherever we find them, savages have some- thing in common with the other, and the most civilized races have not so far outgrown their ancestry as to have entirely got- ten rid of every savage trait." For example, Dodge maintained, cruelty was a trait both natural and common to all human be- ings. In their propensity to engage in it, the savage and civilized man were equals. The only difference came in the *nature* of their cruelty:

> The savage dances with delight at the groans wrung from his enemy, by physical torture; the enlightened gentleman plunges a dagger of courteous words into the heart of his friend and smiles blandly at his mental torture. I know kindly disposed and esti- mable savages, who would tie their enemy to the ground, and

pleasantly warm themselves by the fire built on his naked breast. I know accomplished gentlemen standing high in the estimation of society, who never use an angry tone, yet whose wives have cause to envy the victim of the savage. . . .

The progress of enlightenment of a people would seem to be measurable by their greater abhorrence of physical torture and the ingenuity and politeness with which mental torture may be inflicted. The actual cruelty is possibly about the same in either case . . . but it is the case of the savage that comes up for judgment.[12]

John Bourke, who filled his campaign journals with details of Indian cultures and eventually became president of the American Folk-Lore Society, took this line of thought one step further. He was less certain that civilized people felt a greater abhorrence toward physical torture, charging that "we have become so thoroughly Pecksniffian in our self-laudation, in our exaltation of our own virtues, that we have become grounded in the error of imagining that the American savage is more cruel in his war customs than other nations of the earth have been." Bourke listed atrocities of the Assyrians, Israelites, and Romans, and even the English within the last century. "Certainly," he concluded, "the American aborigine is not indebted to his palefaced brother, no matter of what nation or race he may be, for lessons in tenderness and humanity."[13]

In recognizing the Indians' basic humanity and in acknowledging the deleterious effects that contacts with white civilization had had on Indians, officers moved beyond a dichotomy of savagery and civilization. Although they continued to use these terms, their meaning and usefulness actually became even more blurred. These men acknowledged that Indians were capable of vicious acts, but so, they said, were whites. Indians had vices, but they were often learned from whites. Thus, in attempting to describe the reality of Indian savagery, character, and life, officers continually turned to a discussion of Anglo-American civilization, character, and life, and frequently found that the savage and the civilized man had more in common than simple stereotypes or labels would suggest.

General George Crook neatly encapsulated these ideas in his address to West Point's graduating class in 1884. "With all his faults," Crook said, "and he has many, the American Indian is not half so black as he has been painted. He is cruel in war, treacherous at times, and not overly cleanly. But so were our forefathers." Crook went on to say that the Indian's nature "is responsive to treatment which assures him that it is based upon justice, truth, honesty and common sense; it is not impossible that with a fair and square system of dealing with him, the American Indian would make a better citizen than many who neglect the duties and abuse the privilege of this proud title." Further, Crook told the cadets that the savage was hemmed in by civilization, and he knew it. As a result, he was ready to abandon the old ways and accept civilization. Unlike Trobriand, then, Crook did not accept the idea that Indians were doomed. Just as the cadets' forefathers had demonstrated savage characteristics and had risen above them, so could today's savages. The movement from savagery to civilization was fluid.[14]

General Oliver O. Howard made similar comparisons. While he did not deny that Indians were treacherous, secretive, and capable of cruelty, he believed they exhibited these tendencies only in war. Moreover, "after the war was over none of them ever entered into a deliberate plan to deceive and injure me . . . as many an educated white man has done." As for thievery, he wrote, they only stole from their enemies. "I cannot recall any case within my personal experience," Howard testified, "where Indians robbed their friends, or manifested toward them any greater secretiveness than we white men do to each other in ordinary business life." Howard believed that, as a rule, when an Indian made a promise, he kept it. And when asked if he found Indians especially treacherous, he replied, "No, not so much as the Anglo-Saxon."[15]

General Nelson Miles went even further in his use of Indians as a device for social criticism, celebrating the simplicity of savagery and disparaging the contrivances of civilization. "The most striking fact to be noted of the American Indian before he degenerated through contact with the white man, and anterior to the race war that was waged for centuries before his final overthrow," he wrote in the 1890s, "was the dignity, hospitality, and gentleness of his demeanor toward strangers and toward his fellow savages." Plains Indians—expert equestrians and skillful hunters—particularly appealed to Miles and symbolized all that was noble about savage life. "They were grateful for the abundance of the earth—the sunshine, air, water, all the blessings of nature," Miles claimed, "and believed that all should share them alike." Plains people deplored a grasping disposition and celebrated a generous one. They demonstrated "courage, skill, sagacity, endurance, fortitude, and self-sacrifice of a high order." Furthermore, they "had rules of civility." A few of these, Miles added, "we could copy to our advantage." And, he affirmed, it was "the inexorable needs of a higher civilization, too often in haughty contempt pushing its conquests and gratifying its desires regardless of justice, plighted faith and the finer and purer instincts and emotions that actuate and move the best elements of our nature," which had spoiled this primitive paradise.[16]

Miles was joined in his sentiments concerning Plains Indians and in his thoughts on civilization's destructive tendencies by an officer who waxed poetic about the contrasts between primitive and civilized life. In 1890, G. P. Putnam's Sons published a book of Captain E. L. Huggins's poetry, including a rather lengthy piece entitled "Winona: A Dakota Legend." In the opening lines, Huggins pits savage image against civilized one:

> How changed, fair Minnetonka, is thy face
> Since first I saw thee in thy pristine grace.
> Electric lights fantastically grow,
> Swarming like fire-flies on the shores where long,
> Through countless summer nights a vanished throng,
> Only the Indian camp-fire flickered low.
> The odor of the baleful cigarette
> Assails us now, where the mild calumet
> Around the circle like a censer swung.
> The notes of Strauss intoxicate the air,
> And dainty feet in cadence twinkle there.
> Where in rude strains the warriors' deeds were sung,
> And where the Indian lover's plaintive flute
> Lured to the trysting-place the dusky maid.

Such an introduction should leave no doubt that Huggins's Indians were noble. They were also virtually extinct, largely because of civilization's heavy hand:

> Save a few stately names, the vanished race
> Whose dust we daily trample leave no trace
> Or monument. None who that race have known
> Ere poisoned by the vices of our own,
> Deem it ignoble; but the white man's breath,
> To him a besom of consuming death,
> Sweeps him like ashes from his natal hearth,
> E'en as one day some race of stronger birth
> Will sweep our children's children from the earth
> More noxious than the fabled upas tree,
> We blight his virtues first, and then with scorn
> Repel the hands extended once to save
> Our exiled fathers, fleeing o'er the wave.
> Yet in our deepest fall, the warrior born
> Of warrior lineage fetterless and free,
> Retains unquenched in his unyielding soul
> A secret flame in spite of all control.
> He brooks no slavish, ignominious toil,
> By scourger driven to till the white man's soil. . . .[17]

It is noteworthy that Miles and Huggins, in line with the romantic tradition, described Indians who lived in the time before white men arrived and sullied their idyllic native existence. These people, while primitive, were heroes and worthy of respect, even emulation. The surviving Indians were pitiful because the higher, conquering civilization had reduced their lives to tragedy (although Huggins allowed contemporary Indians some dignity in their spirit of resistance to an agricultural life). What was compelling, even beautiful, about Indian life, these officers claimed, was dead. Inspired by romanticism and the cult of primitivism, these depictions of Indian character were sincere but sentimental. More important, adopting such a view of Indian character allowed these men to compare native life quite "favorably with the pretense, sham, and decadence of civilized society," as William B. Skelton put it. Noble savages operated as vehicles through which these people reproved their own culture.[18]

Military men assumed the natural superiority of white civilization, yet experience proved that its vices influenced Indians more profoundly than did its virtues. In the end, they could not conclude that their own civilization represented a decline in man's virtues or worth, and they certainly did not recommend replacing civilization with savagery. But neither could they maintain rigid standards of what constituted civilized, as opposed to savage, behavior. They were not ready to discard concepts like savagery and civilization, for these concepts, slippery as they might be, ultimately helped the officers to justify their participation in the conquest of the Indians. But many officers' thoughts on Indian character, and their civilization's impact on it, were clearly troubled. Their acknowledgment of tribal differences, as well as their personal relationships with individual Indians, would only complicate matters even more.

3 / Tribes and Chiefs

*These Indians [Hopi, or Moqui] although thrifty, do not
inspire the respect commanded by the Apaches, who in
every manly trait and virtue are far superior to the
effeminate Moqui.* —CAPTAIN JOHN BOURKE

On a late June day in 1868, Ada Adams Vogdes, five months an
army lieutenant's bride, made her way toward Fort Laramie. The
hot, dry days and the desolation of the plains lowered her spirits.
When the party broke from the railroad, Ada confided to her
journal, "my heart sank within me. . . . I thought of all the miles
to be gone over with only mule power, and no rail road to call
upon in case of necessity. Oh! It was a fearful feeling for me, in
the midst of an Indian country, and far from home." Even after
Mrs. Vogdes reached Fort Laramie, she continued to fear Indians, particularly when she left the security of the post to accompany her husband to the wood-detail camp twelve miles
away. "I am frightened nearly to death every evening, when the
sun goes down, until it comes again the next a.m.," she wrote,
and "I rather enjoy it, were I not so afraid of Indians all the
time."

Two months later Mrs. Vogdes welcomed Sioux leaders Red
Cloud, Red Leaf, and Big Bear to the fort. She shook their hands,
said a few words in their language, helped entertain them in the
sutler's dining room and accompanied them to the parlor, where
they "sat themselves down in rocking chairs and on sofas, with
as much *ease* and *grace*, as if they had been born there, and
knew no other life." Now on more familiar terms, her attitude
had changed. Red Leaf, she noted, had "a good fatherly countenance" and looked like "one to whom you would go in trouble,
were he in different circumstances." Big Bear—his buffalo robe
thrown across his torso, exposing "the most splendid chest and
shoulders I ever laid my eyes upon"—particularly appealed to
her. But it was Red Cloud, reputedly one of the most militant and
fearsome Sioux of her time, who became Mrs. Vogdes's friend.

Over the next two years, at Forts Laramie and Fetterman, she delighted in his attentions and invited him to dine at her home. During one of these luncheons, Mrs. Vogdes showed Red Cloud a photograph album that included a portrait of herself:

> After looking at it a moment, in the most affectionate manner, he kissed it, and said I was a "washta squaw." . . . He is really very polite, and dignified in all respects, and when he smiles I never saw a sweeter, his whole face lights up beautifully and the smiles play all over it like the sun when it has been obscured for a time behind the cloud.

The woman who before had been "frightened nearly to death" of Indians was now transformed into the gracious hostess of a famous Sioux fighter, writing about him with affection and marveling at the picture she would make to her eastern friends as she entertained "this naked man."[1]

Military men and women wrote about a universal Indian character in their search for meaningful generalizations, but they also understood that to see one Indian was not to see them all. They made distinctions among individuals and among tribes. Ada Vogdes found Indians in general frightening but befriended particular Indian people. William Parker wrote about "the Indian," yet he declared, "we must remember that while the term Indian conveys to our mind a certain idea as to general characteristics, Indian tribes differ from each other in appearance, manners and customs as widely as the tribes of 'pale faces' differ from each other." Parker allowed that there were four to five hundred different tribes, all with distinctive marriage, death, housing, and eating customs. In fact, he believed, practices varied so widely that people should view with caution any books with statements about "the American Indian," although he failed to see the sins in his own work. Colonel Richard Irving Dodge noted, too, that since there were hundreds of different tribes, no general description was applicable to all Indians "except that all are savage, all are swindled, starved and imposed upon."[2]

There was, then, an almost immediate breakdown of stereotypes and a more refined attempt to discuss Indian life on a tribal and individual basis. Of course, military people continued to speak in sweeping terms, for even tribal characteristics conveyed a sense of uniformity that did not account for faction, band, or individual differences. Nevertheless, these nineteenth-century people used the idea of a tribal character in an attempt to say something significant about native life in the West. If such generalizations could not impart a precise knowledge of the wide variety of characteristics to be found among Indian people, they were at least an alternative to the usual broad-gauge generalities about "Indian character."

When differentiating among tribes and assigning particular characteristics to particular groups, of course, military people continued to evaluate tribal people in moral terms. They used concepts similar to those employed in their discussions of Indian character, with judgments about a tribe's worth often determined by the degree to which its culture approximated that of the officers. Army people favored, for example, tribes that adopted "civilized" economic activities and religious and cultural practices. Some, of course, preferred those who peacefully accommodated themselves to the Anglo-American presence. As a result, some tribes consistently fared better than others in the Anglo-Americans' estimation. Yet the fundamental ambivalence that colored so many military people's accounts of Indian character emerged in their assessments of tribal groups as well. A willingness to resist also sparked admiration. Plains Indians who refused to capitulate to civilization's demands, who refused to substitute plow for bow without a fight, undeniably appealed to some army people.

Among the regularly favored, of course, were the so-called Five Civilized Tribes—the Cherokee, Choctaw, Creek, Chickasaw, and Seminole people—which were transplanted to the trans-Mississippi West from the Southeast in the 1830s and 1840s. They were deemed civilized because many of them had adopted Anglo-American institutions, manners, and economic systems. And, of course, by 1848 warfare with these people was largely a thing of the past.

Erasmus Darwin Keyes, an 1832 West Point graduate from Massachusetts who participated in the military removal of the

Cherokee, clearly respected that tribe. He later remembered that "the repose and dignity of their appearance could not have been excelled by an equal number of our race." Other officers encountered these tribes only after their removal to the West, but they reacted the same way. Colonel Benjamin Grierson, a Civil War veteran from Illinois, described them as semi-civilized and remarked that they posed quite a contrast to the "wild Indians" of the Plains. Similarly, Lieutenant R. G. Carter noted the difference between the Cherokees and the Kiowa. "The Cherokees," he wrote, "seemed to be the largest, best formed and altogether the best type of Indians we saw." They were "quiet, peaceful, industrious farmers and herders" quite unlike the "uneasy, restless, wandering nomads of the plains who had for so many years, been giving our little regular army so much trouble." The Cherokees had once been fierce warriors, Carter admitted, burning, pillaging, and murdering in the Atlantic states, "but now they were revelling, so it seemed, in the fat of the land, with no thought but peace and comfort on the magnificent farms which fronted on the roads along which we were now marching."[3]

At the time he observed the Cherokees, Carter was escorting Satanta and Big Tree, Kiowa men, from the Texas state prison to Fort Sill, where they would be released. This underscored his impression of the distinctions that separated the Cherokee from the Kiowa. Noticing that "our two savage chiefs from the Texas Plains gazed with equal curiosity" at the Cherokee with their plentiful demonstrations of "independence and good thrift," Carter concluded, "the two types seemed as wide apart as the two poles of the world."[4]

Richard Irving Dodge also compared the "wild Indians" of the trans-Mississippi West to the Cherokees. According to this officer, however, there was one exception to western "wildness." That exception was the Nez Perce, a people who, as Dodge understood it, had started advancing toward civilization due to missionary influences.[5] Others shared Dodge's enthusiasm for the Nez Perce. To them, the Nez Perce demonstrated several attractive qualities that set them apart from supposedly more savage tribes. First, these people had welcomed the Protestant missionaries Henry and Eliza Spalding in the 1830s and 1840s, and many of them had converted from their own religion to Christianity. In the process, they adopted other aspects of Anglo-American life. Perhaps more important, the Nez Perce established a tradition of friendly relations with whites from the outset of contact.

When Lieutenant Lawrence Kip encountered the Nez Perce in the 1850s, he noted these attributes. Finding them interested in war and the chase, he added that they are also "blessed with a more tractable disposition than most of their brethren . . . willing to be instructed, not only in the arts of civilization, but also in the precepts of Christianity." Kip did note, however, that they had altered Christianity to suit their own needs, creating "an odd mixture of this world and the next . . . an equal love of fighting and devotion." They combined, he wrote, "the wildest Indian traits with a strictness in some religious rites which might shame those who profess to call themselves Christian."[6]

More than a decade later, Lieutenant George Templeton, who had little admiration for most of the Indians he encountered in Bozeman Trail country, praised the Nez Perce he met at Fort C. F. Smith. They had come to trade horses and blankets for the Crows' robes and lodges. He thought the Nez Perces the best-dressed Indians he had ever seen. He pronounced them "a much better class of Indians" than the Crows and Sioux, since they attempted "some pretences of making themselves clean." Also, the fact that the Nez Perce believed that the Sioux would have their hands full should they try to wipe out the troopers at Fort C. F. Smith probably enhanced Templeton's affection for them. Such confidence was undoubtedly welcome during that perilous winter of 1866, when Captain William Fetterman and a good number of his men would be killed in the vicinity of Fort Phil Kearny, not far distant. Templeton failed to indicate, however, what either the Nez Perce or the Crows thought of his ice skating on the Big Horn River—a pastime he claimed to have introduced to the wild country. He merely noted that several Indians "looked on in silent wonder."[7]

Even the outbreak of hostilities between the army and the Nez Perce did not destroy this tribe's favorable reputation. In fact, in some ways the war enhanced it. In his reminiscences, General Nelson Miles presented the Nez Perce as peaceable, strong, and intelligent. He defined their 1877 troubles as "another cruel injustice" against them, observing that the Nez Perce's friendship and loyalty to the United States government dated back to the Lewis and Clark visit. Before the 1877 conflict, Miles wrote, they could "boast that in nearly a hundred years of intercourse with a superior race no white man had ever been killed by a Nez Perce."[8]

The officers' commentary on the Nez Perce reflects the complexity of their attitudes and the complexity of their situations. People such as the Nez Perce were neither all good nor all bad. However, if one stressed the Indians' relative innocence and the United States' venality, or that of its citizens, that would reflect too harshly on the army and its officers. General Oliver O. Howard of Freedmen's Bureau fame, sidestepped this dilemma by distinguishing between factions within the Nez Perce tribe. Of course, his discussion of factions was not mere manipulation to preserve his own favorable self-image; the factions were real. Howard was one of the few officers who discussed them. Nevertheless, in drawing out the character of each faction, he tended to vilify those who did not share his perspective. Howard judged the Nez Perce to have few superiors among the North American tribes but distinguished between those who remained on the reservation during the 1877 war and the "renegades" who did not. The latter, under the "unhappy effects of superstition and ignorance" of the Dreamer Cult, brought near ruin to their tribe. However, he maintained, the majority of Nez Perce were not only friendly Christians but also steadfast strivers "on the path in which they were started by the worthy, self-sacrificing missionary." These people remained contented inhabitants of their reservation. The troublemakers, he somewhat inaccurately reported, were the non-Christian minority.[9]

While some Nez Perce embraced Christianity and displayed a consistently friendly temperament, the Pueblo Indians epitomized other virtues—particularly an agrarian way of life. One officer wrote, "the Pueblo is purely a farmer, and has been so from time immemorial. All his tastes and inclinations are peaceful. He is the model farmer of America and reminds one of all he has ever heard of the patient husbandmen of Egypt and China." Not only were Pueblo men and women good agrarians but also, according to various officers, they lived in orderly dwellings, demonstrated gentle manners, and appeared clean. They seemed, in short, to incorporate many of the virtues of the Jeffersonian yeoman farmer.[10]

Major George McCall asserted in an 1850 official report that Pueblos were "intelligent, moral, sober and industrious" and "generally speaking . . . better off than the lower class of Mexicans." Furthermore, their superiority was evident in that many spoke Spanish and some of the principal men could read and write the language for simple business transactions. Several officers' wives made a point of visiting the Pueblos and were impressed with various aspects of their lives. Eveline Alexander found that the cleanliness of Taos Pueblo would "put Fort Garland to shame," and Martha Summerhayes was surprised that the road to Tesuque Pueblo was not lined with tourists. Instead, "they pass all these wonders by, in their disinclination to go off the beaten track."[11]

Even Lieutenant James Steele, not normally given to praising Indians, claimed that if "Lieutenant General [Philip Sheridan] of the United States Army ever made the epigrammatic remark . . . that the only good Indian is a dead one, it is probable that he was not at the moment thinking of that lone and solitary variety of the Child of Nature in the West who has never given the military any trouble"—the Pueblo. Steele declared them "the only ones of the original race who have always been friendly to the white man," continuing to toil in their gardens even "with the predatory Apache and the tyrannical and covetous Spaniard, and latterly the Yankee stranger ever peering over [their] garden wall." This officer apparently did not know about the Pueblo Revolt of 1680. But the point here is that by the mid-nineteenth century, the agrarian Pueblos no longer threatened military men, and the military men generally praised them for it.[12]

Evaluating the Navajos was a bit more problematic for army people, particularly during the 1850s, when the army and the Navajos clashed. In some respects, this typified army ambivalence toward many tribal groups. On the one hand, officers found the Navajos attractive, diligent, and involved in semicivilized pursuits, such as sheepherding. Yet the Navajos preyed upon the Pueblos and other settlements in raiding that disturbed the peace and, in the officers' view, required chastisement. As a result, military views of the Navajos were mixed.

In 1854 Lieutenant John Van Deusen Du Bois, a New Yorker, described the Navajos as "a wonderful people." They demonstrated what he defined as semicivilized qualities, raising corn, knitting stockings, and manufacturing tightly woven blankets that would hold water. Yet, he continued, they "have no God and no idea of a future state," and they were "the best thieves in all the country." George McCall agreed that the rapacious Navajos had greatly reduced the number of sheep in New Mexico by 1850, yet he admitted that the Navajos were not as warlike as the Apaches and were certainly "more provident."[13]

In the wake of the Navajo War, the Long Walk, and the tragic Bosque Redondo Reservation experiences, which ended most Navajo raiding by the close of the 1860s, officers and officers' wives presented primarily favorable impressions of the tribe. John Bourke liked their "square shouldered, sinewy, compact, and well-proportioned figures, with straight limbs, square jaws, flashing eyes, and intelligent, good natured faces." Irish-born army surgeon Bernard Byrne declared them superior to the Utes, who, he said, continued to cling to a savage way of life by living in tipis and wandering for the hunt. He found the Navajos, who earnestly looked after their herds, less savage and more intelligent.[14]

It is not surprising that army officers and officers' wives responded positively to the usually friendly farming tribes. Yet they also wrote favorably of those who showed little inclination toward assimilation or agriculture. Indian people who openly resisted white incursions into their territory also received a measure of positive treatment. Actually, some officers seemed especially attracted to Indians who exhibited a spirit of defiance. They demonstrated a healthy respect for the marksmanship, horsemanship, and other martial skills of their Indian foes. But beyond matters of military prowess, which will be explored below, officers commended the characteristics of resisting tribes in general. John Bourke, for instance, acknowledged that the Apaches did not know or practice the Moqui or Hopi industrial and domestic arts. Yet to Bourke, Hopi men appeared "not so noble as the Apache." He admired the Apache as a formidable foe, one not easily terrified into submission. The "naked Apache," he proclaimed, "with no weapons save his bow and arrows, lance, war-club, knife and shield, roamed over a vast empire, the lord of the soil—fiercer than the fiercest of tigers, wilder than the wild coyote he called his brother." Furthermore, he said, although mercy should not be expected from them as enemies, they could be made to be firm friends. While Bourke resorted to animal imagery in describing the Apaches' military talents, he understood that they were people, not beasts. He also described the Apaches as extremely honest, witty, intelligent, gregarious, trustworthy, and kind to children.[15]

Similarly, Joseph Sladen, who lived among Cochise's people for several weeks in 1872, found the Apaches scrupulously honest and believed that these "wild Indians . . . had some characteristics that would have done credit to their white enemies." Sladen explained that they were clean and well groomed, free of licentiousness, always generous, and only mildly superstitious. Fully aware of popular notions that Indians were considered cold, reserved, and humorless, this officer argued that the Apaches were quite the opposite—always cheerful, and full of fun. Further, he wrote in a passage notable for its presentation of whites as stoical and Apaches as lovable:

> They were very affectionate in their disposition, annoyingly so sometimes to our cold-blooded Anglo-Saxon temperament.
>
> We were never free from their displays of affection. They were forever leaning upon us, or putting their arms around us, or feeling of our person or our hair, or examining our clothing, or getting into our pockets, until it became exasperating and one would push them away in excess of irritation.[16]

Sladen acknowledged that they acted the same way with one another, so such behavior was not intended to annoy. It was simply a genuine outpouring of natural feelings.

Some officers, then, not only praised warring tribes, they preferred them. Bourke preferred the manly Apache warrior to
the "effeminate" Hopi farmer. Likewise, other military men
scorned coastal tribes of the Pacific Northwest and California
precisely because of their peaceful dispositions and apparent
lack of martial ardor. They found them deficient when compared to the "wild" Plains tribes. Lawrence Kip sounded a typical note of dismay in contrasting the Plains Indians, who lived
on horseback and looked like warriors, with the coastal tribes,
who, "engaged only in their canoes, or stooping over the banks,
are low in stature, and seem to have been dwarfed out of all
manhood. In everything noble they are many degrees below the
wild tribes of the plains." Similarly, Major Granville O. Haller,
a Pennsylvania native, compared the "energetic, independent
and warlike spirits" who lived east of the Cascades with the
Puget Sound people, who, he claimed, were "docile and timid
fish-eating Indians . . . cowed by the more powerful Indians from
the North" and thus reliant "for their protection upon the white
settlers around them.[17]

To these officers the Plains warrior cut a more imposing, impressive, and romantic figure than did the coastal fisherman.
Plains Indians *looked* like Indians. They rode horseback. They
chased buffalo. The nomad of the Plains, far more than the salmon fisherman of the Columbia River or the farmer of the
Southwest, appeared noble, dignified, even heroic.

More than this, officers were drawn to Indians who fought to
preserve their homeland. As warriors themselves with a military code of ethics, to fight for home and family was honorable,
so they admired a warlike spirit. They respected the traits they
most revered in their fraternity. Moreover, their self-esteem
could be raised if they saw the enemy as brave, determined, and
intelligent.

Such attitudes distinguished officers from many other observers living on the frontier. It would be difficult indeed to find
civilians who admired those Indians who chose warfare over
nonviolent methods of coping with Anglo-American settlement. Military men evidently were more inclined than civilians
to praise other military men, regardless of racial or cultural

boundaries or abstract notions of savagery and civilization. In the process, of course, they reaffirmed themselves and their profession.

Further, the Plains wanderers' existence seemed to provide freedom from civilized restraints and responsibilities. It represented a life of primitive liberty and independence. For this reason, some officers acknowledged the attractions of the nomadic life and appreciated the Plains Indians' resistance to its end. "No tribe enjoying its accustomed freedom has ever been induced to adopt a civilized mode of life," Lieutenant Colonel George Custer explained. And, he admitted, "If I were an Indian, I often think I would greatly prefer to cast my lot among those of my people adhered to the free open plains rather than submit to the confined limits of a reservation, there to be the recipient of the blessed benefits of civilization, with its vices thrown in without stint or measure."[18]

Such remarks hint at what Lee Clark Mitchell has called the "deep sense of foreboding" that accompanied American empire building. Expansion meant the destruction of wilderness at an alarming rate, and underneath the optimistic rhetoric of progress lingered "the suspicion that much, perhaps too much, was being sacrificed to the future." Indians, symbolizing the human dimension of wilderness, were also threatened. Anxiety about the vanishing wilderness and Indians led Americans to question progress's cost and even their own culture. Such doubts revealed "the ambivalence felt among even those who participated in the nation's triumphant conquest of the wilderness" and demonstrate that "issues that we assume are modern—conservation, native rights, and questioning the price of progress—actually originated early in the nineteenth century."[19]

So some officers presented the Plains Indian's life of supposed simplicity, freedom, and independence as natural and healthy. Sounding more like a back-to-nature advocate of the twentieth century than civilization's defender of the nineteenth, General Nelson Miles explained that the Plains people acquired food, shelter, and clothing from wild deer and buffalo. The flesh of these animals gave them an abundance of wholesome food, the buffalo robes made them comfortable, and "[b]uffalo and elk hides furnished excellent lodges that were . . . healthful at all seasons of the year." Further, they worshipped a God of nature and believed that all shared equally in nature's blessings. "For one to wish to monopolize any part of the earth," according to Miles, "was to them the manifestation of a grasping disposition."[20]

It would be folly, however, to assume that the officers possessed a universal admiration for Plains Indians, or that an individual officer would be consistent on this matter. Indian resistance could lead to admiration, but it could also lead to anger, for officers understood that they risked personal annihilation. If the Plainsmen were dignified, they were also treacherous. If kind to one another, they were also mercilessly vicious to enemies and distrustful of strangers.

An individual's perspective depended partly on his circumstance at the time he penned his opinion. In a memoir, Oliver O. Howard described the Sioux as "the finest physical specimens of Indians" that he had seen, and he revealed a fundamental respect for these people, who were "free from fear . . . being ever ready for war" and who "were not easily mastered by force." In his 1876 field journal, however, Lieutenant James Bradley indicated that his men had vandalized a Sioux grave and had found a white woman captive's note, in which she said the Indians were kind but that she had "to do their bidding." The officer railed against this "fate worse than death" and called for "so complete an overthrow of the hell-hounds called Sioux that never again shall poor women be made the victims of such barbarity at their hands."[21]

Yet even here no simple rules apply. Personal, contemporary accounts could be more charitable than public, retrospective ones. In a personal diary entry, Captain Albert Barnitz, eventually breveted for his role in the Battle of the Washita, remarked on the Cheyennes' "truly grand and formidable appearance" at the 1867 Medicine Lodge Council. Years later, Captain Charles King remembered the Cheyenne as "beggarly, treacherous rascals" for whom "the love of rapine and warfare" was the "ruling passion."[22]

As much as anything, an officer's own taste and temperament

determined his reaction to a tribe. General Philip Sheridan both respected the Cheyenne above all other tribes and held a personal vendetta against them. Sheridan probably knew more about them, too, because a scout named Ben Clark tutored him on these people and prepared a Cheyenne dictionary and grammar for him. But in Sheridan's case, knowledge of the Cheyenne did not lead to compassion for them. He feared their military capabilities, their independent spirit, and the disquieting effect he believed they had on other Indians. Sheridan, in fact, thought that the Cheyenne rather than the Sioux were responsible for Custer's defeat at the Little Big Horn.[23]

Hugh Scott admired the Cheyenne too, but with much less hesitation. So taken was Scott with these tribesmen that he even rated them above the Nez Perce. In a letter to his mother written at Fort Abraham Lincoln in November 1877, the young Lieutenant Scott indicated that the recently captured Nez Perce had been shipped off to Leavenworth and that he would send a photograph of Chief Joseph once the photographs went on sale. Chief Joseph, Scott admitted, was good looking. Then he added,

> The Cheyennes are the Indians I like thou[gh]—braver—cleaner and more manly in every way than any I've seen in the Northwest and I've seen nearly all of them. The Nez Perces are too much like the Crows and of all the horrible cowardly wretches the Crows are the worst. The Nez Perces are not cowardly, but in stature, appearance, dress, hair & filth they are very much alike. The Yanktonais Sioux don't pan out well or the Assinaboines or the Rees, Mandans, or Gros Ventres, the Cheyennes beat them all.[24]

Like a choosy customer at a produce stand, Scott casually tossed aside those groups that fell short of his standards—standards based largely on outward appearance and individual appetite.

Further complicating assessments of tribes and obscuring distinctions between savagery and civility was the officers' recognition, once again, that contact with their own presumably higher culture corrupted tribal life. Time and again they deplored the destructive effects that white contact had on friend and enemy alike. The dregs of white civilization living on the frontier polluted Indian existence. Not atypically, James Rusling lamented the fate of the formerly attractive, peaceable Yuma, who "all seem[ed] corrupted and depraved by contact with the nobler white race." He blamed their degradation on the "open and unblushing looseness and licentiousness of the riff-raff of Arizona City." And Bourke remembered the Papago (now known as the Tohono O'odham) as "honest, laborious, docile, sober, and pure" but assumed they would degenerate after twenty years' contact with his white countrymen.[25]

In the end, military people's attitudes toward particular tribes thwart any attempt to form neat or simple patterns. The officers and their wives demonstrated a capacity to see Indian tribes, whether friendly to the army or not, in multidimensional terms. In part, their comments reflected their circumstances. Certainly in the heat of battle or from the confines of a Bozeman Trail post under virtual siege, officers tended to stress the more negative aspects of their enemy's "tribal character," and they even suspected their Indian friends. But army wives could find Indians more interesting when the Indians did not pose a threat to the women or their families. In calmer moments, army men and women at least attempted to present evenhanded portraits.

None of this, however, is meant to suggest that their images of particular tribes matched reality. That officers and their wives cited positive and negative characteristics in discussing both friend and enemy does not mean that they were either accurate or objective observers of tribal life in the trans-Mississippi West. Not given to careful analyses of Indian cultures, they reacted to Indian behavior, manners, and physical appearance on a cursory, superficial, nonethnological level. They were not ethnologists or anthropologists in the twentieth-century mold; they did not transcend their own values and worldviews and assumptions about savagery and civilization to meet tribes on their own terms.

What the military people's comments about tribes do suggest, however, is that their experiences on the frontier with actual Indians made it more difficult to resort to simple, monolithic stereotypes of good and bad Indians. Even the wild, fierce Apache could be gregarious, witty, and kind to children. Even the Blackfoot, with a reputation for implacable hatred of whites, could be honest, hardy, good humored, emotional, attractive, and affectionate.

Just as generalizations about savagery and civility, or good and bad Indians, proved inadequate in characterizing tribes, so too did such judgments fall short in accounting for individual Indians. Officers exhibited greater empathy for individual Indians than for groups. They sometimes attributed human emotions, motivations, and tendencies to solitary souls. Simultaneously, they often failed to portray native people in terms they would apply to themselves or to people of their own culture. In fact, officers usually revealed a detachment from Indians, a sense that Indians were not only very different but also inscrutable and, all too often, inferior. They relied frequently on classical, mythological, and even biblical imagery in describing individuals, which reflected a habit of thinking about Indians as abstractions. Army officers, then, certainly understood that Indians were humans, but they did not stress Indian humanity, and they resisted identifying too closely with them.

Officers wanted, perhaps needed, to maintain a distance between themselves and Indians. As a result, they rarely developed personal relationships with Indian men. (Their relationships with Indian women will be discussed in the next chapter.) Perhaps opportunities to develop friendships with Indian males proved rare. But more likely, inclinations to befriend Indian men, whether friend or former enemy, were scarce. At any rate, officers' comments about individual men betrayed a restraint, a conscious detachment, and an inability to penetrate racial barriers in order to achieve much genuine communication, sharing, or understanding.

This was true even of officers who took Indians into their homes as guests or as members of their household staff. Lieutenant William Woods Averell came as close as any officer to befriending a former Indian enemy. After dangerous hand-to-hand conflict with a Navajo leader ("I realized that if ever I lost hold of his right wrist," he wrote, "my life would go"), one of Averell's colleagues shot the Indian in the arm and ended the struggle. Upon taking the man back to the post, where the surgeon set the Navajo's broken arm, Averell entertained him in his quarters and "made him some presents of things he fancied." It is certainly interesting, perhaps even remarkable, that there was no lasting animosity between these men. On the other hand, while they became companions, they were never friends. In part, language barriers posed a serious impediment to effective, meaningful communication. In addition, suspicion and caution no doubt undermined potential bonds of fellowship, if not friendship. The Navajo, after all, was virtually a prisoner of war. But Averell's reaction indicated neither malice nor affection. The Indian man was at most a curiosity to him.[26]

Similarly, French-born Colonel Philippe Regis de Trobriand considered a Gros Ventre named Crow Belly an object of amusement. The officer agreed to have some repairs done on the man's single-barreled guns, so "the chief" and several other men waited for the weapons in Trobriand's quarters. After a pantomime conversation concerning combat, Crow Belly requested something to eat, and Trobriand offered a repast of corncakes, bread, and molasses. The Gros Ventre then smoked the Frenchman's pipe while the latter showed him his full-dress epaulets, his arms, and a photograph album of the Army of the Potomac's principal generals. Upon reaching General Ulysses S. Grant's portrait and hearing that he was the commander of all chiefs, Crow Belly

> examined it closely, then putting the open book on his chest, he lowered his head, closed his eyes, and seemed to give himself up to a mental invocation. Several times he went through this "medicine" routine at different places in the book, and I understood by this mystical application, he sought to infuse in himself the bravery, wisdom, and talents of those of our generals whose faces he admired most.

Finally, the repaired guns arrived, and after an emphatic handshake the Gros Ventre took his leave. This encounter entertained Trobriand on a winter's day at Fort Stevenson in Dakota Territory. But when it ended he remarked, "at last I was rid of my visitor." According to this officer's account, Crow Belly perceived the soldier as a comrade-in-arms, a confrere, an equal.[27] Trobriand probably did not return the sentiment.

Erasmus Darwin Keyes, the officer who found the Cherokees so attractive, demonstrated reserve in his relationships with individual Indians. He allowed that his conversation with a San Joaquin man, Chief Pasqual, "tended to prove the unity of the human family." This opinion was encouraged, no doubt, by Pasqual's "uncommon intelligence" and the fact that he spoke Spanish. But there was no indication of rapport between the officer and the Indian—only a comment that their meeting *tended* to suggest a human bond. Neither did Keyes express any particular feeling for a twelve-year-old Mono boy whom he acquired as a servant, proclaiming the youngster "an untutored savage in the broadest sense of that term." Keyes took an interest in Sam's moral development "to observe the characters which the lessons of civilization inscribed most easily on a blank human mind." The officer remarked that Sam had left his parents with no emotion or apparent regret, appeared deficient in curiosity, and rarely laughed. As Sam grew up, according to Keyes, he "hated work and loved whiskey, and ere long he became a drunkard, and I then lost sight of him." In the case of Sam, Keyes perceived him as a "blank human mind," an experiment in civilization and savagery rather than a young boy who could have felt pain at separation from his parents even if he failed to show it, a youngster who thought writing a wonderful mystery even though the West Point–educated Keyes would not teach him letters, or a child who perhaps rarely laughed because there was little reason.[28]

Apparent indifference to an individual's fate was one way an officer could distance himself from an Indian man. Another way was to use imagery that transported the person to the distant past or even to the realm of fiction. Averell's description of a young Navajo who surrendered to the troops during the 1858 Navajo War reflected this approach. "His attitude was a natural expression of dignity and submission," Averell wrote. "No Roman orator ever wore his toga with more ease and grace than did this savage in his splendid blanket." Even an officer not usually impressed with Indians could lapse into such positive, yet impersonal, language when writing about an individual warrior. Army surgeon Rodney Glisan, for example, found the Indians of Washington Territory to be unworthy of the name "noble red man" because their "treachery and ingratitude soon effaced from those who know [them] best, all romantic notions of the elevated traits of [their] character, as imbibed from Cooper's novels." Yet Glisan believed that there were some exceptions to this rule. "Old Tom," of an undisclosed tribe, was "one of the noblest specimens of an Indian I have ever seen." "Bold as a Spartan," Glisan continued, "and with a stentorian voice, he is the *beau ideal* of a warrior."[29] A flattering portrait, perhaps, but not a particularly human one.

Army wives' relationships with lesser-known Indian men could be as detached as those of the officers, but there was an additional element here, one tinged with sexual implications. Ellen Biddle was ill at ease with her servant, an Apache named Charlie. In fact, she felt downright threatened by him. Although she described him as "tall and slender, not very dark, with quite a good expression of countenance," she also related an uncomfortable, even intimidating, incident concerning him. The young man entered her room uninvited, and she ordered him out. Instead of obeying, he picked up a chair, placed it in front of her, and then sat down as if to say, Biddle remembered, " 'I like you very much!' " "I was very much frightened," she wrote, "but I did not wish him to know it." So she escorted him to the door and told him never to enter her room without permission. "[A]lthough he seemed docile and fond of us," she recalled, "I was never quite at ease when alone with him."[30] This incident, along with other women's fears of captivity and the presumed consequent rape, indicates an underlying, unstated sexual tension that permeated officers' wives' perceptions of Indian men.

Yet some, like Martha Summerhayes, admitted a refreshingly candid physical attraction to particular Indian men, although they intended to admire them only from afar. Summerhayes described a servant named Charley as "a handsome naked Cocopah Indian, who wore a belt and a gee-string." Charley, she explained, "appealed to my aesthetic sense in every way. Tall, and well-made, with clean-cut limbs and features, fine smooth copper-colored skin, handsome face . . . this was my Charley, my half-tame Cocopah, my man about the place, my butler in fact." While patronizing, this description indicates that Mrs. Summerhayes found her "man about the place" attractive. He apparently did not return the sentiment, but he "could do nothing but gaze on" Summerhayes's friend, Alice Martin. Martin laughingly asked Summerhayes, " 'Why on earth don't you put some clothes on him?'" Summerhayes replied that her friend needed to "cultivate her aesthetic sense" so that "in a short time she would be able to admire copper-colored creatures of Nature as much as I did."[31]

Interracial flirtations apparently occurred, but they rarely developed into love affairs or sexual involvements, at least among officers' wives. Ione Bradley marveled at the Navajo men she saw at Fort Wingate, "stripped to a breach-cloth, moccasins, and a gay head band, their matchless figures shining in the sun like pieces of bronze statuary." Sarah Canfield admired three Sioux leaders who visited Fort Berthold. Their robes were "only held by the hands [which] had a way of slipping down and displaying their splendid brown shoulders. They were magnificent specimens of manhood." And at a dance at Fort Apache, Martha Summerhayes noticed Chief Diablo's "great good looks" and added that Diablo, entranced with one of the officers' wives, asked the army man how many ponies he would take for her. On another occasion, she noted that the "bucks looked admiringly at the white women." Even women who rarely praised Indian people admired some Indian men's physical appearance. Frances Roe begrudgingly granted that a Cheyenne man she met at Camp Supply in Indian Territory, was "very dignified, and very good-looking too for an Indian." Finding Chief Joseph's Nez Perce band "horrible, dirty looking things all rolled up in blankets," Emily Fitzgerald nonetheless thought their leader "a splendid looking Indian."[32]

Exceptions to this detached view of Indian men came with accounts of more famous individuals. Interestingly, in these cases both officers and wives emphasized the individual's humanity. Rather than grandly exalting or thoroughly disparaging them, military people presented these Indian leaders as approachable, sensitive, reasonable, sometimes emotional, even normal people. A number of military men, for example, afforded Apache leader Cochise this kind of treatment. One man noted that while Cochise was determined to defend his people, he also bore a kindly, even melancholy, expression. Another thought that the Apache had a pleasant face and under normal circumstances was quite courteous. It was only when "Apache wrongs were touched upon, that he became terribly severe in aspect."[33]

Joseph Sladen, who was left in Cochise's camp in 1872 as a hostage while General O. O. Howard returned to Fort Bowie to order a halt in the pursuit of Cochise's people, remembered an interesting exchange with this famous man. As he watched Howard's party disappear from sight, Sladen recalled:

> I suppose I must have had a somewhat sober look upon my face, for the old chief [Cochise] looked earnestly at me and then turning to Jefferds [an interpreter] said,
>
> "Captaine triste."
>
> I laughingly replied, "O, No, not at all. I never felt better in my life."
>
> He said to Jefferds, "Tell the Captain not be triste. He is perfectly safe here. He can leave his saddle in one place, his blanket in another and his pistol in another. . . ."
>
> Later he said to Jefferds, "Tell the Captain that we will have some 'tiswin' here, by and by, and we will all get drunk and have a good time.

Sladen did not greet his invitation "with a hearty second," because his "idea of a good time was not to be in the midst of a camp of drunken Indians." Nonetheless, Sladen admired Cochise. He was, according to the officer, "a striking looking man [who] showed in his person and carriage the force and dignity that gave him an autocratic power over the people whose chief he was."[34] But beyond that, in relating this episode Sladen intended to portray Cochise as a sensitive human being who was aware of Sladen's position and emotional state. He presented Cochise as sympathetic and kind.

Other officers boasted of friendships with illustrious Indian leaders. They had a perhaps understandable inclination to impress their readers with their acquaintance, even intimacy, with celebrities. Whatever the reason, this boasting is certainly significant, given the tone of detachment so typical in accounts of lesser-known Indian men. Along these lines, Lieutenant Charles Gatewood, a Virginian with much scouting experience in Arizona, engineered Geronimo's surrender in 1886 and wrote his wife that he had become "great friends" with his former foe. Upon laying down his arms, Gatewood claimed, Geronimo gave him a "hearty shake of the hand" and told him he would go anywhere with Gatewood, as the officer had never harmed him.[35]

Similarly, Lieutenant C.E.S. Wood befriended Chief Joseph. After the Nez Perce's surrender to the army, Wood received immediate charge of Joseph, and for a time the two men discussed "fully and freely the whole matter" of the Nez Perce conflict. In the process, Joseph and Wood became friends. Years later, after Wood had resigned his commission to begin a Portland, Oregon, law practice, the army officer sent his oldest son, Erskine, to visit Joseph. Joseph adopted the boy, who became a member of the tribe. Even Howard, Joseph's symbolic conqueror, believed he was the leader's friend. Reminiscing about his first meeting with Joseph, Howard wrote, "Joseph put his large black eyes on my face, and maintained a fixed look for some time. It did not appear to me an audacious stare; but I thought he was trying to open the windows of his heart to me, and at the same time endeavoring to read my disposition and character . . . I think Joseph and I became then quite good friends."[36]

Officers' wives repeated the pattern of befriending prominent Indians rather than ordinary ones. As already indicated, Ada Vogdes enjoyed a friendship with the Sioux leader Red Cloud. Anson Mills's wife, Nannie, liked Spotted Tail "from first sight" and frequently invited him to dinner, sometimes in the company of other respected elders. According to Mills, a captain at the time, Spotted Tail offered to paint some pictures of his war exploits for Mrs. Mills. Among the drawings he produced was one of Spotted Tail killing a captain of the United States Army! This indiscretion did not, however, end the friendship.[37]

Several military people thought that the Shoshone leader Washakie resembled various notable Americans, including George Washington and Henry Ward Beecher. (*Wyoming State Archives, Museums and Historical Department*)

The Shoshone leader Washakie was a favorite of Fanny Corbusier, who thought he resembled George Washington, and of Elizabeth Burt, who believed his "features were strikingly like those of Henry Ward Beecher." Martha Summerhayes found that Winnemuca, a Paiute, had a "gentle and dignified demeanor."[38] Of course, Red Cloud, Spotted Tail, Washakie, and Winnemuca were considered friendly to the army by the time these women made their acquaintance.

Why would officers and their wives exhibit detachment for more or less anonymous individuals yet empathy, even friendship, for famous ones? Perhaps they had more opportunity to interact with leaders and to communicate with them through interpreters. Certainly as spokesmen for their people's interests, officers and Indian leaders met and talked. Further, officers may have been inclined to befriend leaders rather than common warriors because they believed these men shared their social status. They may have presumed, perhaps mistakenly, that an Indian leader's relationship to other Indian warriors was analogous to an officer's relationship to enlisted men. Therefore, a prominent individual was worthy of an officer's attention whereas a regular warrior was not. Finally, individuals such as Cochise, Geronimo, and Chief Joseph *were* famous and in some corners of the country even respected. Both army men and women could expect an interested audience when these names appeared in their letters or their published works. Officers may have hoped to enhance their reputation through association with heroic Indians. Friendship connotes mutual respect, and the respect of a notable man, perhaps especially that of a former enemy, was no doubt attractive to some who wore the United States uniform.

Fame alone, however, did not insure an individual Indian a positive portrait in an officer's writings or a potential friendship with him. Sitting Bull, for one, did not appeal to officers. General Nelson Miles acknowledged that he was "a thinking, reasoning being," but he also claimed that the prominent Sioux's appearance when aroused to anger "was more like that of a wild beast." Trobriand pronounced him "one of the most dangerous and evil Indians in Dakota." Another officer thought that Sitting Bull throughout his life had practiced cruelty to animals

and humans alike and "was always imperious and insolent toward our generals" and "as if conscious of a wicked heart and
fearing some punishment . . . was afraid of death, and always
terrified when defeat stared him in the face." Sitting Bull, he
opined, was a coward. In a rare exception, army wife Anna Maus
offered a more charitable picture of Sitting Bull, claiming in her
memoir that he was "noble-minded." She preferred to dwell
upon his "good qualities," which included "obedience to his
mother and loyalty to his father as well as the few acts of mercy
attributed to him." "May all his good deeds," she concluded,
"be examples to be followed by the young men of his tribe, and
all the unworthy things be forgotten."[39]

Of course, an officer's perception of an individual Indian depended partly on that individual's attitude toward him. Some
officers believed that particular Indians liked them, and so, apparently flattered by their affection, they returned the feeling.
Joseph Sladen indicated a certain reluctance to befriend "Na-
Chise" or Natchez, Cochise's son and one of the men who later
joined Geronimo's resistance. But the young Apache was so persistent that Sladen finally succumbed. An "ever present companion" to Sladen while the latter stayed in Cochise's camp,
Na-Chise examined every article of Sladen's dress and saddle-
bags. He would "paw [Sladen] all over," examining the soldier's
hands and hair. But Na-Chise reciprocated. He taught Sladen
the habits and condition of the Apaches, including how to make
a fire by rubbing sticks together. He also taught the officer that
the Apaches went hungry quite often and were continually pursued by army troops. In spite of this, Na-Chise would frequently
approach, Sladen recalled, "and resting his hand on my arm, or
if I was seated, leaning upon me, he would say 'bueno Amigo'
and at my last parting with him . . . he said sadly, 'adios bueno
Amigo.'"[40] Such affection won over Sladen, and he remembered
Na-Chise with great fondness.

An intransigent Indian who openly and consistently despised
whites, on the other hand, would not endear himself to officers.
Such was the case with a number of Pacific Northwest tribesmen. Consequently, officers' accounts of them seem especially
severe. Lieutenant Lawrence Kip, for example, believed that

Yakima leader Owhi and his son Qualchin were addicted to murder and brutality. They were, he pronounced, "the two worst Indians this side of the Rocky Mountains. The son is even more notorious than the father." Kip did not alter his view of them when they came in, on their own accord, to make peace. Within an hour of entering Colonel George Wright's camp, Qualchin was hanged. The young man's pleas for his life only disgusted Kip:

> Bound as his arms were, he fought and struggled till they were obliged to throw him down on his back to fix the noose, he shrieking all the while . . . "stop my friends . . . do not kill me . . . I will give much money, a great many horses." The rope was thrown over the limb of a tree, and he was run up. . . . He died like a coward, and very differently from the manner in which the Indians generally meet their fate.[41]

Rather than prompting sympathy, Qualchin's desperation only reinforced Kip's view of the young man.

Erasmus Darwin Keyes, who observed the same scene, took a different view. "As soon as his hands and feet were bound and the preparations for his death concluded," Keyes remembered, "resistance was out of the question and love of life was the sole motive of his conduct. He was still young, not over twenty-five years of age, and his physical constitution was apparently perfect—that, and his renown as a prince and warrior, gave to his life a charm and value which he was unwilling to surrender." Yet this New Englander expressed a chilling indifference to the father's death. Shot while trying to escape, Owhi suffered for two hours, lying across his horse, as Keyes put it, "like the carcass of a dead wolf" and looking "like a dying bull dog," before he finally succumbed. The officer found it a "gloomy" though "not terrible" end.[42]

Keyes displayed a similar callousness at the death of a Klickitat leader named Kanaskat, although Keyes did admit that the latter's demise haunted him even after a lapse of twenty-seven years. Keyes maintained that Kanaskat "was not only noted for the ingenious devices of torture that he would practice on his victims, but for the ferocious pertinacity with which he began and continued the war." During the conflict, a soldier shot Kanaskat and brought him in, wounded but not yet dead. When the warrior reportedly shouted, "'My heart is wicked toward the whites, and always will be, and you had better kill me,'" Corporal O'Shaughnessy "placed the muzzle of his rifle close to the chieftain's temple, blew a hole through his head, and scattered the brains about." Keyes went on:

> Never before did I gaze on a human countenance in which hate and blasted hope were so horribly depicted. It seemed to me, while I was regarding the fierce contortions and burning gaze of the chief, that I was in the presence of a defiant demon whose fitting habitation was the most fulgent cavern of Hell. . . . There was a diabolical fascination in the massive jaw, fixed scowl, and bronzed skin of the monster's visage, that drew me to cross the field several times to gaze on it where he lay, face up and eyes wide open. . . . There was no line that pity or tenderness, or holy meditation has ever traced upon it. It presented a scene of absolute moral desolation more awful than the Dead Sea or the Crater of Etna.

Keyes acknowledged that Kanaskat was a "model Indian patriot," but he was also, in Keyes's view, obstinately sulky, ferociously persistent in war, and ultimately the greatest foe of whites, so he deserved no respect in death. In fact, Keyes did not even bury the Indian's body. "Regarding the carcass of the dead chief as that of an unclean animal that men hunt for the love of havoc," Keyes wrote, "we left it in the field unburied, and went on our way to fight his people."[43]

Somewhat less heartless and certainly less dramatic, Luther Bradley dismissed Crazy Horse's death with a few words: "So ends a troubled life." He believed that the Sioux leader "was active for mischief and his death is a good thing for his own people as well as for us." Several days later, Bradley noted that many of the Indians expressed satisfaction at Crazy Horse's death and were relieved that he was "out of the way."[44]

Military men and women did not deny the Indians' humanity, but neither did they consistently confirm it. All acknowledged that Indians belonged to the human species, yet their language and imagery undermined such assertions. With the exception of notable native leaders, army people tended toward abstract or impersonal depictions of Indian men. To be sure, officers' ideas about Indians served their own emotional and psychological needs far more than they provided realistic information about Indians. A degree of detachment was perhaps necessary to carry out military duties. In their comments about and relationships with Indian women, however, the tone of detachment would often slip away.

4 / Indian Women

*The squaws do the work . . . but their life is unquestionably
far happier than the do-nothing, thankless, dyspeptic life led
by a majority of American women.*
—COLONEL ALBERT BRACKETT

As Lieutenant John Bourke sauntered through the Santo Domingo Pueblo one day in 1881, he came upon a young couple
mending a quarrel, "for which each was heartily sorry." The
man was especially good-looking and the woman shapely,
pretty, and well dressed. Bourke watched them surreptitiously.
When the youthful Pueblo drew closer to the woman, he "was
received with a disdain tempered with so much sweetness and
affection that he wilted at once, and, instead of boldly asserting
himself, dared do nothing but timidly touch her hand." Finally,
she relented by accepting his grasp, and "he with earnest
warmth was pouring into her ears words whose purport it was
not difficult to conjecture."

Bourke, who pursued Indians not only with a soldier's rifle
but also with an ethnographer's notebook, thus presented an
unconventional glimpse of Indian people in a very human pose.
He believed this view to be rare. "So much stuff and nonsense
have been written about the entire absence of affection from the
Indian character, especially in relations between the sexes," he
commented, "that it affords me great pleasure to note this little
incident, in which the parties acted with perfect freedom from
the restraint the known presence of strangers imposes."[1]

This officer's acknowledgment of romantic love between Indian men and women was exceptional, for nineteenth-century
stereotypes conveyed a grim image of Indian relationships, one
more bestial than human. Yet Bourke's assertion of Indian humanity in the context of writing about Indian women was not
uncommon among army accounts. In fact, the worlds of Anglo
military men and women and Indian women were not as separate as one might expect. This meant, of course, that army

people had to reconsider their preconceptions about native women—expectations of "Indian princesses" or "dirty squaws" shaped by schoolbooks, captivity narratives, and Cooper's novels—because noble savagery had its feminine component. The noble Indian woman was an archetypal Indian princess, a Pocahontas. She was virginal yet primitively passionate. She was childlike, naturally innocent, and inclined toward civilization and Christianity. She was drawn to white men, helping and mating with them. And, of course, she was beautiful.[2] Conversely, the savage woman was a squat, haggard, ugly, papoose-lugging drudge who toiled endlessly while her husband sported on the hunting grounds or lolled about the lodge. She lived a most unfortunate, brutal life. Furthermore, she fought enemies with a vengeance and thirst for blood unmatched by any man. Both princess and squaw operated as symbols, devoid of flesh and blood. Naturally, these widely accepted notions about Indian women obscured their humanity.

It is notable that officers and their wives applied neither the princess nor the squaw motif to all Indian women and were particularly reluctant to use the princess image. Lieutenant C. A. Woodward did identify a Comanche chief's daughter as "one of the most comely Indian maidens of the wild tribes I have met," noting that she was beautifully garbed in bright colors and sat astride her horse "as only the queens of the forest can do." And Colonel James F. Rusling praised a Ute girl—the princess, the beauty, the pet of the tribe, he claimed, who was "resplendent in paint and feathers" and who had "a rich and musical laugh."[3]

More common, however, was Lieutenant James W. Steele's description of the squaw:

> She is beaten, abused, reviled, driven like any other beast of burden. She is bought and sold; wife, mother, and pack animal, joined in one hideous and hopeless whole. Nevertheless, in all that is peculiarly Indianesque, she excels her master. In cunning, hatred, and revenge, in the specialties of cruelty and the refinements of torture, she has no equal on earth or in Hades. There is really no more beauty to be found among Indian "maidens" than there is among gorillas. . . . More false than ever Cooper's wonderful tales, are the poems which descant upon the charms of dusky

love and the romance of wilderness affection. . . . The man who invented those charming but phenomenally false Indian ideals, and first crowned the universal squaw—squat, angular, pig-eyed, ragged, wretched, and insect-haunted—with the roses of love, ought to see the woman once, and as a punishment, to be subjected for a session to her indescribable blandishment.[4]

Army wives agreed that comely females were rare. They repeated the theory that Indian women were unattractive because of hard work and continual exposure to the elements. Ellen Biddle considered the Cheyenne women she met at Fort Lyon "repulsive in appearance; their faces were full of deep lines, showing the hardships they must have endured," and another found that Indian women in Texas "looked more like men than women," their countenances "unattractive and inexpressive . . . not troubled by any useless sensibility."[5]

The white women, of course, insisted that the occasionally attractive Indian women were princesses. One officer's wife, for example, believed that Wauk, an Arapaho, must have been a princess by birth, since she was tall, slender, and "very unlike the short, fat squaws one usually sees." Elizabeth Custer identified Mo-nah-see-tah, a Cheyenne woman whom her husband found attractive, as a "Princess, the ranking woman of them all." She "had not been married long enough," Mrs. Custer explained, "to fade and grow old with manual labor."[6]

Both men and women complained that Indian men enslaved their women. Such treatment, they argued, was an inevitable condition of the Indians' savage state. A society's treatment of its women served as a barometer measuring its level of civility. Civilized people pampered women; savage people enslaved them. Most officers would have accepted Kentucky-born West Point graduate Richard Johnson's maxim that "[t]he higher the human family rises in the scale of civilization, the more deference is paid to woman. Among educated and refined people in America she is queen, and all men bow to her as they should."[7] Among Indians, in contrast, she is a slave.

Such pat images of Indian women as either beautiful princesses or haggard slaves naturally seeped into army accounts of

frontier life. Indeed, given their wide acceptance and use in the
nineteenth century, their absence would have been remarkable.
In spite of their all-pervasive influence, however, some military
people discarded these concepts. A significant number of them
established meaningful and genuine communication with Indian women. They achieved a measure of understanding that at
least temporarily transcended notions of civilization and savagery or the roles of the conqueror and conquered. "In fact,"
wrote Texas-born Lieutenant Britton Davis about Chiricahua
and Warm Springs Apaches with an almost unbelievable naivete, "we began to find them decidedly human."[8] Such a revela-
tion was not Davis's alone. Others shared his discovery that Indian women's actual experiences were richer, more diverse, and
simply more human than the conquest mythology allowed, and
they discovered and wrote about this more frequently with respect to Indian women than men. Also, the officers made this
discovery more often than did their wives.

In the process, some men simultaneously expressed thinly
veiled doubts about Anglo-American cultural superiority. They
presented Indian women's lives in very positive terms and even
asserted that these women had advantages over Anglo-American women. In fact, a few claimed that the latter should emulate
the former. Some praised the primitive virtues of a feminine
out-of-doors life and criticized genteel women's aversion to it.
Some lauded Indian women's power in the family or even the
tribe. Some considered native childbirth practices healthier
than those of Anglo-American women. Army wives most assuredly did not agree. In all cases, however, comments about
native women served as vehicles through which military people
reflected upon themselves and even engaged in debate about
women's proper role in society, the value of outdoor exercise for
women, the "civilized" institution of marriage, and nineteenth-
century middle-class methods of childbirth. Of course, officers
were not relating accurate anthropological observations about
these women, nor were they able to shake off all their stereotypes. As with Indian men, their comments on Indian women
reveal more about Anglo-American civilization's ideas of cul-

ture, savagery, and in this case, women's proper sphere than they do about the realities of Indian women's lives.

Even officers who emphasized the drudgery and degradation of Indian womanhood wrestled with a puzzling dilemma: Indian women did not despise their lives; rather, they enjoyed themselves. Why were these women, living apparently brutal and desperate lives, happy? Why did they appear content with endless, wearisome servitude, and why did they submit to their fate without complaint? Admitting that "a happier, more light-hearted, more content woman cannot be found" than an Indian woman, Colonel Richard Irving Dodge concluded that her bliss was due either to ignorance of alternatives or constant work that kept her from reflecting on the horrors of her life. But Colonel Albert Brackett offered a different explanation. The Shoshone and Ute women he met labored continually, pitching and packing up tipis, carrying wood and water, cooking, and engaging in "all the drudgery of the camp." He also declared their lives to be "unquestionably far happier than the do-nothing, thankless dyspeptic life led by a majority of American women." One might be inclined to pity them for their lives of hard work, Brackett argued, but their health and happiness stemmed from living the out-of-doors life and getting plenty of exercise. These practices constituted the "main points in the pursuit of happiness."[9]

To come to such conclusions, these military men had to adjust their standards of appropriate behavior for women—at least for Indian women. White women riding astride mounts, rather than sidesaddle, for example, scandalized them. But they accepted, even admired, the practice among Indian women. Retired captain Joseph Sladen thus rhapsodized about Apache women, their long hair dangling down their backs in dark braids: "I have seldom seen a prettier picture than that of one of these young women sitting astride a horse and riding like the wind." Captain Randolph Marcy admired Plains Indian women equestrians who, riding astride their horses, were every bit as skillful as men. He was especially impressed with two Comanche women who lassoed several antelope with "unerring precision" from horseback.[10]

Sladen and Marcy may not have urged their wives or daughters to adopt Apache or Comanche horsemanship practices, but Brackett unquestionably meant his comments on the outdoor life as a criticism of white, middle-class women's indoor life. And his was not a lone voice. In matters of matrimony and maternity, some officers believed that Indian women compared favorably with white women. This was especially so of south-western tribal women who lived in permanent villages where men shared the agricultural work, and so more closely approximated the Anglo-American division of labor between the sexes. Consequently, officers less frequently presented them as slaves and drudges, and beyond this, they even claimed that some southwestern women had economic advantages, marital rights, and political privileges unknown to white women. Lieutenant William Woods Averell, for example, noted that the Navajo chiefs' wives were respected and that sometimes "their voices were heard in the councils." Captain John Bourke reported that Hopi women not only managed but owned their houses, and husbands could not sell household goods without their wives' permission.[11]

Even Lieutenant James Steele commended Pueblo women as "creatures . . . whose dignity would not suffer by comparison with some of the queens of civilization." Furthermore, he believed that unlike the white women who demanded rights but engaged in no productive labor, Pueblo women demonstrated that they had "rights all along because they engaged in manly labor," and so deserved them. He continued:

> It is a question whether the much-discussed subject of woman's rights really had its origins in the minds of cultivated and highly-educated people. Among all the aboriginal tribes of America, women have had their "rights" time whereof the memory of their brutes of husbands runs not to the contrary. And the truth is that those rights entail upon the sex, as well in civilization as in savagery, that concomitant of equal drudgery which the Logans and the Stantons and the Miss Dickinsons would be very unwilling to assume. To the privileges and labors of masculinity, the conditions of civilization seem to be an eternal bar.

To underscore his point, Steele mentioned a Pueblo woman who sold piñon nuts on an Albuquerque street corner while juggling her two-day-old baby on her hip. "Such women as these," Steele snapped, "are alone physically competent to maintain rights."[12]

Others noted Indian women's marital rights without offering a similar commentary on whether white women also deserved such prerogatives. At the same time, these men implied that the Indian way undoubtedly offered advantages to women, advantages that they found attractive. While visiting the Shawnee and the Delaware, Captain Randolph Marcy learned that their marriage contract bound a couple only as long as husband and wife wanted it so. If a woman left her husband, she was authorized by their law to take all the personal property she possessed at the time of the marriage, and the husband had no claim on it. This army explorer found such practices very just, for they made a woman somewhat independent of her husband and probably deterred husbands from behaving tyrannically and abusing their wives.[13]

In a comment that may have shocked some of his more genteel readers, Colonel Richard Dodge maintained that Indian women were virtually owned, like property, by their husbands, who could beat or even kill them with impunity. Yet, he wrote, "the domestic life of the Indian will bear comparison with that of the average civilized communities." Husbands were generally kind; wives generally faithful, obedient, and industrious. Moreover, Indian women did have the right, according to Dodge, to leave one husband for another, suffering no social stigma in the process. Rather than viewing this separation and remarriage process as barbarous, he regarded it as beneficial, a practice that probably ameliorated the condition of Indian women. They could simply leave cruel husbands for kinder ones. Civilized women did not have this option, or at least it was obtained less easily and at greater social cost.[14]

Musing about Indian marriages prompted similar comparisons plus an unusual statement of cultural relativism from the pen of Colonel Trobriand. He believed that Indian liaisons were principally commercial propositions whereby Indian men bought and sold women "almost as they buy or hire a horse." Yet, he argued, young girls sought out these transactions, and if they became mothers in the process, suffered no shame or embarrassment among their people and eventually found husbands who willingly adopted children born out of wedlock. They were not perceived, nor did they see themselves, as debauched. They were not expelled from their community or society in the way a "civilized" woman would be. Trobriand stated that, although Christians may consider such behavior immoral, neither the Indians nor he saw it that way. "[E]verything in this world is relative," he philosophized, "nothing is absolute but mathematical truth, which has nothing in common with philosophical truth." That was the lesson he had learned from studying Indian customs firsthand. In fact, his studies had opened "visions of great scope," as he examined the relationship between the causes of particular behavior and its effects.[15] For some army officers, then, the institution of marriage and the status of women opened up "visions of great scope," suggesting alternatives to their culture's manners and morality.

The same was not true of officers' wives. They most assuredly did not turn to native models of marriage. Further, they certainly did not share Trobriand's or Dodge's or Marcy's views about Indian women's greater rights or political power. Such opinions would have annoyed, perhaps even infuriated, the army wives, who firmly believed in their unequivocal superiority to Indian women. They never described Indian women's position or status as more advantageous than their own.

Instead, they held firm to the idea that Indian men enslaved their wives. In this mold, Elizabeth Burt remembered that "her first impression of domestic life among the Indians was intensely disagreeable and prejudiced me greatly against the lordly chiefs." She watched a woman struggling with a heavy sack while a man followed behind, prodding her with a stick. "The brute," she gasped, "[h]ow I wished for a good, strong soldier to knock him down." Mrs. Custer deemed Cheyenne women "servile squaws" and rather remarkably explained away polygamy as an advantage for Indian women because it meant that the wives would divide the heavy labor. Fanny Corbusier did acknowledge that among the Nevada Paiute, women ruled the household and if a husband did not behave, he could be tossed out.[16] Such a view was rare. Most often, officers' wives presented Indian women as terribly oppressed. They seemed, in fact, more intent on stressing their supposed enslavement than did the officers.

Apparently officers' wives did not discuss the issue with Indian women. They merely assumed that Indian women were, and even perceived themselves to be, oppressed. Perhaps if they had talked with native women about such matters, they could have broadened their view of the Indian women's status and power within their own cultures. Recent anthropological and historical scholarship challenges as ethnocentric the belief that Indians themselves considered women subordinate to men, but none of the army wives questioned this assumption in the nineteenth century.[17]

Why would white women, more than white men, insist on Indian women's supposed enslavement and degradation? They did not seem to be making a statement about oppressed womanhood in general. There is little indication that the officers' wives experienced any sense of the twentieth-century idea of "sisterhood" or a shared female culture with native women (although several exceptions to this, particularly in the matters of childbirth and child rearing, are noted below). Instead, officers' wives preferred to set themselves apart from and above Indian women. They seemed compelled to assert their superiority and appear to have been more rigid than men in setting civilized standards for women.

Indian women's work obviously did not mesh with white culture's prescribed female behavior, which some historians define as "the cult of domesticity," the belief that woman's sphere is in the home, where she provides domestic tranquility for her husband and children and where she communicates moral and cultural values to the family.[18] To do other than to deplore Indian women's physical labor, outdoor life, and general position within their society would have involved eroding an ideology that provided middle- and upper-class white women, such as officers' wives, with an important place and purpose on the western frontier. When officers such as Brackett or Trobriand challenged civilized standards of marriage and morality, they challenged the very foundation of these white women's lives. The women were not prepared to have that foundation shaken, particularly when the proposed alternative came from the "savage" world of "inferior" Indians.

The wives would not have responded any more favorably to those officers who admired Indian women's vitality in childbirth and concluded that the "Indian way" of bringing children into the world was preferable to the civilized way. Several men extolled the virtues of native women's stamina, physical endurance, and capacity to continue working right up to, and almost immediately after, parturition. They indicated that white women should emulate Indian women on this matter. Childbirth practices, then, became another vehicle by which officers could reprove civilization and its women—particularly those of their own social set.

Trobriand, for example, declared Indian women's childbirth practices "extraordinary." To him, working up to the onset of labor pains and returning to work the day after giving birth was natural and appropriate. Civilization, he complained, had replaced this natural and easy process with "long torture, medical attendance, intervention of chloroform, puerperal fever, two weeks in bed, thirty days in the bedroom, and such precaution." Civilized people created artificial environments for themselves and their bodies and in the process, "physically and morally . . . corrupted the work of nature." As a result, white women became weak and often died in the course of childbirth, while Indian mothers gathered up their babies and healthily, vigorously went on their way.[19]

William T. Parker, a soldier who eventually became a medical doctor, also praised Indian women's stamina, especially regarding "womanly functions." A great admirer of their "fortitude, perseverance and unflagging devotion to womanly duty," particularly maternal duties, Parker attributed their supposed ease in childbirth to large hips, "capacious" pelvises, and robust health. Unfortunately, he added, Indian women were beginning to consult white doctors and acquire white methods of child-bearing, to their detriment. "From an out-of-doors life of activity with plenty of fresh game and wholesome food and clear water, with a healthful te-pee for home, the change has been made to log cabins with overheated close air." The result was that the Indian women's naturally healthy constitutions were deteriorating, and miscarriages and disease were increasing "to the surprise and disgust of the Indian mothers and grandmothers." Parker meant not only to praise Indian women but also to criticize, albeit gently, the civilizing program that taught native women the useless pastimes of genteel ladies: "embroidery, poetry, music, sentimental and religious readings."[20]

Unfortunately, Indian childbirth practices did not merit much attention in army wives' writings, so the subject did not develop into a debate between the white men and women. Perhaps Victorian sensibilities prevented these ladies from more open expression of thoughts about childbirth, at least on paper. Whatever the reason for their reticence, there is certainly no indication that they shared Colonel Trobriand's opinion that Indian childbirth practices were extraordinary or William Parker's contention that they were superior to white women's.

Explaining that Apache women treated their newborn babies to an ice-cold bath, Lydia Lane merely noted, "it must have been disagreeable." She was not impressed with mother's or baby's fortitude. While Katherine Gibson's husband was escorting a number of Ponca prisoners, one woman dropped out of the line, disappeared behind a bush, and eventually emerged with a baby in her arms. The officer placed the woman in a wagon so she could rest and brought her water. Mrs. Gibson offered no judgment on either the woman's methods or her physical strength. Nevertheless, her husband's attentions toward the Ponca woman proved consequential. When Mrs. Gibson gave birth to their first and only child, the Ponca husband brought several beaver skins for the baby, a gesture that deeply touched the officer. His kindness to a former captive was now returned. "In parting," Gibson wrote, "the captain said, gripping the rough hand in a warm clasp, 'Again let me thank you for your gift. Also my squaw thanks you, and may the Great Spirit prosper you and bring you good hunting.'"[21] This story is especially notable for the roles the army officer and the Indian father played in joining the two families around the experiences of childbirth and motherhood—events usually envisioned as women's affairs.

To be sure, Indian and white women breached barriers through the bonds of motherhood without a man's intervention, and if army wives did not celebrate Indian methods of childbirth, they did occasionally acknowledge that motherhood could forge a link with native women. Martha Summerhayes remembered one such occasion. She was languishing in her quarters, feeling rather weepy and quite uncertain how to cope with her new, fretting baby:

> The seventh day after the birth of the baby, a delegation of several [Apache] squaws, wives of chiefs, came to pay me a formal visit. They brought me some finely woven baskets, and a beautiful papoose-basket or cradle, such as they carry their own babies in. . . . [I]t was their best work. I admired it, and tried to express to them my thanks. These squaws took my baby (he was lying beside me on the bed), then, cooing and chuckling, they looked about the room, until they found a small pillow, which they laid into the basket-cradle, then put my baby in, drew the flaps together, and laced him into it; then stood it up, and laid it down, and laughed again in their gentle manner, and finally soothed him to sleep. I was quite touched by the friendliness of it all.[22]

In at least one case, such beneficial interaction worked in the opposite direction. When presenting his wife's description of the following experience in his autobiography, Captain Richard Pratt explained that it demonstrated "the delicate perception of the Indian woman, the strong mother love in all races." His wife, working in her quarters at Fort Arbuckle with the outer door open, noticed a "most miserable and repulsive squaw" approaching. As the Kiowa woman scooped up the Pratt baby in her arms, the officer's wife sprang forward and reclaimed her daughter:

> The poor miserable woman looked at me in the most pitiful manner, then gathering up the corner of her blanket she held it as one would hold a sick infant, at the same time crooning a mournful cry, she made a sign that her baby had died, and to tell how great

her grief, she showed she had cut off her little finger at the second joint, which was one of the extreme mourning customs of the Kiowas. . . . [M]y sympathies were so moved that almost unconsciously I replaced our baby in her arms. Tenderly and carefully, the bereaved Indian mother handled her as she passed her hands over the plump little limbs. After some moments she handed her back with a grateful look and with a hearty handshake she departed.

One week later the Kiowa woman returned with a basket of wild plums for the Pratts. Again she held the Pratt child "and this time with signs asked permission and was permitted to kiss the child, for this sorrowing Indian mother was no longer repulsive."[23] Another week passed and she returned with two buffalo tongues, asking only the chance to hold the baby. This was the last time Mrs. Pratt saw the Kiowa woman.

The Apache delegation to Mrs. Summerhayes's quarters and Mrs. Pratt's kindness for the mourning Kiowa woman demonstrated the capacity of both Indian and white women to help one another. Captain Gibson's treatment of the Ponca woman and the Ponca father's return gesture indicate that men could be equally sensitive. That such kindnesses related to matters of motherhood suggests that both sexes, as well as both races, recognized it as a universal experience, one that led to at least temporary reciprocal compassion and understanding.

These experiences demonstrate the complexity of relationships between military and Indian people. They also indicate the folly of assuming that women were more likely to exercise compassion or perceive Indians in notably more positive ways than men. At the same time, they should not overshadow the barriers that continued to exist between Indian and white on the military frontier, and the most obvious barrier was the warfare between army and Indian—warfare that sometimes included native women fighters.

The question of the role of Indian women in warfare proved a sticky one for army officers. The officers' code of gentlemanly conduct did not condone shooting at women or children. On top

of that, word that women and children were among the casualties in engagements such as the battles of the Washita or
Wounded Knee or Major Eugene Baker's 1870 attack on a Piegan
village inflamed critics of Indian policy and the army's role in it.
Stung by eastern humanitarians' charges that they were brutal,
blood-thirsty renegades of the border and resenting insinuations
that they purposefully killed women and children, officers insisted that these deaths were accidental rather than intentional.
No one deplored these incidents more than the troopers, some
maintained. Others argued that Indian women took up arms
against soldiers and consequently became fair targets for troopers' bullets.[24]

In defending themselves against critics who charged them
with murdering Indian women, officers frequently resorted to
standard squaw stereotypes. Once a native woman became en-
raged, Lieutenant Robert G. Carter explained, "[n]ot a gleam of
pity entered her feminine breast. She was a cold-blooded, thirsty
vulture, only intent upon her prey, as good as the warrior himself." For the soldier, he continued, "[t]here was little or no time
for false sentiment, courtesy or knightly gallantry in the face of
a 'gun' in the hands of an infuriated squaw intent on 'getting
somebody.'" Carter acknowledged that love and fear for the children's safety motivated Indian women to take up arms and that
white mothers would certainly share this instinct. Yet, in an
Indian woman, Carter insisted, it partook more of "savage devotion and instinctive traits of the wild animal." When cornered,
she fought with all the strength of her savage nature and with
the "desperation of a tigress." Carter, who would later receive a
Congressional Medal of Honor for distinguished service against
Indians along the Brazos River in Texas, added that "There were
few or none of the 'peace-and-order' loving members of the
pussy-footed pacifists of that period, or members of the press,
who oftentimes referred to her as the *'poor defenceless squaw,'*
who would have cared to put themselves in her way under any
conditions of battle." After the battle, he went on, Indian
women could be found scalping and torturing the wounded, cutting off the fingers and toes of those still alive, and indulging in
other barbarous practices.[25]

Yet even on this matter, officers did not agree. One individual provided an explanation for such practices, indicating that it was a way to express contempt for an enemy and also a way to keep the enemy's spirit "from entering the Realms of the Blest." He certainly did not condone such behavior, but in offering spiritual or religious reasons for its practice, he mitigated the "savagery" of it. Others openly showed respect for Indian women who defended their homes and families. During the Gila Expedition of 1857, a native woman's valiant attempt to carry her wounded husband off the battlefield greatly impressed Lieutenant John Van Deusen Du Bois. He was sickened when troopers killed them both. Cochise's sister, a fifty-year-old widow with "strongly marked, unprepossessing features giving evidence of a strong will," impressed Joseph Sladen. She was, he said, the "presiding genius" of an Apache outpost overlooking the road to Fort Bowie. While it was unusual for a woman to have such responsibility, this English-born officer wrote, Cochise had great confidence in his sister, and the army officer agreed that her "independence and force seemed to justify this faith in her ability." Finally, Lieutenant Britton Davis later recalled that while fighting Apaches in 1882, he heard groans from a wounded enemy firing on troopers. Charging the sharpshooter's position, the soldiers discovered a young woman shielding an infant. She drew a knife and fought the men until they finally overpowered and disarmed her. She had a bullet-shattered leg, Davis remembered, but did not utter a single groan when, without anesthesia, her leg was amputated. "She stood it," he noted, "without a murmur."[26]

Although officers publicly maintained that Indian women were not the intended targets of army bullets, their personal papers reveal that the army did not always take great care to protect noncombatants during a fight. Lieutenant Walter S. Schuyler, on a scouting mission from Camp Verde to Fort McDowell in Arizona Territory in 1873, noted in his field journal that upon finding a camp of Indians, his men woke them by firing into their homes without warning. "Two bucks and one squaw got away," he calculated, without indicating how many other women or children did not. The previous year Schuyler, a

Toos-clay-zay, a Chiricahua Apache, was married to Cochise and was the mother of Natchez. (*American Heritage Center, University of Wyoming*)

member of one of New York's most prominent families, almost casually reported to his father that in an attack on an Apache-Mojave village, forty Indians were killed. Any children who survived the fight were left on the battlefield to be picked up later by their kinswomen or whoever would care for them.[27]

Even if officers gave precise orders to spare women and children, soldiers sometimes either deliberately or accidentally disobeyed them. Such was the case in an incident John Bourke, a lieutenant at the time, related in his diary during an 1872 Apache conflict. "Orders were given to make no charge upon the works, to pick off every Indian showing his head, to spare every woman & child, but to kill every man." After the battle, Bourke and others charged the spot where the Apaches were entrapped, however, and found "a horrible spectacle" of seventy-two bodies. Although Bourke did not state the number of women and children among the dead, it is unlikely that they avoided the soldiers' fire. Five years later, on reaching the place where the Nez Perce had defeated Colonel John Gibbon's forces, army doctor John Fitzgerald wrote his wife that they found thirty dead Indians, mostly women and children. "I was told by one of General Gibbon's officers," he explained, "that the squaws were not shot at until two officers were wounded by them, and a soldier or two killed. Then the men shot every Indian they caught sight of—men, women, and children. I saw five or six children from 8 to 12 years old, as near as I could determine."[28]

Fitzgerald's explanation mirrored the most common justification that officers recorded on the matter of Indian women casualties. Once Indian women took up arms against soldiers, they became fair game for trooper retaliation. Others insisted that Indian depredations brought the army down upon the natives to punish them for their misdeeds. If women and children died in the process, that was the regrettable but necessary result of a well-deserved punishment.

Further, the devastatingly effective technique of surprise attacks on Indian villages for the purpose of destroying property as well as lives unfortunately allowed no means by which women and children could escape. By the end of the Civil War, the army had established two important and related strategies that it could apply to western Indians. The first concerned winter campaigning. Winter was a season when Plains Indians, for example, were more sedentary and also more vulnerable. If their food stores were destroyed, the effects could be disastrous for the entire group. The second strategy involved total war. This meant waging war not only against combatants but also against noncombatants. If women and children were not deliberately killed, they could certainly die when food, housing, livestock, and other material necessities were destroyed. The enemy was left destitute, demoralized, and defeated in total war. Neither gender nor age could protect a person from these consequences. Total war posed moral dilemmas, however. It meant that either directly or indirectly, officers were limiting noncombatants' chances of survival, short of surrender. But those who favored total war argued that the strategy could bring about a quicker resolution to the conflict. War, to these men, was a business, and the best way to end it was to speed up the process by waging war against the enemy's civilians as well as the enemy's soldiers.[29]

Along these lines, Captain Lewis Thompson asserted that finding dead women and children after a battle was terribly sad but inevitable. In a bit of doggerel, he explained, "But things like that we know must be, / After a famous victory." No one deplored these incidents more than the troopers, Thompson argued. As for critics who censured the cavalry for taking advantage of surprise attacks, he posited, "By any code which society ever instituted to protect its citizens and punish outlaws, these Indians were guilty of death; yet their crimes were forgotten in the face of their terrible punishment."[30]

Such apparently hard-hearted explanations, however, do not hint at officers' occasional acts of mercy, toward Indian children in particular, after such battles. Several men discovered children either orphaned by the fighting or lost in the melee. They took them in, sometimes temporarily, sometimes permanently. During the Bannock War of 1878, after Umatilla scouts attacked a camp and killed about fifteen Indians, army surgeon John Fitzgerald's men "found a poor, little, black-eyed, Indian baby girl, about 8 or 10 months old, that had been abandoned by its savage mother," Fitzgerald explained to his wife. He agreed to care for her and fed the baby its supper. "I want you to tell Bess and Burt [their children] all about this and ask them if they would like to have a little Indian baby sister. Shall I bring it home to you, dear?" he asked, using the impersonal pronoun in referring to the child. Then he quickly added, "(I confess I have not the remotest idea of such a thing so rest easily)."[31]

In his diary, Bourke related a similar tale about a five-year-old girl orphaned by the Battle of the Slim Buttes. Taken with her beauty, he brought her to headquarters, where, "in spite of her vociferous screams which quieted down very soon after she saw our dinner set out upon the piece of buffalo robe . . . our little Indian child, speedily recovered her composure and ate as heartily as the rest of us." Captain Charles King told the same story, claiming that the girl was so pretty, wet, cold, and hungry that "Bourke's big heart [w]as touched." Following the same battle, Captain Anson Mills's men found a three- or four-year-old girl. After comforting and feeding her, Mills took her to see the captives and the dead in an attempt to find her mother. Upon seeing two "fine looking half-breed squaws, only partly dressed, bloody and mangled with many wounds," the little girl began to scream until Mills placed her on the ground, whereupon she ran and embraced one of the dead women. "On returning to my station," Mills later wrote, "I told Adjutant [Henry] Lemly I intended to adopt this little girl, as I had slain her mother." It was only later, when the adjutant asked how Mrs. Mills would react, and perhaps after the wrenching pain of that scene had begun to fade, that Mills realized he had not "given that side of the matter a thought and I decided to leave the child where I found her."[32]

Other officers overcame concerns about their wives' displeasure and brought Indian children home. Although he never formally adopted the child, Captain S.B.M. Young took in an Indian baby that soldiers found trying to nurse her dead mother in Arizona. Initially, his wife was horrified to see the child, but she finally agreed to care for "Ogarita," who remained part of the family until her death at age four.[33]

Those who did take in Indian orphans demonstrated little-

Captain S.B.M. Young brought the Apache girl at left home after a
battle in which soldiers discovered her trying to nurse her dead
mother. (*U.S. Army Military History Institute*)

known incidents of individual compassion. Such acts hardly
counterbalance the pain and suffering of the Indian wars, but
they do serve to remind us that military men could be moved in
the presence of such pain to attempt some mitigation of it—
slight, even insignificant, as their gestures might seem. Perhaps
more important, Anson Mills's statement that he intended to
adopt the Indian child because he had killed her mother indicates a sense of personal responsibility for the tragedy. That
momentary confession of individual accountability certainly
occurred to others as well.

Most army men and women experienced their most prolonged
encounters with native women not on battlefields but in camps
or on reservations near military garrisons. These encounters
provided an opportunity to observe the Indians in domestic

situations and to establish relationships with individuals. Officers' wives rarely pursued friendships with Indian women, however. In fact, they reserved most comments about individuals to prominent men, perhaps perceiving the men as more powerful and more interesting. In ignoring individual Indian women, officers' wives were acting in accord with what one anthropologist describes as "the pervasive European idea that women constitute the passive, inferior, and hidden side of humanity." Consequently, "Plains Indian women [were] rarely visible as individuals."[34]

It is also possible that Indian women did not welcome intimacy with army wives. One officer noted that when a party from Fort Sill picnicked near a Kiowa camp and then decided to tour it, their "very inquisitive manner disgusted the squaws who look with disdain on white women and their airs."[35] There is no doubt that many officers' wives considered themselves the social and racial superiors of Indian women. Indian women certainly discerned this, and such sentiments did not, of course, encourage friendship. Indian women may have returned the sentiment, seeing the white women as *their* inferiors. Unfortunately, military men and women did not record Indian women's perceptions of white women with any regularity, so the best one can do is speculate on the extent of their interest in interaction.

Occasionally, however, army wives and Indian women established a temporary rapport, although the native women remain largely anonymous in the wives' accounts. For fleeting moments, at least, these officers' wives sensed connections beyond the maternal ones already noted. Elizabeth Custer, for example, sympathized with a Cheyenne widow she encountered after the Battle of the Washita. The woman, one of the captives from that fight, approached Lieutenant Colonel Custer with her two sons in tow and explained that their father had been killed in the battle. Mrs. Custer felt tears rise in her own eyes. "I could not but look at the promise of athletic strength in the children," she wrote, "and wish with all my soul that instead of these embryo warriors she might have had daughters who would never be reared to go to war."[36] At the time, Mrs. Custer may have viewed the boys as potential threats to, and future enemies of,

her husband. But the passage also suggests another interpreta-
tion, particularly since Elizabeth Custer wrote it after her own
husband's death. In remembering the incident, she felt a connection with this Cheyenne woman—in the love of a wife for a
husband and in the heartrending costs of war to a family.

On a lighter note, Alice Baldwin found common ground with
Navajo women in matters of grooming. She helped a number of
them curl their hair with crimping pins and concluded that
"feminine vanity and tastes are much the same the world over,
no matter what the race or color." When Mrs. Baldwin traveled
to Fort Keough in 1877, she discovered that her costume aroused
the interest of Crow women and so agreed to undress as they
crowded around her:

> the crinoline and corsets they marveled at, but did not admire.
> . . . The voices of Indian women are naturally soft and melodious,
> as I sat or stood among them, listening to their chatter and laugh-
> ter and no doubt passing uncomplimentary comments about me,
> I felt that it all meant sincerity, which does not always prevail in
> a cultured and fashionable society.[37]

But not all army officers' wives were as obliging as Alice
Baldwin in satisfying Indian women's curiosity about them.
Ellen Biddle did not enjoy Cheyenne women's interest in her:
"They put their hands on [me] and felt my cheeks and hair and
insisted upon my taking it down for them to see." She was afraid
of them, in fact, as they climbed onto her wagon, begging for the
feather in a hat and for a string of beads.[38]

It was, in the end, Indian children who most appealed to
officers' wives and who most successfully eroded barriers between white and Indian on the military frontier. "The papooses
came the nearest of anything in that strange place to making me
forget my trepidation," Elizabeth Custer wrote of the Cheyenne
captives' camp on the Washita. And while she feared that the
Cheyenne woman Mo-nah-see-tah, who was rumored to be
Lieutenant Colonel Custer's mistress, might stab her, she found
that the woman's baby "disarmed" her. While stationed at Fort
Laramie, Frances Carrington befriended some Indian young-

sters. "Children intuitively recognized their friends," she explained,

> and these Indian children were no exception to the rule. . . . I was sitting near my window one day . . . when a dark cloud seemed to obscure my vision. Looking up I found the window space covered by little brown faces, to which I gave a smile of recognition, and with a friendly word . . . I beckoned them to the door and dispensed with generous hand some ginger-snaps.

Indian children, like other children, have ways of conveying information readily, and very soon both windows would be crowded. Anna Maus remembered that during her years among the Sioux she found the children most attractive. Their mothers, recognizing her sincere interest and affection for them, sought out her nursing skills when the children became sick. Officers' offspring could help break down barriers too. Maud Allen, the little daughter of Colonel Harvey Abner Allen, would run up to a "horrid, big Indian" at Fort Sitka in Alaska Territory, according to her mother, and hit him. The man would look angry until he realized who had struck him. Then he and all others around would laugh. "They all know her," Mrs. Allen reported about the native people, "and think she is a wonder."[39]

Both Indian and white families feared that their children's admirers would steal them. This is a testament to the high value they both placed on their children and the mutual distrust with which they regarded one another. Captain Parmenus Turnley's wife permitted a Sioux woman to hold their child, but the family nurse "was always in trepidation of such times lest the old squaw would make off with it." On the other hand, Mrs. Orsemus Boyd admired a particularly dark-eyed baby boy and found that, at first, her frequent visits pleased the boy's mother. But one day she brought him a little garment she had sewn herself and noticed that the mother's attitude had changed; now she feared that Boyd had "sinister designs upon her prize." On subsequent visits, "no trace of the baby could ever be found," Boyd reported. "Had his sex been different," she claimed, "I probably could have obtained complete possession; but boys are highly prized among the Indians."[40] It is noteworthy that Mrs. Boyd would never allow Indians to touch her own baby.

Some of the military men shared the army wives' affection, even delight, in native youngsters, although the women commented on the presence of children more often than did the men. Nevertheless, officers were not immune to Indian children's charms. A few officers, as already noted, even brought Indian children into their homes, sometimes as adopted children and sometimes as servants who practically became family members. One army doctor employed an Apache-Mojave boy who especially endeared himself to the family. He studied with the officers' children and showed such academic promise that he was sent to school in Lawrence, Kansas.[41] Officers did not always find their wives eager to accept Indian children, however. General Winfield Scott Hancock wanted to adopt a young Cheyenne boy, a survivor of a white-perpetrated massacre. But Almira Hancock flatly refused to give her consent. Although the boy professed a horror at returning to Indian life after three years among whites and although she found his reluctance "pitiful," she would not take him in permanently. As if to emphasize his second-class status and her determination on this issue, Mrs. Hancock would not even permit him to sit at the dinner table with the family.[42]

One cannot argue that army officers' wives proved more compassionate toward Indian children—or adults, for that matter—than officers. An Almira Hancock always throws a wrench into such generalizations. When it came to relationships with individual Indian women, however, there was a clear and important disparity between military men and women. Sexuality made the difference. Some army officers were not simply friendly but intimate with native women, in ways that army wives could never be and in ways in which the wives were not involved with individual Indian men. The nature and frequency of these sexual encounters and love affairs is difficult to ascertain, however. Some men discussed friendships with native women but declined to elaborate on their level of intimacy. Nineteenth-century officers were exceedingly discreet about all sexual liaisons. On top of that, middle-class Anglo-Americans of their time did not condone miscegenation, so officers hesitated to publicize their personal acquaintance with it.

The most common area for miscegenation between European men and Indian women, of course, had been the fur trade, where a situation of mutual dependency between European traders and Indians led to significant economic relationships, cultural exchanges, and sexual interaction. The army officer and the fur trader, however, encountered different conditions concerning the availability of white women. For many decades a ban on European women in the Canadian West led to widespread intermarriage between traders and Indian women. The norm for sexual relations there, according to Sylvia Van Kirk, "was not casual, promiscuous encounters but the development of marital unions which gave rise to distinct family units." Such marriages produced a large number of mixed-blood children, and as the daughters matured they were favored over full-blood Indian women for matrimony. With the nineteenth-century appearance of European women in western Canada, Van Kirk argued, a "sharp rise in the expression of racist sentiments" emerged, and these white women, "lovely, tender exotics," became the most desired women of all.[43] This suggests that, in part, fur traders married Indians because the preferred white women were not available. With the emergence of mixed-blood women and the arrival of white women, intermarriage stopped.

Unlike fur traders, army officers stationed in the nineteenth-century trans-Mississippi West could find white female companionship, although white women were not necessarily readily available. Some married officers left their wives in the East, but others brought them along to frontier garrisons. Bachelor officers looked to nearby towns or fellow officers' unattached female relatives, who visited the posts, for female society. As a result, between commonly accepted norms that strongly discouraged open racial mixing and the greater availability of white women than fur traders had found, intermarriage rarely occurred. Most sexual encounters between officers and Indian women were extramarital, perhaps casual, and from the white men's perspective, promiscuous. Sometimes the encounters were sordid and exploitive; sometimes they were tender and romantic.

Whatever the nature of these sexual episodes, officers wrote little about them, making it difficult to document or analyze them. Unfortunately, most official documents limited their remarks on these matters to enlisted men. Disturbed over reports of miscegenation on the frontier, for example, Congress convened the Banning Committee in 1876 to investigate the problem of immorality at frontier army posts. The committee assumed that the problem was between enlisted men and Indian women, and nothing was said about officers. Post surgeons' records indicated that venereal disease was a common ailment among enlisted men, with syphilis ranking fourth among infectious diseases of soldiers at Forts Buford, Randall, and Stevenson between 1870 and 1874. Post laundresses and camp followers shared some responsibility for spreading venereal diseases. But most post surgeons believed that Indian women were a major source of infection and recommended that they be kept away from posts whenever possible. Like the Banning Committee testimony, surgeons' venereal disease records remained silent on officers.[44]

The army made an exception to this rule of silence when officers shamelessly cavorted with prostitutes—whether white, Mexican, or Indian—in the presence of enlisted men. Officers found guilty of this offense could be cashiered. For the most part, however, officials preferred to discourage the documentation of scandalous behavior. It took Captain Nicholas Nodt four years to file successfully a report concerning an incident at Fort Fauntleroy that involved officers' "favorite squaws." In 1861 a horse race between officers and Navajos deteriorated into a dispute when the Navajos claimed that the officers had cheated. In the chaos that followed, some Navajos were killed. Needless to say, the experience left relations with the Navajos severely strained. The only Navajos who remained at the post were several officers' Navajo mistresses. The commanding officer sent these women as emissaries to their tribe, where they were not well received. Thus, not only were sexual relations with Indian women a reality, but army officials were willing to exploit these relations in moments of crisis. Even more important, however,

This tense Chiricahua Apache captive was taken in a fight on August 22, 1885. She was wounded in the right arm. (*American Heritage Center, University of Wyoming*)

was Nodt's difficulty in reporting the experience. Officials preferred to suppress such evidence.[45]

In private correspondence, officers were occasionally more open about sexual relations with native women. The Seventh Cavalry's Captain Myles Keogh, who would perish in the Battle of the Little Big Horn, informed his brothers in a letter penned from Fort Hays, "We have here about ninety squaws—from our last fight [the Battle of the Washita]—some of them very pretty. I have one that is quite intelligent. It is usual for officers to have two or three lounging around." In a situation that must have been appalling to these Cheyenne women, a Mexican interpreter who was in charge of the captives procured the women and delivered them to the officers' tents. For his role, the Mexican man became known among the officers as "Romeo."[46] Under these circumstances, officers apparently saw the Indian women as the spoils of war, as sexual conveniences, as powerless and depersonalized objects.

It was the same circumstance that produced the most famous liaison between an officer and an Indian woman: the alleged affair of Lieutenant Colonel George Custer and the Cheyenne woman Mo-nah-see-tah. Retired captain Frederick Benteen of the Seventh Cavalry (who despised Custer, branding him an "S.O.B. . . . murderer, thief, and liar") claimed that following the Battle of the Washita, Custer extended an invitation to officers "desiring to avail themselves of the services of a captured squaw to come to the squaw round up corral and select one!" Custer, Benteen charged, took first choice and lived with Mo-nah-see-tah, who was pregnant at the time, during the winter and spring of 1868 and 1869. Benteen also maintained that an army surgeon had "seen him not only sleeping with the Indian girl all winter long, but [had] seen him many times in the act of copulating with her." Benteen's obvious lack of respect for Custer certainly undermined his objectivity and perhaps even his reliability on this matter. Since many nineteenth-century men argued, at least in public statements, that sexual relations with Indian women degraded the white men, Benteen may have intended to slander Custer's memory by making these accusations. However, Ben Clark, who worked for the army as a scout, and Cheyenne oral tradition both corroborated Benteen's claims. In fact, Paul A. Hutton has claimed that Mo-nah-see-tah's role as Custer's mistress was "common camp gossip in military circles," and "the fact that more was not made of it during the period . . . probably reflects a gentleman's agreement to keep quiet on a not uncommon practice of the frontier military."[47]

Army officers' wives joined in this conspiracy of silence, if not to protect individual officers' reputations, then to protect that of the frontier army as a whole. For women like Elizabeth Custer, who was probably not immune to the gossip concerning her husband's relationship with Mo-nah-see-tah or blind to the practices of other officers, such behavior was undoubtedly painful. Yet it may have seemed easier to ignore it than to confront it. She certainly did not acknowledge it in her published accounts.

Nevertheless, the potential for sexual intimacy between officers and Indian women was clearly an issue between the men and their wives. Several officers mentioned Indian women in their letters home, then quickly added that they had no interest in taking them as lovers. Captain E.O.C. Ord, writing to his wife from Fort Walla Walla in Washington Territory in 1858, said, "tell Mrs. Hardie the capt. is looking extremely youthful & when any good looking squaws come along he looks toward them & sighs—for home." And he added, "remember if Mrs. H. takes this too hard—tell her Hardie is as anxious to get home— home, home! as your affectionate and devoted husband."[48]

After he wrote of admiring the Crows at Fort Phil Kearny, Lieutenant Colonel Luther Bradley wrote his fiancée that "some of the women were even good looking." He hastened to add that such women were rare, however, and that she "need not fear my falling in love with any of them, they are not in my style." Captain Albert Barnitz also reassured his wife that he would not "fall in love with any of their dirty little squaws," referring to Cheyenne and Arapahoe women, and demonstrated his fidelity by claiming that while at the 1867 council at Medicine Lodge, Kansas, an Arapahoe brought a young woman to be his companion for the night. Although she "was elegantly ornamented with vermilion, and seemed to have been especially gotten up for the occasion," Barnitz refused the offer, showed the Arapahoe a picture of his wife, and told him one "squaw" was enough.[49]

Time and again, officers replayed in letters and memoirs Barnitz's scenario of Indian men offering Indian women. Officers firmly, though graciously, refused, maintaining the highest moral standards in the face of such temptation. En route to New Mexico in 1849, Randolph Marcy met a Comanche named Is-sa-keep, who offered him, within hearing distance of about five hundred emigrants and soldiers, a temporary wife. "I was a good deal embarrassed at such a proposition," Marcy recalled, "made in the presence of so large an assembly, but told Beaver to inform the chief that this was not in accordance with the customs of the white people." Whether Marcy was embarrassed by the proposition itself or by the fact that it was made in the presence of five hundred people is unclear. But upon hearing that Marcy had declined his offer, Is-sa-keep told Marcy he was the strangest man he had ever seen, as every other man wanted a woman after traveling for a long time.[50]

Such stories were often self-serving, especially when officers indicated that the Indian women were willing partners. It was only natural, of course, for these men to enjoy the prospect of appearing attractive, even desirable, to members of the opposite sex, regardless of race. It was only human to want the affection of people they met on the frontier, including Indians. In this spirit, James Parker told his brother that when he arrived at Fort Sill in the autumn of 1876—his first post assignment after graduating from the military academy—Comanche women living in the vicinity of the fort "would try to get up a flirtation—without regard to the feelings of their spouses, some of whom did not seem to relish their advances." Since even the best looking of these women streaked their "black faces with a variety of ill assorted paints," however, the young Parker concluded "that my taste was not sufficiently educated to risk an acquaintance."[51]

It is interesting that these men were not thrown into paroxysms of horror at what they would have considered the looser sexual practices of some Indian people. In some cases they acknowledged that contact with whites explained licentious behavior that was not an aspect of precontact Indian behavior. One man even claimed that Indian women were virtuous and faithful to their husbands, except for those who lived in the vicinity of military garrisons! Another blamed the demoralization of Indian women on the reservations, where traditional methods of protecting women no longer held sway and the United States government failed to provide adequate substitutes.[52] Further, these men understood something about the inevitable attraction between men and women. They might not make sexuality a topic of everyday conversation, but neither did they deny its existence.

Some even admitted that they found Indian women tempting but kept them at arms' length, either because they could not quite overcome their scruples about mixing with Indians or because they did not want to risk alienating spouses back home. Among the captives of the 1857 Gila River Expedition, the lively Lieutenant John Du Bois was taken with a spirited and particularly attractive woman whom he identified, of course, as a princess. Gracefully clothed in buckskin, with a sweet voice, curling lip, flashing eyes, and small hands and feet, she was, Du Bois declared, "haughty as an Empress receiving homage." "By jove—I could marry such a wildcat," the New Yorker exclaimed, "if she lived on 5th Avenue & owned half a county." He did add, "*On dit* that the morals of the captives are not irreproachable." Whether he spoke from personal experience was not clear.[53]

Although Marcy declined Is-sa-keep's offer of a temporary wife, he playfully asked a Comanche woman to leave her husband and go home with him. He showed the woman a photograph of his wife, and she, in answer to his jesting proposal, pointed to the photograph and then drew her hand across her throat, "most significantly indicating that, in her judgment, my house would be anything but a safe place for her." And he concluded, "as I was rather inclined in the same opinion myself, I did not feel disposed to discuss the subject any further."[54]

At least one officer acknowledged that Indian women could take advantage of officers' attentions and sentimental or romantic inclinations. After their own families were wiped out by war, several Apache women, according to Lieutenant Britton Davis, "practically adopted" army officers. A seven-year-old girl, with her mother's encouragement, became one officer's special protégé, acquiring finery at his expense. "These romantic friendships," Davis lamented, "should have had the proper romantic ending—when the grateful Indian girl throws herself before the leveled rifles, a la Captain John Smith. But alas and alack! When the hostiles went out in the spring of 1885 the girl and the woman went with them, seemingly not caring a trooper's damn whether I was filled full of lead or not."[55]

Officers' comments about women emphasized the romantic and ignored the sordid implications of Benteen's charges against Custer or Keogh's reports about the Washita captives. The officers hinted at Indian women's sexuality but denied having any personal acquaintance with it. Marriages, of course, were almost unknown, although Lieutenant D. H. Rucker of the First Dragoons married a "civilized" Cherokee, and army surgeon Washington Mathews married a Hidatsa woman.[56] Most maintained in public statements that a sexual relationship or marriage between savagery and civilization threatened civilization. While the Indian would be elevated by the match, the white man would be lowered.

General O. O. Howard believed that white men were "naturally" demeaned by such liaisons. Their personal cleanliness suffered, their clothing turned ragged, their self-respect was degraded, they lost dignity, and they became indifferent to a civilized way of life. Richard Irving Dodge claimed that "squaw men" either lived off their wives or lived off government rations and the largesse of Indian agents. Moreover, they debased their Indian wives, abandoning them or prostituting them for their own gain, and in the process "lowering the tone of the tribes."[57]

If marriage or public acknowledgment of sexual mingling with Indian women was out of the question for officers, however, romance was not. In his novel *An Apache Princess*, Captain Charles King examined this possibility. Natzie, the princess—"a theoretical heathen, but a practical Christian"—falls in love with pale, genteel Lieutenant Neil Blakely. In Pocahontas-like fashion, she saves his life but learns that her love for Blakely will be unrequited, for he loves Captain Robert Wren's

eastern-educated daughter, Angela. Blakely prefers hunting but-
terflies to frontier vices such as drinking and gambling, yet his
army friends believe that he had flirted with Natzie and, in an
ungentlemanly way, had encouraged her attentions. "Even
women who could not find it possible to speak of her probable
relations with Neil Blakely," King wrote, "dwelt much in
thought and word upon her superb devotion and her generosity.
That he had encouraged her passionate and almost savage love
for him, there were few to doubt." An Apache princess was a
suitable companion for a frontier flirtation and even a passionate love affair, but Blakely reserved his ultimate serious love for
the civilized woman. He did flirt with Natzie, but true to the
officer-gentleman's code and contrary to garrison gossip, he was
not guilty of "encouraging her attentions in an ungentlemanly
fashion." In the end, confirming the impossibility of any permanent commitment between an officer and an Indian woman,
Blakely marries Angela, and Natzie marries a Chiricahua man.[58]

To a degree, King's fiction mirrored frontier reality. Though
rare, romances between officer and Indian woman did occur,
and though vague about the nature of these relationships,
officers' accounts reveal that these friendships could have
warmth and be of some consequence. True, they were couched
in Indian-princess imagery and in most cases were never destined to achieve the respectability or sanctity of marriage, but
they nevertheless indicate that, if only for a short time, officers
and Indian women could attain a level of communication, understanding, and affection that transcended concerns of savagery and civilization, of occupying army and conquered native
people. Further, the officers' use of princess imagery does not
necessarily invalidate the friendships or emotional involvements. In a culture that frowned on racial mixing, perhaps these
myths provided the only acceptable means by which they could
write comfortably about romance with Indian women. Perhaps
they lacked the imagination to offer alternative language to describe these relationships. Of course, it is possible that romantic
language and imagery camouflaged the base nature of these relationships, particularly if officers seduced and exploited helpless captives as spoils of war. But it is also possible that the

sexual affairs could be more felicitous, wherein both parties were willing and saw one another as equals. In some cases, one can cut through hackneyed princess stereotypes to find genuine human involvement.

This seemed to be the case in the relationship between a Yuma woman and her admirer, Lieutenant Thomas W. Sweeny. The "Rose of Colorado" had, according to this Irish-born officer, beautiful black, dazzling eyes unlike those of Yuma men, which Sweeny found small, dark, and cunning. Her face was soft and more intelligent, he believed, than any Indian face he had ever seen. But most impressive to Sweeny was her body, which when "almost nude, was truly magnificent, and would have been a glory to a young sculptor." Tall, half bold and half timid, she moved like a gazelle. They became friends. In one touching exchange, the Yuma woman asked Sweeny if white women were beautiful. He answered that they were but assured her that she was every bit as handsome, although white men did not like women who painted themselves. Being painted herself, she looked rather disappointed and asked if he felt the same way. Sweeny gently told her, "It is not wrong in you . . . for it is the practice of your people." But he also added, "believe me, you would look much handsomer without it." He went on to say that God was the best judge of color and complexion, so people should not alter his work. At that point the Yuma woman asked more about God, and Sweeny obliged but then stopped short. "Good heavens muttered I to myself, what am I doing? I am positively preaching—the government ought to have sent me out as a missionary to convert the Indians, instead of fighting them."[59]

Similar warmth characterized William Woods Averell's relationship with a Navajo woman named Ah-tlan-tiz-pa. He found her "undoubtedly the prettiest Navajo woman in the country." It appears that Averell's interest in Ah-tlan-tiz-pa was more than professional. Upon hearing that he had been wounded during the Navajo War, Averell claimed, Ah-tlan-tiz-pa ran into his tent and threw herself on the ground. "It was not until repeated assurances that I was alive and not fatally hurt that she partly raised herself and crept toward my bed." He made arrangements for her to enter the garrison freely and "so, to borrow the idiom of our ancient friend, J. Fenimore Cooper, the Indian maiden occasionally brought the breezy vigor of the piñon-clad mountains and the ruddy glow of savage life, unfettered by any conventionalities, into the . . . cabin of the wounded paleface." Unfortunately, Ah-tlan-tiz-pa's point of view is not recorded, so we must rely on the officer's romanticized view of things. If he is to be believed, the Navajo woman demonstrated some feeling for the officer, and the relationship was important to both people.[60]

Philip Sheridan lived with a Rogue River Indian girl named Frances for several years while he was stationed in the Pacific Northwest in the 1850s. She visited him after the Civil War in Washington, D.C., but eventually returned to Oregon, married a Hudson's Bay Company trapper, and moved to Canada. Sheridan never mentioned the relationship directly, but when President Grant promoted him, Sheridan asked that he not be sent to the Northwest, "for many reasons some of which are personal."[61]

Of course, there was also Lieutenant Colonel George Custer's admiration for the Cheyenne woman Mo-nah-see-tah. A beautiful chief's daughter, she agreed to act as an interpreter for the army in the negotiations with other Cheyenne and with the Arapahoes. Belonging "to the cream of the aristocracy, if not to royalty itself," according to the famous Indian fighter, she was "an exceedingly comely squaw . . . possessing a bright, cheery face, a countenance beaming with intelligence . . . bright, laughing eyes, a set of pearly teeth, and a rich complexion." In addition, "her well shaped head was crowned with a luxuriant growth of the most beautiful silken tresses . . . extending, when allowed to fall loosely over her shoulder, to below her waist." Custer's passages about Mo-nah-see-tah reveal attraction, but like Averell he only admitted that "she became a great favorite with the entire command."[62] The rumors of a sexual relationship, however, suggest that Mo-nah-see-tah may have meant more to the lieutenant colonel than he indicated.

The overall effect of this military commentary on native women was a more humanized view of Indians. Why would women rather than men elicit these reactions from officers and their wives? Perhaps they saw all women, regardless of race or culture, as more approachable, more emotional and less inscrutable than men. Also, they defined Indian women in terms of their relations with others—their husbands, their children, or the army people themselves—which reinforced concepts of native women as humans. It was in this pose that Bourke presented the Santo Domingo woman and her lover who opened this chapter.

In addition, while an occasional woman took up arms to defend home and family, Indian women were not perceived by officers or army wives as the enemy. Their husbands, brothers, and fathers most directly threatened officers' well-being. Indian women appeared to the soldiers more nearly as passive bystanders in times of conflict, bringing to bear on the situation their own expectation of appropriate behavior for women and men. Men did the fighting; women, for the most part, did not. Finally, military men and women probably saw Indian women as more easily "redeemed" for civilization. They most likely accepted their culture's assumptions about white women as a civilizing influence on the frontier and perhaps assumed that Indian women could play the same "gentle tamer" role in their own cultures.

Attitudes such as these, of course, reflected Anglo-American expectations and assumptions about woman's role in society. They were not based on a recognition, let alone an understanding, of the Indian cultures' roles for women. Further, although these attitudes demonstrated that army people could change their opinions based on their experiences with actual Indian women, this did not alter their actions. An acknowledgment of Indian women's humanity and personal relationships with individuals could make their tasks as soldiers, however, more complicated. It could even render them ineffective. In the final analysis, most officers considered Indians inferior beings who were obstructing their nation's advance across the continent. The officers' ultimate purpose was not to understand, communicate with, or care for Indians but to clear the countryside of these supposed obstacles to civilization's aspirations.

Indians were not just frontier curiosities, sexual substitutes, or useful tools to reflect upon Anglo-American civilization and its practices. They were also a problem, as many nineteenth-century Anglo-Americans construed it, demanding some resolution. It fell to the federal government to formulate a policy, a plan, a resolution. And it fell to army officers to enforce it. Not only their livelihood but sometimes their very lives rested on that policy. It is no wonder, then, that their thoughts sometimes turned to the shape and substance of Indian policy and their role in it.

5 / Thoughts on Indian Policy

Savages cannot be civilized without first being taught to respect the power which civilization promotes, and the only argument which avails with them is the one they employ— the argument of force. —MAJOR ALFRED E. BATES

General Alexander McCook announced in 1865 that there were only three alternatives for federal Indian policy: preserve the country west of the Kansas settlements and east of California and Nevada for Indians alone, place Indians on reservations and use armed forces to keep them there, or exterminate them. He concluded that the first alternative would not work because "the country west of Kansas must be settled, and the mines of our great mountain ranges . . . must be developed." As for the third option, McCook wrote, it "is so cruel and inhumane that the idea of it cannot be entertained."[1] That left the second option—the one that focused on reservations—as the most realistic and the most moral. The majority of his fellow countrymen and fellow army officers came to the same conclusion.

United States Indian policy during the last half of the nineteenth century centered on the reservation system. On reservations, policymakers hoped, Indians would begin the acculturation process that would eventually usher them into the Anglo-American world. There they would learn the English language, Anglo-American values, and (for the Plains people and other nomads or seminomads) an agricultural way of life. Civilian agents would supervise reservation activities, particularly after the transfer of Indian affairs from the War Department to the Interior Department in 1849. After the Civil War, President Grant inaugurated the Peace Policy, wherein churchmen served as Indian agents in the belief that men of a religious bent would prove less corrupt and more energetic and dedicated to instituting the civilization program than their predecessors in office. The army would enforce federal policy. Physical suppression was therefore not a policy goal, but the federal government would rely upon its military might to coerce Indians onto reservations and keep them there. It was also expected to provide Indians some protection from Anglo-Americans who did not observe reservation boundaries.

As the government implemented its policy, many native people resisted, sometimes through armed conflict. That resistance dominated army-Indian relations between 1846 and 1890, but it did not lead to any reexamination of Indian policy. In fact, "neither in objectives nor in execution," according to Robert Utley, "were whites to challenge [the reservation system] seriously until well into the twentieth century."² Neither did army officers question the broad goals and direction of nineteenth-century Indian policy. However, in private and public statements alike—military etiquette concerning political comment notwithstanding—officers vigorously criticized civilian control of Indian affairs, and after the Civil War certain aspects of President Grant's Peace Policy. They lobbied, at least informally, to defend and even expand their own role in the West. Officers did not quarrel with the ends of federal policy, but they did debate the methods and management of that policy.

It was fairly easy to criticize civilian management of federal Indian policy, and military men found the solution to be equally simple: return control of these affairs to the War Department. Officers believed, first of all, that inept government officials, ignorant about frontier conditions and Indian people, sparked Indian wars by making decisions that only exacerbated frontier tensions. They also argued that corrupt officials, whom they labeled "the Indian Ring," formulated policies that promoted bureaucrats' self-interest and undermined the welfare of Indians, frontiersmen, and army officers.

One officer rather typically charged that the Indian Ring embraced "all the rascality perpetrated upon the nation's wards" by furnishing inferior provisions for which the government paid high prices and by withholding these supplies until the Indians, facing starvation, went to war. At that point, he complained, the army was called in to "punish the poor Indian." In an 1877 article, Colonel John Gibbon insisted that corrupt agents drove Indians to desperation by their swindling and neglect. He added that "even a Christian will fight before he will starve." After all, the Indian, "although a savage, is still a man, with probably quite as much instinctive sense of right and wrong as a white man." Yet the blame for the Indian wars fell upon the army, "supposed by the 'Indian Ring' to be so bloodthirsty as never to be contented unless engaged in the delightful task of chasing roving bands of Indians for thousands of miles."[3]

Lieutenant Frank Baldwin, a Michigan native with a long career in the post–Civil War army, was also disgusted with agents who appeared "anxious to line their own personal pockets with a majority of the immense appropriation annually made for the support of the Indians." In addition, he claimed that government agents and traders offered arms and ammunition to Indians that were eventually employed against the military. The Interior Department distributed weapons to certain tribes with the understanding that the arms would be used only to kill buffalo. But officers believed that Indians purchased guns in excess of their hunting needs and then turned them on army men. All this went on, according to Baldwin, "with the knowledge and consent of these damned, miserable thieving Indian agents."[4]

The inauguration of the Peace Policy in 1869 brought negligible improvements, according to army men. They identified several problems with the system. First, churchmen could be corrupt too. Captain John Bourke, for one, doubted the churchmen's presumed morality. He pointed out that "abundant" was a term churchmen and Apaches could not agree upon—"the wicked Indians laboring under the delusion that it was enough food to keep the recipient from starving to death." "To the credit of the agent," Bourke sardonically added, "it must be said that he made a praiseworthy but ineffectual effort to alleviate the pangs of hunger by a liberal distribution of hymn-books among his wards." The Chiricahuas, "not being able to digest works of that nature," understandably left the San Carlos Reservation.[5] Bourke believed that paltry pay and the precarious tenure of

their office caused agents selected on the basis of denomination
to be of an even "lower average than the political dead beats
who managed the Indian between 1849 and 1867." Dividing religious appointees into two classes, the incompetent and the
"fanatical sanctimonious rascals," Bourke elaborated:

> The first class includes good and well-meaning old men who have
> failed in every business enterprise ever undertaken by them but
> whose religious fervor and general probity of character must be
> admitted by everybody. This class is just "nuts" for the contrac-
> tors and other cormorants hanging around the agency. . . . The
> other class of agents are those who steal the livery of heaven to
> serve the devil in—the most sanctimonious of the whole congre-
> gation, they are most anxious to go out among the *Indians* for
> the mere pleasure of evangelizing them; this category is not in
> general terms looked upon with favor by the contractors who
> find the lion's share of the spoils system from the Indian appropri-
> ations claimed by the "pious fraud" who had wiggled his way
> into his position by the influence and under the patronage of
> some Christian church.⁶

But even more serious was the officers' concern that Indians
would perceive churchmen as weak and unwilling to employ
force on the reservation. Indians, being warlike according to this
line of thought, respected only soldiers and would obey only
those willing to use force to assure obedience. Christian-ap-
pointed agents were "a fitting climax to the preposterous acts
which for a century have stultified the governmental 'control
and management' of Indians," according to Richard Irving
Dodge. To appoint Nathan Meeker, however faithful, honest,
and Christian in bearing he might be, to an agency "in charge of
a set of wild brigands like the Utes, is simply to invite massacre." Christian feeling and sentiment were hardly suitable
characteristics for an effective agent. Rather, a forceful demeanor and the ability to control were of paramount importance. Finally, he noted incidentally that appointing churchmen
to government positions was probably a violation of the Constitution because it united church and state and discriminated

against potential agents who were not members of Christian churches. This officer was not concerned, however, with the violation of Indians' religious freedom.[7]

Army officers, of course, were not especially objective observers of civilian Indian agents. From 1849 until the end of the century, military officials were attempting to regain control of Indian affairs, and their frequent criticism of civilian management certainly served that purpose. Yet, while clearly interested in enhancing their own power, some army men also earnestly and sincerely argued that the military, with its years of frontier experience and careful disbursement of appropriations, could more honestly and effectively manage Indian affairs than could civilians.

Protestant churches and the Board of Indian Commissioners opposed the transfer of Indian affairs back to the War Department, however. They believed that Indians disliked the troopers and that soldiers undermined the morals of Indians. Also, they maintained, the army acted arbitrarily and inflamed Indian wars by their penchant for forceful solutions. Civilian agents, of course, opposed the transfer of Indian affairs back to the War Department because they stood to lose their jobs. The military received strong support, on the other hand, from westerners and occasionally from easterners. *The Nation*, for example, recommended the return of Indian affairs to the War Department after the Fetterman fight, in which Captain William Fetterman's entire command of about seventy men died in an 1866 engagement with Sioux and Cheyenne warriors near Fort Phil Kearny in Dakota Territory. But perhaps no group advocated transfer more vigorously than did the officers themselves, putting forth arguments that touched on economic and practical matters as well as on the more philosophical issues of what army officers perceived as the "Indian character" and the army's ability to cope with it.[8]

From a practical point of view, officers insisted that military control would be more economical because the army monitored its expenditures closely. Moreover, officers would operate beyond the reach of corrupt politicians as quartermasters replaced political hacks and military professionalism supplanted

political spoils.⁹ In addition, army partisans presented the officer as simply more honest by virtue of his professional code and
calling. One man argued that although some officers might attempt to acquire Indian appropriations for their own pockets,
military law was so strict and just that they would not last long.
Besides, "the heart felt desire to retain peace with the Indian as
well as the great aim and ambition of all army officers to keep
up to and elevate the already high standing of army officers,
would cause almost every one of them to be honest and to ad-
ministe[r] Indian affairs honestly and justly." Another asserted
that a military man would be more honest than a civilian agent
because he "holds his position by a life of good conduct tenure;
has a recognized place of prominence in society; [maintains] the
hope of promotion and distinction as a reward of faithful service
and feels that the pettiest act of peculation is certain to be traced
home to him."¹⁰

Officers' attributes as managers, these men argued, brought
benefits not only to the taxpayer but to the Indian as well. Honest and just management meant the end of starvation, and thus
of one of the major sources of provocation for Indian wars.
Further, because officers understood both Indian people and
frontier conditions, they were, according to General William T.
Sherman, "the least prejudiced" of frontier operators, and they
commanded soldiers who could frequently "defend the Indians
against manifest wrong, and . . . sometimes interpose before
war is inevitable." Officers commanded the warriors' respect,
another argued, because of their "wholesome application of real
restraint and active force"—actions much more calculated to
bring results than the trickery, treaties, and soft persuasion that
civilians used.¹¹

Just as most army officers agreed that the War Department
should manage Indian matters, so did the majority concur on a
fundamental maxim about the nature of that management: Be
fair but firm. With the advent of President Grant's Peace Policy
and its expectation that Indians would be conquered through
kindness rather than warfare, officers heightened their rhetoric
that only force would achieve the goal of concentrating Indians
on reservations. "There is no more ineffective treatment for

savages," retired lieutenant James Steele asserted, "than the rec-
ipes of philanthropy."[12]

Of course, by insisting on the necessity of force, these officers
were insuring a place for themselves in the arena of Indian affairs. Diplomacy largely fell to others, but who else could apply
force? Also, such assertions provided justification for army actions, past, present, and future. But more, officers believed that
a policy based on force coupled with fairness was destined to be
most successful because it was based on what they believed was
a realistic assessment of Indian character. While officers did not
often speak with one voice, on this they demonstrated a remarkable consensus, sharing the assumption that, regardless of tribe,
most Indians required a demonstration of power. So pervasive
was this sentiment that even those who empathized with Indian
resistance assumed that force was ultimately necessary in order
to "save" the natives for civilization. In fact, the judicious use
of force could bring about a quicker resolution of difficulties
and a longer life for Indian and officer alike.

Here again, according to this line of thought, it would ultimately be in the best interest of the Indian people to treat them
severely at the outset. The gentle touch should come, but only
after final conquest. Granville O. Haller asserted that the Indians' conquest was inevitable, so "forebearance and generous
conditions" would "only procrastinate the final result." Indeed,
he warned, generosity and leniency should prevail only after Indians had been "paralyzed by fire and sword" and after "absolute
submission to the will of the strong Race is effected." Somewhat more sympathetically, Lieutenant Walter S. Schuyler
explained to his father in 1874 that Indians on the Verde Reservation "have to be forced to work by military force. I suppose
they will see the 'why' of it all in time but they do not now."
Turning down an opportunity to leave Arizona, he chose to stay,
explaining, "I can not leave now where I have the first glimpse
of a successful issue to my labors. My hard earned experience
would be lost not only to myself but to the Indians and people
of the country." Not the least of his accomplishments to date,
Schuyler claimed, was the fact that in eleven battles with the

Indians he had never been defeated or even lost a man. His military prowess, he believed, encouraged Indian respect for him and Indian willingness to work for him in the fields.[13]

A few argued that Indian wrongdoing had to be met with swift and severe retribution because Indians lacked moral principles, so only force, or the fear of it, would insure correct behavior. William Parker believed that Indians did not understand the concept of "moral suasion" and read it as cowardice. Others argued that Indians were basically childlike and so required discipline. But most often, military men maintained that Indians were fundamentally warlike and respected only the same in others. Kindness or patience would be interpreted as fear or weakness. Only warfare, or at least a willingness to go to war, would cow Indians into submission. Native people simply did not appreciate alternatives such as moral suasion, diplomacy, or simple kindness.[14]

Some officers said that they had tried these alternatives only to find that force proved most effective. Philip Sheridan, for example, in command of the Department of Missouri under Lieutenant General William T. Sherman in 1867, later remembered that he had hoped to maintain peace between the Indians and encroaching pioneers by "resorting to persuasive methods," including an abundant supply of rations. So, he wrote, "I fed them pretty freely, and also endeavored to control them through certain men, who, I found, had their confidence." But, he claimed, this method did not work, and by July 1867 the Cheyenne, Sioux, and Arapaho had begun raiding white settlements. In fact, the Indians, Sheridan testified, engaged in "murder and rapine, which for acts of devilish cruelty perhaps has no parallel in savage warfare." The warriors would imprison the men and ravage the women until they "became insensible . . . all the women who fell into their hands were subjected to horrors indescribable by words." In 1869, Sheridan directed Colonel Benjamin Grierson to hang all Indians guilty of murder and send all those guilty of robbery to Fort Leavenworth. "The trouble heretofore with Indians," Sheridan explained to Grierson, "has been caused by the absence of all punishment for crimes committed against the settlements. No people, especially those in a wild state, can be expected to behave themselves where there are no laws providing punishment for crime."[15]

Similarly, Colonel Henry B. Carrington arrived in the turbulent Powder River country in 1866 prepared to treat Indians kindly and fairly without resorting to violent confrontation. In a special order penned while en route to Fort Laramie, he cautioned his men against mistreating Indians, asserting that it would be considered a "very gross offense for a soldier to wrong or insult an Indian." But in the wake of the Fetterman disaster later that year, Carrington reported that the Sioux and Cheyenne "must be subjected and made to respect and fear the whites," for "the Indian, now desperate and bitter looks upon the rash white man as a sure victim, no less than he does a coward."[16]

Officers preferred to emphasize the necessity of employing force from their standpoint as military professionals, yet their writings indicate that personal considerations influenced them as well. They could become frustrated and angry with Indian resistance and anxious to assert their dominance. Consequently, officers sometimes urged violence out of simple pique. An individual might publicly justify warfare in order to keep Indians on reservations, civilize them, and protect them from encroaching white settlers, but he could also interpret an experience with Indian resistance as a personal affront. Such experiences frustrated army officers accustomed to the rigors of military life, where an individual's wish could be a command. An enlisted man who refused to obey orders met swift punishment. An Indian who refused to obey an officer's command posed more of a problem. He might respect neither the individual officer nor the army itself. In this context, physical force (or the threat of it) could prove the only apparent recourse to preserve an officer's dignity. The upshot was that sometimes private reasons reinforced the officers' professional opinion that Indians required demonstrations of power and firm discipline.

Philip Sheridan related such an event in his autobiography. While serving in the Pacific Northwest in the 1850s, he was ordered to fetch sixteen men from the Rogue River Indian reservation. But the Indians reacted to his demands to accompany him with "contemptuous laughter," and he returned to his post without the men or his pistol. Describing himself as crestfallen, he was also angry, embarrassed, and determined that such defiance would not go unpunished. Anxious to chastise these people, he explained, "I at once set to work to bring about a better state of discipline on the reservation, and to put an end to the practices of the medicine men (having also in view the recovery of my six shooter and self respect), by marching to the village and taking the rebellious Indians by force." Eventually the sixteen men came in without a demonstration of force and were made to labor "until their rebellious spirit was broken." Once they recognized the power of the United States, Sheridan concluded, "a course of justice and mild force was adopted, and unvaryingly applied." Undoubtedly, Sheridan also found some satisfaction in their recognition of his personal power.[17]

William T. Sherman's correspondence, too, revealed outrage with Indians who resisted American policy and a tendency to interpret an Indian refusal to obey his orders as a personal insult. He cautioned one officer about allowing "any Indian [to] be saucy or insolent inside a Fort—make him respect & fear the flag." Upon learning that the Kiowa leader Satank had been shot while trying to escape, Sherman wrote, "Hanging would be better, but we can be certain that he is now extinct."[18] While Sheridan and Sherman insisted that Indians, by their very nature, acted like children and so required a strong hand to command respect and obedience, their private experiences and correspondence betrayed an anger with recalcitrant Indians who challenged their authority. Admitting only that Indian character required officers to be firm, their indignation and exasperation disclose less a sense of professional detachment than a personal, angry compulsion to overpower and punish Indians.

The link between anger and the desire to punish Indians was demonstrated not only by men of high command but also by those who believed in the necessity of domination but doubted their capacity to realize it. Here the additional element of fear underscored wrath and heightened the desire to thrash soundly those natives who challenged officers' authority. Lieutenant

Thomas Sweeny recounted such an episode in 1851 with some Cocopa and Yuma principal chiefs at Camp Independence in California. They demanded to know the intentions of his small delegation. He replied that it was the will of the "great father at Washington" that he remain to protect his children, Indian and white. Promising to reward those who obeyed him, he warned, "the moment they disobeyed . . . I would punish them with the utmost severity, destroy their planting grounds, and drive them beyond the Colorado towards the 'rising sun!'" Sweeny then confided to his diary, "Big talk, this, from an officer in command of a *detachment* consisting of a non-commissioned officer and nine men." Feeling vulnerable and perhaps a little sorry for himself, Sweeny declared,

> Nothing but fear restrains them, and nothing but ceaseless vigilance on our part can keep them in check, and prevent them from trampling me and my small command into nonentity. At some unguarded moment, for nature cannot watch forever, I shall be surprised, I suppose, cut off, massacred, minced sans remorse, by wretches who would no more face a stricken field [an open and fair battle] than leap into the crater of a volcano. To such end will most probably my aspiration after glory come.[19]

Lieutenant William Schuyler confessed to similar fears of Indians he identified as Yumas and Mojaves. These people had not been "thoroughly punished." He believed that they "can be ruled for the present only with a hand of iron, which is a manner of governing totally unknown to the agents of the Indian Bureau, most of whom are afraid of the Indians, and are willing to do anything to conciliate them, thereby making them lose all respect and confidence in them [the Indian agents] and only sowing the seeds of insurrection." He added that he was afraid of these Indians himself, for he had "seen enough of them to know that the only way to insure my safety and their future civilization and prosperity, is to make them afraid of me." Schuyler insisted that Indians knew only two emotions, fear and hate, and "unless they fear a person they despise him, and show in every way their contempt for his authority."[20]

Colonel Benjamin Grierson was the exception that proved the rule on the issue of force. A number of other things also set Grierson apart from his fellow officers, however. He was, as his biographers noted, a rather unlikely cavalry officer, because a childhood incident left him afraid of horses. He had been a talented musician and band leader but a failure at business, so when the Civil War began, Grierson was deep in debt, living in his parents' home with his wife and children. By the end of the war, his fortunes had improved. Hailed as a national hero for his daring 1863 raid through Mississippi at the head of 1,700 men, Grierson attracted the attention and support of Grant and Sherman. In 1866 he received a colonelcy in the Tenth Cavalry, a regiment of black soldiers. The colonel became a staunch supporter of their military abilities in an era when many officers doubted the capacity of blacks to serve effectively.[21]

He was also an officer who believed that diplomacy and a willingness to live up to treaties rather than a resort to the sword would preserve peace in the West. Grierson's duties on the Southern Plains between 1868 and 1871 sorely tested his devotion to a bloodless accommodation between Indian and white interests. In the spring of 1869, for example, Grierson informed his wife that the Indians at Camp Wichita in the Indian Territory had not received sufficient provisions and that those they did receive were of the poorest kind. These people could not be expected to remain on the reservation, starving, when buffalo roamed nearby. Yet he had instructions to keep them on the reservation by force, if necessary, though he believed that doing so was a gross injustice. The following year he wrote his brother, "What is required to settle the 'Indian question,'" is not force but "strict fulfillment of all government obligations."[22]

Grierson did not keep his concerns about the use force within the family circle, even though he understood that his inclination toward peaceful solutions caused him professional difficulties. In fact, his enthusiasm for the Peace Policy brought him into disfavor with Sheridan.[23] Nevertheless, in September 1869 Grierson assured the Quaker agent Lawrie Tatum of his solid support, "let the consequences be what they may." He confided to Tatum that it "seems . . . from recent development, that I too must be considered *too much of a Quaker* or a *peace man* to be left here in charge of military affairs on this Reservation." Referring to General William B. Hazen's recent appointment as commander of the District of the Lower Arkansas, including the Kiowa and Comanche reservations, Grierson continued:

> If I had launched out and killed a few Indians—on the principle of the Irishman at the *Fair*—which was "wherever he saw a head to hit it"—I would no doubt have been considered *successful* and it would then have been unnecessary to place another officer over me as an intermediate commander between me and Dept. Hdqrs. So long as I have command, you may rest assured that, I will pursue such a course as to control the Indians & prevent depredations without losing sight of the object contemplated by the philanthropic and good people of the land—without *bringing in a man for the purpose of gaining an opportunity of killing off Indians,* let those who may wish it done (either on account of material interests or *personal advancement*), grumble as they may. I will do only what I believe to be just & right, even at a sacrifice of my position and Commission in the Army.

Three years later, Grierson still supported the Peace Policy, informing Felix Brunot, chairman of the Board of Indian Commissioners, that he was "confident that with judicious management—with a sufficient and effective military force properly made use of—the wild Indians about Sill or in that section of the country—can be thoroughly controlled & kept peaceable & quiet without *war or bloodshed*."[24]

Grierson understood that the humanitarians appreciated his support of the Peace Policy, and he was not above asking Tatum to use his influence among Quakers and the Peace Commissioners to defeat those who conspired to remove him from control of military affairs at Fort Sill. He also asked Brunot to endorse him for the position of brigadier general in charge of military affairs in the Indian Territory. But such maneuvering was neither uncommon in the frontier army nor an indication that Grierson was seeking this position simply to catapult himself into higher rank. He was sincerely sympathetic to the Southern Plains Indians' predicament.

Grierson's faith in the Peace Policy did receive a jolt in 1870, however, when Kiowa and Comanche raiding resumed. Fort Sill and Tatum's livestock became targets, and settlers along the north Texas frontier became victims too, losing not only livestock but sometimes their lives. Under these circumstances, the colonel took a more aggressive stance, demanding the return of livestock, captives, and order. Sporadic raids continued anyway. Even Sherman, Commanding General of the Army, nearly became a casualty when he visited Texas in the spring of 1871. Finally, Grierson agreed with Tatum that Kiowa leaders such as Big Tree, Satank, and Satanta, who openly admitted their part in raiding, should be arrested and incarcerated. That summer Grierson joined Colonel Ranald Mackenzie in a joint campaign to chastise the Comanches who were off the reservation. Yet, maintaining his faith that accommodation was preferable to bloodshed, Grierson ended the brief campaign without exchanging blows with the Comanches. At that point, Sheridan transferred Grierson away from Fort Sill and eventually off to West Texas. Finally, in the summer of 1874 Sheridan received the secretary of war's permission to wage war against the Kiowas, Comanches, and Cheyennes (even onto the reservations), a clear indication that one of the major principles of the Peace Policy had ended on the Southern Plains. When the Red River War of 1874–75 was over, the Kiowas and Comanches were defeated, never again to disrupt white expansion.[25]

If Grierson's approach to Indian affairs was not celebrated by Sheridan, he did have supporters among fellow officers of lesser rank. When Grierson returned east on personal business in the spring of 1869, Lieutenant Henry E. Alvord kept him informed of events in Indian Territory and agreed with Grierson that the surest way to insure peace was not to rely on violence but to "keep their bellies constantly full." The following year, Alvord reported that Grierson was being "heartily abused" by frontier newspaper correspondents who preached extermination and "by men in the ranks who are or pretend to be spoiling for a fight." But, Alvord said, "I have no doubt your work and its results are well understood and appreciated at the places where it is of most consequence that they should be."[26]

The fact remains that Grierson did not typify the officer corps. Most believed in judiciously applied force to subdue Indians and accelerate their acculturation. Unquestionably, they emphasized the necessity of force more than fairness in their public statements, but one can find testaments to the necessity of the latter, too. George Crook's 1884 commencement address at West Point provides a good example. In fact, the address can be seen as an officer's guide to the fair treatment of Indians and also as a rare note of advice to young officers about to leave the banks of the Hudson for the trans-Mississippi West:

> Make them no promises which you cannot fulfill; make no statements you cannot verify. When difficulties arise, as they occasionally will, endeavor to be so well informed of all the circumstances of the case that your action may be powerful and convincing, because just and impartial. Let the Indian see that you administer one law for both the white-skinned and the red-skinned, that you do this without regard for praise or censure, and you will gain his confidence because you have shown yourself worthy of it. . . . You will find that the Indian has no rights which our people are compelled to respect. The benefit of laws which protect the white man are not extended to the Indian. Even the Courts are closed to him, and to secure him common justice and protect him from outrage will frequently require all your intelligence, courage and energy.[27]

To say that the majority of officers emphasized force over fairness, moreover, is not to suggest that officers advocated extermination. As others have demonstrated, although eastern "friends of the Indian" branded officers as exterminationists, few military men advocated or tried to effect it. Genocide was neither the policy nor the result. They did, however, favor the extinction of Indian cultures and ways of life. Many even believed that Indian cultures were doomed and that the Indians' only hope of survival rested with their acceptance of civilization and Christianity. The Indian "will be as the Arab, or the Ismaelite," Colonel Henry B. Carrington pronounced, "unless rescued by some new and well nigh miraculous agency . . . and the rising generation transformed by the sole agency which can rescue the Indian . . . genuine Christian faith."[28]

Army men insisted, in fact, that it was their nation's moral obligation to provide some means of survival for Indian people, since Americans had forcefully acquired Indian property. The United States owed Indians the opportunity to assimilate. To Colonel Richard Pratt, the government's role in wresting property from the Indians meant that "his place and needs were preeminently a righteous burden on us, in which the integrity of enforcing our national principles was being tested." Randolph Marcy was equally adamant on the matter of moral obligation, claiming that the Indians had "been despoiled, supplanted and robbed of their just and legitimate heritage by the avaricious and rapid encroachments of the *white man.*" He went on to say that numerous Indian nations had already been exterminated by "unjustifiable war" and by the effects of white men's vices. "It is not at this date in our power to atone for all the injustice inflicted upon the *Red Man,*" Marcy concluded in 1866, "but it seems to me that a wise policy would dictate almost the only recompense it is now in our power to make—that of introducing among them the light of Christianity and the blessings of civilization, with their attendant benefits of agriculture and the arts."[29]

According to the policymakers' plans, reservations would be the natural place for Indians to acquire the blessings of civilization and learn the skills to survive in the Anglo-American world. A few officers, of course, criticized the reservation system from a purely military vantage point, claiming that reservations served as supply bases for Indian warriors. Such remarks most often came from contemporary letters or diaries written by frustrated officers in the field. Benjamin Grierson told his wife that the Mescalero Apache Agency had become "merely a hospital and supply camp for the Indians who are out upon the war path." Only old men, women, and children remained on the reservation, while young warriors slipped away at nightfall with the best horses and mules. In addition, the Indian women would collect rations and turn them over to "hostile Indians."[30]

The idea of the reservation as a human transformation agency certainly had its detractors among army ranks as well, though these critics were in the minority. Colonel August V. Kautz lambasted the reservation system as "one of the most fatal and destructive to the Indian race in a humanitarian view." The problem, according to Kautz, was that the government provided Indians with their subsistence. As a result, they did not need to work and instead had leisure time to learn all the white man's vices, to which they had "such a natural tendency." After several years of government support, they lost all independence and capacity to make war. They became vagrants, "living by begging and prostituting [their] women and children." The only Indians to escape this pattern, he maintained, were those bands that had not been subjected to the reservation system.[31]

Colonel Richard Pratt was perhaps the most vocal and persistent critic of reservations, charging that Indians "were made desperate by the enforcing of our obnoxious prison reservation policies." He assumed that Indians wanted to acculturate. "I have ever found that Indians everywhere have had," he wrote, "a perfect willingness to begin to accomplish that purpose." Comparing Indians to former black slaves and recent European immigrants, he believed that all three could be educated and assimilated into the mainstream of American society and culture if they were only given the proper opportunity. The reservation system, however, segregated Indians. Consequently, it impeded assimilation and excluded Indians from "participation in our American family." By forcing blacks to live with and among whites, Pratt argued, "slavery became a more humane and real civilizer, Americanizer, and promoter of usefulness for the Negro than was our Indian system through its policy of tribally segregating them on reservations and denying this participation." If taken out of the reservation and forced to live in the midst of a civilized community where he could observe the industrious farmer working in his fields or the mechanic building houses, an Indian could observe firsthand the benefits of such industry—an experience, Pratt explained to Senator H. L. Dawes, that "is worth more as a means of implanting such aspirations as those you desire for him in his mind than ten years, nay, than a whole lifetime of camp surroundings with the best Agency school work that can be done."

Pratt incorporated these ideas into his program at the Carlisle

Indian School in Pennsylvania, particularly through his "Out-ing" plan, whereby Indian boys and girls lived with a white fam-ily for a time to learn farming or other skills. In his extremely defensive autobiography, published in 1923, a time when ideas about cultural relativity were beginning to eclipse assimilation-ist ideas and when the allotment policy was undergoing very critical review, Pratt argued that the "Outing" feature of Car-lisle's education enforced participation in the dominant culture and so was "the supreme Americanizer." In concert with other assimilationists, Pratt clearly wanted to detribalize Indians. To this army officer turned educator, the complete civilization of the Indian meant absorption into national life, including citi-zenship, and denial of any Indian identity or tribal affiliation. "The sooner all tribal relations are broken up; the sooner the Indian loses all his Indian ways, even his language," he wrote, "the better it will be for him and for the government and the greater will be the economy to both."[32] He never doubted the wisdom or righteousness of such a course of action.

Most officers, however, apparently had no problem with the reservation as a place to work out what they presumed to be the necessary transformation of Indians, and most believed Indians were capable of becoming Americanized, although they rarely offered panaceas for the civilizing process. Given their general ambivalence about the virtues and vices of Indians' lives, and those of civilization as well, perhaps their reluctance to provide proposals was understandable. Most argued that Indian "recla-mation" was only a matter of time. They were, however, suit-ably vague about how much time was required to transform Indians into American citizens and farmers. Thus Crook nebu-lously maintained that Apache "regeneration could be a work only of time and of the most patient watchfulness and care," while Major Alfred E. Bates wrote, "It is probably safe to say that few of them realize that, according to 'Darwinian theory,' it will take some generations of their race to supply the connect-ing links, of which they are one, between the 'anthropomor-phoid ape' and the European settler."[33]

General Nelson Miles agreed that the change "must be gradual, continuous, and in accordance with nature's laws."

Reflecting the naturalist mood of his generation and its ideas about progress, Miles posited that the "history of nearly every race that has advanced from barbarism to civilization has been through the stages of the hunter, the herdsman, the agriculturalist—and had finally reached those of commerce, mechanics, and the higher arts." Once nomadic Indians were induced to become farmers and mechanics, and once they accumulated property and learned industry, strong incentives to remain peaceful would emerge, "namely, occupation, the fear of confiscation of property, and the loss of the comforts of life."[34]

Officers based their claims for the Indians' ability to change on two arguments. A few pointed to examples of Indians who had embraced white ways. Others offered "scientific" explanations loosely based on ideas about environment and evolution. Army surgeon Rodney Glisan, for instance, insisted that while an Indian could be most barbarous in warfare, "yet, that he is capable of civilization, the history of a large number of tribes most fully attests." He mentioned the civilized tribes of New York and the "half-civilized" Cherokee. In response to those who believed that the extermination of Indians was both the most humane and the most effective way of solving the Indian Problem, Colonel Richard Irving Dodge answered that the Indian had never had a fair chance to demonstrate his ability to become civilized, although the condition of the Cherokees, who were more advanced than most Indians, certainly demonstrated their ability to improve. Dodge expanded his argument. Believing that Indian intelligence was at least equal to that of the lower classes of the American South, black and white, Dodge dismissed any possibility of inherent, irreversible racial inferiority. "Their civilization," he asserted, "is not a natural growth, but it is the result of their circumstances and surroundings."[35] Under the proper circumstances—that is, a civilized environment—Indians could change.

Officers did assume that reservations operated only as temporary devices that would disappear once Indians became assimilated. Most believed in the ultimate goals of detribalization and acculturation, so they also welcomed allotment in severalty as a logical next step in Indian assimilation. In 1888, Benjamin

Grierson claimed that the Mescalero Apaches had been advancing toward civilization and in the near future would be ready for
allotment. This would undermine tribal relations and open
large sections of their lands to white settlement "without detriment to their [the Mescaleros'] interests." Several years earlier,
George Crook had maintained that the Apache wanted to own
land in severalty and that he should be made a citizen as well.
"This plus land will give him a stake in the community," Crook
wrote, and at the same time weaken his Indian identity.[36]

A noteworthy fact about officers' discussions of policy is their
distance from Indians themselves. They wrote about Indians as
if they were impersonal subjects in a social experiment rather
than human beings. In so doing, officers were no different from
the humanitarian reformers and most other observers of their
day. For all their talk about being realists and for all their experience with actual Indian people, they did not demonstrate a capacity to transcend their culture's deeply ingrained habit of
treating Indians as abstractions or even troublesome obstacles.

What is also notable about officers' comments on policy is
the fact that they shared all the assumptions and goals of their
presumed nemesis—the eastern "friends of the Indian," the
philanthropists. The squabbles between officers and reformers
revolved around issues regarding who would manage Indian policy, not what direction such policy should take. In the end,
officers and eastern humanitarians shared much more than
either group apparently recognized. Moreover, like eastern
philanthropists, policymakers, and congressmen, officers never
suggested consulting with Indians on the nature of policy. They
assumed the same paternalistic pose of knowing what was best
for the Indians and presumed that their good intentions would
excuse any suffering that might result. Finally, both the officers
and the philanthropists assumed that Indian cultures were easily altered and that whites possessed the power to mold the native people in ways the whites thought appropriate. Once the
army ended military resistance, they believed, all resistance
would stop. Military conquest would supposedly render Indians
totally powerless to oppose acculturation.

Again, a lone exception proves the rule. Lieutenant John

Bigelow, former West Point cadet, suggested in 1886 that the Indians retained some powers that whites had to recognize. The advocates of the allotment policy, he believed, were premature. He addressed those people who regarded reservations as "a causative peculiarity of Indian savagedom, and [who] propose to regenerate the Indians by the abolition of the reservations and their establishment in severalty." Bigelow pointed out that land held by the tribe still belonged to the Indians, "as far as anything guaranteed to them by our Government can be." What if Indian people preferred to continue holding land communally? "Having for generations been fraudulently debarring them from civilization, are we now to commence fraudulently imposing it upon them?" The fact is, he insisted, that attempts to civilize Indians and the severalty policy itself could be successful only if Indians wanted it. Yet policymakers had always evaded the central problem of Indian reluctance to give up their own ways of life and to adopt the white man's, and the absence of a solution to this problem "means nothing more nor less than peaceful, or forcible, extermination."[37] Unless the Indians chose to cooperate with the policymakers, all attempts to save them for civilization would fail.

Bigelow did not question the wisdom of acculturation, as others who followed several generations later would. He merely meant to point out that without Indian acceptance of that goal, all attempts to achieve it would be doomed. Indian people possessed some power in their relationships with whites, and that must be recognized, he claimed. But like many of his colleagues in the officer corps, he questioned the means rather than the ends. So steeped were these men in the conventions of their time regarding savagery and civilization, progress and evolution, vanishing red men and expanding white men that they could not challenge the general course of Indian policy. They could only decry its corrupt management and insist that military management based on a fair but forceful approach would ease the inevitable transformation of Indians into Americans. They stood poised and ready to provide the military muscle to see this policy through to its end.

6 / Explanations of the Indian Wars

Our sympathies were with the Indians.
—GENERAL GEORGE CROOK

In 1852, Colonel Ethan Allen Hitchcock, a Vermont-born, West Point—educated army officer and grandson of Revolutionary War hero Ethan Allen, commanded the Pacific Division of the United States Army in California. He had fought the Seminoles in Florida and the Mexicans at Contreras, Churubusco, and Molina del Rey. He was an accomplished soldier. He was also a man of literary bent who, in four years' time, would resign his commission to become a fulltime writer. In the meantime, Colonel Hitchcock kept a diary wherein he recorded his musings on theological, moral, and philosophical matters. Besides his concerns with "the unfathomable mysteries of life," Hitchcock occasionally turned his attention to Indian affairs, and sometimes the metaphysical and the practical collided.

"I called to see the Methodist minister today," Hitchcock wrote on July 31, 1852, and he "had the audacity to say that Providence designed the extermination of the Indians and that it would be a good thing to introduce the small-pox among them!" Hitchcock took leave of the clergyman and his "savage sentiment" and noted in his diary that, regrettably, that "is the opinion of most white people living in the interior of the country." He was convinced that such attitudes, along with white abuses and mendacity, provoked most Indian wars, and this conviction did not make his job any easier. Hitchcock once confessed to Reverend William Greenleaf Eliot, the prominent humanitarian and reformer, that frontier service "is harder on me than on most others, for I know the cruel wrongs to which the enemy has been subjected, so I cannot help wishing that the right may prevail which is, to use your own language, 'praying for the Indians.'"[1]

Though better read in Spinoza, Bacon, Leibnitz, Plato, Goethe, and Hegel, and more inclined to ponder religious and philosophical issues than most of his fellow officers, Colonel Hitchcock was not alone among army officers in concluding that Anglo-Americans bore the heaviest responsibility for inciting Indians to acts of violence and even full-scale war. Of course, Hitchcock did not speak for all military men. A few insisted that unprovoked Indian depredations sparked bloodshed. Others argued that blame rested with both Indians and whites, explaining that evil whites attacked innocent Indians, who in turn retaliated by assaulting innocent whites. The irresponsible elements from both sides escaped punishment while inciting and escalating violence. Yet the majority of officers concluded that Anglo-Americans, by expanding westward, were pressing Indians into fighting to protect their homes, property, and families. It was a position with which officers could empathize and even identify. It was also a position destined to cause consternation among the more thoughtful officers, who attempted to reconcile such sentiments with a duty, at times, to wage war against Indians.

Individual military men were not, of course, consistent in fixing blame for the outbreak of Indian wars. Sometimes opinion changed as time passed. An officer might express anger toward Indians in a contemporary field journal yet sympathy when he settled down years later to write his memoirs in the comfort of his home. This was the case with Major Granville O. Haller. In his 1855 diary he dismissed the Yakimas' reasons for resistance as "the old song of tampering with their women and beating and ill treating them." Haller's subsequent list of Indian grievances revealed impatience with, rather than empathy for, the Indians. Forty years later, however, while writing reminiscences of the Yakima War that he intended for public consumption, he concluded that the conflict was caused by aggressive emigrants, miners, and a government that "does not consult the Indian whether he wishes to sell but fixes the price it will give him, then, for years, fails to pay the annuities, or price agreed upon, in the treaty." The retired officer claimed that the Yakimas warred, not out of savagery, but out of love for their homes and their own way of life. He even went on to say:

And if we are candid we must admit that the Indians of Washington and Oregon are entitled to some commendation for their patriotic spirit in resisting the tyranny of civilization—if our Revolutionary Fathers were in resisting the tyranny of Royalty—for we find they were loyal to their Indian customs, and rights—fought for them—were individually brave—but lacking the cohesion of disciplined [troops] and the materials for war, they . . . had to yield to the iron hand of Destiny.[2]

Thus, over time, Haller curbed his harsh judgment of Indian resisters and, in taking the longer view from a desk well removed from battle, came to acknowledge the role American expansion and deception played in provoking Indians into wars.

The majority of officers, in fact, simply could not neglect the role the white presence played on the turbulent frontier. They lived and worked too close to the violence, and they were too intelligent to reduce conflicts to uncomplicated scenarios of evil Indians and blameless whites. Some did insist that Indians, rather than whites, initiated violence, or more precisely, subversive elements within a tribe or band agitated for war and prevailed over more peaceful, acquiescent tribesmen. In the process, these officers largely avoided soul-searching discussions of white men's aggression and consequent moral responsibility for Indian wars. But neither did they hold all tribal members responsible.

General Oliver O. Howard, for example, claimed that the Nez Perce divided into what he called the "progressive" and "reactionary" factions. The former embraced a civilized life and Christianity, while the latter clung tenaciously to their savage ways and "superstitious" religions. Howard maintained that no Christian Indians took part in the war, while the reactionary element instigated it. He avowed that Chief Joseph and White Bird participated with misgivings, knowing they would lose all they had gained through the efforts of white missionaries. They could not, however, rise above the pernicious, wicked influences of those who raged for war. Howard focused special attention on the "Dreamers," who taught that the earth should not be disturbed by cultivation or other improvements that would interfere with its natural processes. In addition, they believed that a leader from the east would bring all Indians back to life, unite them, and see that they retook the land once the whites were expelled from Indian country. Howard was referring to the preaching of a Shahaptian man named Smohalla, who began prophesying the resurrection of Indians in the Columbia River region in the 1850s. According to the tenets of the Dreamer religion, whose followers spent long periods in deep meditation, Indians would eventually form a mighty force to destroy whites and recreate their Indian world. Smohalla was not a particularly important figure until after the Civil War, when the federal government began to enforce its reservation policy in the Pacific Northwest. At that point, his message took on a decidedly militant bent as he urged Indian people to resist the reservation movement and the government's acculturation efforts.

As a supporter of acculturation, Howard disapproved of Smohalla's efforts, but he could not ignore the fact that while the Dreamers may have figured in the outbreak of war, a more fundamental cause explained the conflict—namely, government efforts to force the Nez Perce out of the Wallowa Valley and onto the Nez Perce reservation at Lapwai. In opposing this move, Howard admitted, they demonstrated "the natural and persistent resistance of independent nations to the authority of other nations." Joseph and the other "renegade" Nez Perce refused to accept either the jurisdiction of the United States or the white man's schools, churches, farms, and houses, because they preferred absolute independence, including cultural independence. "This was, indeed," Howard pronounced, "the fundamental spirit that actuated every wild Indian in whose soul slumbered the fire of Indian manhood—a manhood after their ideas."[3]

But this was not a manhood after Howard's ideas, for to acknowledge that would be to call into question the very civilization for which he fought. He was not prepared, or even inclined, to take that step. Howard did recognize the presence of factions, and he tried to vindicate those Nez Perce who cooperated with the government's program. Yet he still viewed the matter in simplistic and inaccurate terms. He did not take into consideration the complications of a decentralized tribal power. He did not understand that in some cases the peaceful and the militant could even live side by side in an Indian village. To be fair, it would have been the rare army officer who understood these matters. At least Howard indicated that the situation involved several different Nez Perce points of view.[4]

Colonel Philippe Regis de Trobriand was another officer who recognized the role of factionalism in nineteenth-century Indian politics and warfare. Trobriand posited that young fighting men made up the turbulent faction of every tribe. Often leaders had difficulty maintaining control over them. Warfare, he explained, provided young men with the means of acquiring influence, power, and status within the tribe. Blind, brute, savage instincts did not compel these men to fight. Rather, their political culture demanded that they prove themselves through warfare in order to participate in tribal decision making.[5] This assessment was certainly more sympathetic than Howard's, yet both Trobriand and Howard presented Indians as the initiators of hostilities. Consequently, they sidestepped the issue of white—even army—complicity.

Most officers, however, did not dodge the issue of the white people's role in frontier conflict. Noting the provocative impact of Indian attacks on frontier settlements, they also discussed the incendiary effect that the Americans' presence had on Indians. They concluded that the blame for warfare rested on both sides, with neither Indians nor whites being totally innocent or totally culpable. Whites, for their part, pushed farther and farther west, often directly onto Indian lands. On the Plains, the pressure of advancing settlement, along with the activities of buffalo hunters, led to the rapid disappearance of buffalo herds and made preservation of the peace exceedingly difficult. Even New Englander Robert G. Carter, who detailed grisly accounts of events such as the Salt Creek Massacre—in which the Kiowa had stripped, scalped, and mutilated the white victims—admitted in his memoirs that for the Indians to "sit idly by and witness the disappearance of their meat supply at the hands of the heartless skin-hunters was beyond the[ir] endurance." In looking at particular events of his frontier service during the

1870s, then, Carter portrayed Indians both as aggressors and as victims. They broke treaties and disturbed the peaceful advance of the frontier because they were angry over "the encroachment of the whites on their lands and the slaughter of buffalo on what they considered their own hunting ground." In fact, he wrote, the troops at Fort Wingate were often called out to prevent white men from trampling on the rights of Navajo, Hopi, Zuni, and other "semi-civilized Indians of the area who occupied lands by right of inheritance."[6]

It was not the representatives of the best elements of white America who instigated Indian wars, but rather "the reckless, the idle and the dissolute," according to John Bourke. Likewise, it was not the wise, peace-loving Indians who started conflicts, but rather young warriors anxious to gain renown through war. "The worst members of the two races," Bourke explained, "are brought into contact, and the usual results follow; trouble springs up, and it is not the bad who suffer, but the peaceably disposed on each side."[7]

Some took this line of reasoning even further, excusing Indian atrocities upon whites by arguing that, while horrible, these actions remained the normal response of a supposedly savage people. Civilized people, they said, should rise above brutality because their intellectual abilities and moral sense were more highly developed. As General Philip Sheridan put it, the Indians' "savage nature modified one's ideas . . . as to the inhumanity of their acts." But when white men engaged in similar acts, "no defense can be made for those who perpetrated the crime, if they claim to be civilized beings." Army surgeon Rodney Glisan agreed that "we ought to make some allowance for Indians' barbarous acts" since they were "not educated to the high sense of right and wrong possessed by our more enlightened people." Glisan understood Indians' "natural" resentment toward repeated efforts to move them around the countryside in order to accommodate white settlers, but he took care to exonerate permanent settlers, pointing his finger instead at nomadic miners who abused Indian women and a distant Congress that opened land to settlement before extinguishing Indian title. Glisan even asserted that permanent settlers treated Indians kindly not only because of moral considerations but also because they knew "the danger of maltreating the revengeful savage." He sympathized, however, with those settlers who, aroused by the "indiscriminate slaughter by the savages," called for extermination of the Indians. Glisan concluded:

> Still there is no reason for attaching the blame to either party exclusively, for the notions, habits, and moral relations, of the Indians and whites are so diametrically antagonistic that it is simply impossible for them to live side by side for many years without contentions. This has been the case ever since the earliest settlement of North America.[8]

Many other officers offered more decided doubts about their fellow countrymen on the frontier. Some could not conceal their contempt for the shadier elements of Anglo-American society that flourished beyond the reach of law or generally accepted modes of civility. One captain who denounced the frontiersmen in a letter to his wife written during the Rogue River War explained that Indians of the Sierra Nevada had killed an army lieutenant. But he quickly added that the natives could not be blamed, because "rascally whites" frequently killed their people "out of sport." In disgust, this veteran of the Seminole and Mexican wars contended that "I do think our race of Western Missouri men, commonly called Pike's County Men, are the most unmitigated, mean, rascally race I ever met with. They have all the meanness of the low Yankee, combined with the ignorance and laziness of the negro and the brutality of the Indian." He deeply resented the white emigrants, land-grabbers, and adventurers out for personal profit yet demanding government protection. Soldiers served as expendable pawns in the political game, forced to risk their lives for the benefit of this "rascally race."[9]

James Parker blamed Texas cowboys, buffalo hunters, and horse thieves for upsetting the Comanches and Kiowas. In fact, he claimed, a recent party had killed seven Indians with impunity. In a ringing indictment that included the Indian Department, the military, horse thieves, and miners, he maintained that Indians had a very difficult time. "As for me," he wrote his mother from Texas in the 1870s, "I would like to go on a scouting expedition after renegade Texans and hang up every scoundrel I caught."[10]

Miners became a favorite target of officers who believed that these often transient men murdered Indian men and children, raped Indian women, and then moved on—leaving the army to deal with the repercussions of their outrages. Miners ignored treaty provisions, trespassed on Indian lands, and as a shiftless and irresponsible group of money-grubbers, represented the basest element of white society in the frontier areas. Major John Sedgwick, writing to his sister from the Pikes Peak region in 1860, typically contended that "there never was a viler set of men in the world than is congregated about these mines." He believed that half the murders on the Plains attributed to Indians were actually committed by miners.[11]

A good number of officers accused speculators and merchants of instigating Indian wars so that they could profit from the influx of military troops and, in the long run, also profit from the new communities that would develop on previously Indian-owned lands. That soldiers' lives were sacrificed for others' financial gain infuriated military men, and the merchants' tendency to ingratiate themselves with political leaders by arguing that the whole nation's interests would be served by such warfare only made matters worse. In 1856, Brigadier General John Wool reported to Lieutenant Colonel L. Thomas that all was quiet in Washington and Oregon territories and that he did not expect any hostility on the part of the Indian inhabitants. However, he added, if war resumed, political and "pecuniary" speculators would be responsible. These people "will spare no efforts to make it appear that the war is not ended . . . for no other reason than to promote their own ambitious ends, under the pretence of enriching the country."[12]

Wool's charges were echoed across the military frontier. In 1854, Captain William Brooks explained in a personal letter that the army was waging a "war of extermination" against the Navajo, for no other reason that I can see than because the people, merchants and others are in hopes of extravagant expenditures of money throughout the Territory—using the plea that our arms have been tarnished, and we must wipe out the stain—General Garland I regret to have to believe, has allowed himself to be more or less swayed by the baneful influence of the aforesaid merchants and others, and especially by the secretary of the Territory now acting Governor—who is one of the principal merchants and property holders of Santa Fe.

Twenty-five years later, Major Alfred Lacey Hough, in writing about the Ute conflict of 1879, lambasted those "elements of the civilian population which constantly irritated the Indians, thereby complicating the problem of the military." From his post at Animas City, Hough told his wife that the local population wanted to bring in money and drive out the Utes through an expensive war. He found frontier people "wholly unscrupulous" and added, "it is an outrage that we of the Army who have all the hardships to encounter should be made such catspaws or mere tools of ambitious men who care only for their own interests, and cater to the public for sympathy."[13]

If the merchants, speculators, and other frontier interests had put country before self, perhaps officers such as Hough, Brooks, and Wool would have had fewer qualms about the wars. Fighting Indians in order to civilize them, to acquire lands that natives did not use in ways whites considered appropriate, to expand the nation's boundaries, or to defend the honor and dignity of the nation and its armed forces were honorable and moral purposes. But fighting Indians to line the pockets of mendacious frontier entrepreneurs did not strike these men as a proper use of army time, energy, talent, and lives. They were ready to risk their lives for the good of the country, but not for the profit of individual countrymen.

Finally, a good number of military men placed the blame for Indian hostilities squarely on the American government, which as Lieutenant Colonel O. L. Hein put it, "had been uniformly unjust to the Indian."[14] As already noted, since 1849 the responsibility for Indian affairs had rested with the Department of the

Interior. Consequently, some officers' motivations for blaming the government—or more precisely, civilian government officials—reflected their strong belief that the responsibility for Indian affairs should be transferred back to the War Department. Political considerations aside, however, many officers sincerely believed that their criticisms of government policy and government agents were valid and justified.

William Henry Bisbee, a retired brigadier general, for example, maintained in a 1903 memoir that the fundamental problem on the frontier had been the federal government's vacillating conduct. It neither fully protected the pioneers nor wholly kept them out of Indian lands until Indian title could be cleared and the Indians had received satisfactory compensation. The result was a seesawing policy in which "Indian rights, if they existed, were set aside [and] bad feeling resulted, with the soldiers as usual in those days, placed on the frontier line to maintain order or do what they could."[15]

Other army officers assigned guilt more specifically to particular government agents or commissioners. West Point graduate Isaac Stevens, having resigned his commission in the Army Corps of Engineers to serve as the civilian governor and Indian superintendent of Washington Territory, became a frequent target of officers' attacks. He convened the Walla Walla conference in 1855 in order to bring tribes to the treaty table to cede their lands. Officers who attended the conference severely criticized Stevens for the manner in which he conducted business, and they concluded that he was responsible for the ensuing outbreak of warfare. Lieutenant Henry Hodges complained to Captain George McClellan in 1856 that the Yakimas resorted to war because of the treaties made by "his Serene Highness, 'I.S.S.,'" which were "hurried through in a very summary manner. Something like the Highwayman, who with his hand on your throat, and a pistol at your head, requests your small change."[16] Hodges avowed that the Indians sensibly asked for time to study Stevens's propositions, but Stevens, who was determined to settle the issue of land immediately, refused their request.

Major Robert Seldon Garnett joined Stevens's critics, complaining in an 1856 letter to his cousin, Robert M. T. Hunter,

that the governor forced "ill judged provisions" upon the natives and that Stevens's "Quixotic pilgrimages" into the interior
were unnecessary, since no whites would settle that region for
another three hundred years. Garnett's predictions on future settlement in Washington Territory, of course, proved faulty, but
his sympathy for the Indians who lived there was clear. He
assured his cousin that if he possessed the power to annul
Stevens's treaties, he could end the war in six weeks without
firing a shot, harming settlers, or making impractical or un-
reasonable concessions to the Indians. He added that infor-
mants told him that the treaties provided the Indians with reservations that were too small even for mere subsistence and that,
if forced to live on them, the natives would starve. "If there is
truth in this," he wrote, "it is in my opinion a just cause not
only of dissatisfaction and complaint but of war. We can't expect
men to change their habits of life, the habits of their race, or to
starve to death quietly merely to satisfy the wild schemes of
white men." The government should provide "nothing more
than humanity demands us to give them, and which common
justice should never have permitted us to take away from
them."[17]

Other officers accused their government of duplicity in dealing with Indians, promising something and not delivering upon
that promise or else failing to spell out the exact terms of a
treaty. Captain Albert Barnitz noted in a journal he kept while
attending the 1867 Council at Medicine Lodge, that the
Cheyenne and Arapaho had no idea what they were giving up in
signing the treaty and predicted that war with the Cheyenne
would soon break out "in consequence of misunderstanding of
the terms of the present and previous treaties." Major Hugh
Scott, who escorted the defeated Nez Perce to Oklahoma, concluded in later years that the Nez Perce were "treated most un-
justly by the government, first as to their lands and secondly in
their deportation to Oklahoma, where they would not live." He
declared that "their treatment by the white man is a black page
in our history."[18]

Officer sympathy for the Nez Perce was not only expressed in
retrospect. In the midst of the crisis brewing between the United

States government and the Nez Perce of the Wallowa Valley, an officer named H. Clay Wood presented O. O. Howard with a report on the status of Young Joseph and the Nez Perce who followed his leadership. Wood heralded the Nez Perce in familiar terms. They were, he wrote, distinguished by their "superior intelligence, their power, and wealth of cattle and horses, their fine physical development, freedom from disease, and comparative virtues." The real turning point for the Nez Perce came with the flow of miners onto their reservation, the government's attempt to provide compensation for the Indians while meeting the white demands for land, and the separation of the tribe into the treaty and nontreaty people. In more than forty-five pages of evidence, Wood provided a concise history of the government's relationship with these Nez Perce and concluded that the causes of their dissatisfaction included miners' trespass, government mismanagement and blundering, and what he saw as "the real cause of the dissatisfaction existing among the Nez Perces with the treaty of '63 . . . a strong and undying love of home." At the end of his treatise, Lieutenant Wood offered the following: "If our Government cannot keep its plighted faith, even with the Indian, if it has no sense of honor left, the civilized nations of the globe will not be slow to find it out, and when they do, there is reason to fear a chapter in our history remains to be written which mankind shall tremble to read."[19]

Of course, Indian agents came in for a full share of the blame for having abused their native wards, defrauded them of their annuities, and instigated Indian wars in the process. Lieutenant Frank Baldwin was one who railed against "these damned miserable thieving Indian agents." If "you have anyone to accuse for the necessity of my being obliged to come into this country to fight the original owners and occupants of this the most beautiful country that I have seen west of the 100th M[eridian]," the Michigan native wrote, "you can with truth and justice accuse the Indian Dept," whose employees he believed were anxious to grab appropriations intended for Indians.[20]

Whether they emphasized Anglo-American aggression and greed or suggested that both treacherous Indians and evil whites shared responsibility for the wars, all officers insisted that the army's presence did not constitute an additional provocation. Rather, they viewed the soldiers' role as primarily peaceful. They defined their role as that of a buffer between aggressive frontier interests and an inept or corrupt federal government on one side and preyed-upon Indians on the other. They held themselves blameless.

In his autobiography, General George Crook typically blamed white abuses for the outbreak of Indian wars. But to make matters worse, he wrote, when whites provoked Indians into hostilities, the army had to punish them. "The trouble with the army," Crook complained, "was that the Indians would confide in us as friends, and we had to witness this unjust treatment of them without the power to help them. Then when they were pushed beyond endurance and would go on the war path we had to fight when our sympathies were with the Indians."[21]

Margaret Carrington, who was married to the man in command of Fort Phil Kearny at the time of the Fetterman affair, expressed similar sympathies. She presented the Crows as victims of both Sioux and white aggression, noting that the Sioux occupied lands to which the Crows had "natural title." In this respect, Mrs. Carrington demonstrated a fairly sophisticated understanding of Northern Plains intertribal dynamics. According to Carrington, the Crows were bound to the land "by sacred legends; endeared by years of occupation and wasting conflicts for its repossession, pressed by the whites from the west and now approached from the east. The Crows still maintain their rightful title, and ask of the white man that he acknowledge it." But even more significantly, Margaret Carrington claimed that many army officers shared her feelings. She went on to say in a romantic yet sincere flourish that in spite of the officer's natural

feeling of bitterness prompting the desire to exterminate his foe and thereby visit upon him some of the horrid scenes he has passed through, there comes the inevitable sentiment of pity, and even of sympathy with the bold warrior in his great struggle; and in a dash over the plains, or breathing the pure air of the moun-

tains, the sense of freedom and independence brings such a contrast with the machinery and formalities of much that is called
civilized life, that it seems but natural that the red man in his
pride and strength should bear aloft the spearpoint and with new
resolve fight the way through to the final home in the Spirit
Land.[22]

Indians fought, people like Crook and Carrington maintained,
in order to stem white aggression, lust, or greed rather than to
provide outlets for a directionless, aimless savagery. In other
words, Indians warred against Anglo-Americans for legitimate,
rational, and even moral purposes. Ironically, military men
seemed more willing to acknowledge this about Indian enemies
than they were about Indian allies, scouts, and auxiliaries. At
the same time, officers' meditations on the causes of Indian
wars also provided them with an opportunity to criticize certain
members of their own society: civilian Indian agents, corrupt
frontiersmen, and members of volunteer regiments. These
groups competed with army officers for power on the frontier,
particularly in Indian affairs. Consequently, the military's view
of them was not always objective. Yet officers' expressions of
outrage against white perpetrators of violence suggests that
political motivations alone do not explain their apparently sincere sympathy for tribesmen.

Such assessments placed the more reflective, perceptive military men in the tenuous position of ultimately defending the
aggressors, particularly those who initiated or ignited hostilities
for immoral and mendacious purposes. These officers expressed
anger, frustration, and contempt for grasping frontier merchants, unscrupulous Indian agents, ragtag miners, and less frequently, even yeoman farmers who provoked wars to enhance
their personal wealth. The consequent bloodshed did not serve
a noble or justifiable purpose. To nineteenth-century army
officers, who preferred to view themselves as agents in civilization's triumph over savagery, this posed a serious dilemma. If
Indians fought defensive wars, then the U.S. Army—as vanguard
and ultimate protector of civilization—fought aggressive, offensive wars. The irony of this point of view did not escape the

more sensitive, thoughtful officers. How did military men deal with the moral consequences of their actions? How did they reconcile decided sympathies for Indians with their military duties, and their personal misgivings with their public actions? How did they justify their participation in the Indian wars?

One must begin by distinguishing between public and private utterances. Many military people, for example, responded forcefully and publicly to eastern humanitarians' accusations that soldiers exterminated innocent Indians. In the face of such critics, they closed ranks, defending the army wholeheartedly. Reformers pushed for peaceful measures to achieve the goals of federal Indian policy. They singled out the military as a major impediment to nonviolent solutions to "the Indian problem" and to the success of any acculturation program, often viewing army officers, according to historian Robert Mardock, as "bloodthirsty border ruffians who hungered for the extermination of the Western tribes." Former abolitionist Wendell Phillips, for example, insisted that the actual Custer Massacre occurred not on the Little Big Horn but eight years earlier on the Washita River when Custer attacked a peaceful Cheyenne village, slaughtering women, children, and unarmed men.[23]

Stung by this kind of comment, officers, a particularly self-conscious group, reacted quickly and with no equivocation. Major General John Schofield claimed that no group valued "more highly their reputation for faithful and honorable conduct in the public service" than army people. He argued that if military justice had prevailed on the frontier rather than that of corrupt Indian agents and greedy frontiersmen, thousands of lives and hundreds of millions of dollars would have been saved. Upon reading Phillips's attack on Custer, Nelson Miles, a colonel at the time, informed his wife in an 1876 letter from Montana Territory that he had publicly replied to Phillips's charge. He wanted to defend Custer. Moreover, he did not "think the Army should knuckle down and allow a man to hold it up to the world as below the level of humanity."[24]

Frustrated and angered by critics who attacked them from the security of Boston, army men, risking their lives on the frontier, insisted that they were fighting to provide westerners with what

New Englanders had achieved several centuries earlier. "It is in New England, the land of the Pequots and the Iroquois," Captain Charles King pointed out, where "the most violent partisans of the peace policy are to be found today." Noting that the further removed he was from actual Indians, the more inclined a citizen was to like them, King went on:

> Each state in turn has elbowed him on towards the Mississippi, and by the time the struggling aborigine was at the safe distance of two or three states away, was virtuously ready to preach fierce denunciation of the people who simply did as it had done. . . . [W]hen we look back and remember how the whole movement was inaugurated by the Pilgrim Fathers, is it not edifying to read the Bostonian tirades against the settlers—the pilgrims and pioneers of the Far West?[25]

Other officers concluded that well-meaning philanthropists simply possessed little knowledge of Indians or Indian affairs and in their ignorance lashed out at the army. Lieutenant Colonel George Forsyth acknowledged the humanitarians' concerns but dismissed them as the fears of a good and truly philanthropic people who knew absolutely nothing about Indian campaigns in the West. He deeply resented eastern critics of the Washita battle who accused the army, the War Department, and General Philip Sheridan of instigating the fight "solely that the Army might have an excuse for its being, never seeming to realize that the Indians had brought the trouble upon themselves by a series of unprovoked murders and outrages upon the frontiersmen and their families almost passing the bounds of mortal endurance." Nelson Miles sarcastically complained to his wife that it "required a peculiar kind of genius to conduct an Indian campaign from West Point—or Boston, although they know a great deal about Indians in that model city—at least they think they do, which is very important."[26]

Officers' wives joined their husbands in responding to eastern critics and defending the army's actions, although their forum was private correspondence more often than public statement. "Surely you do not believe," Elizabeth Custer chastised her aunt after the Battle of the Washita, "the current rumors that Autie and others are cruel in their treatment of Indians? Autie and others only do what they are ordered to do. And if those who criticize these orders could only see for themselves . . . [a]s we see . . . the brutalities of the men, the venom of the squaws. . . . People in civilized conditions cannot imagine it. But we who have seen it know." Almira Hancock fumed about "northern philanthropists" and their "ignorance of a class of human beings, whom they know little about and always seem averse to a closer inspection of, when invited to study the subject on the ground." Of those who criticized the surprise attack on the Piegan band of Blackfoot in 1870, she had these words: "The false sentiment bestowed and entirely wasted upon this treacherous race by a class who know nothing of their character and habits, except from the sentimental brain of the imaginative Cooper, have been and always will be the *bete noir* of the frontier service."[27]

Criticism from eastern philanthropists certainly compelled army people to consider the morality of the means, if not the ends, of Indian policy. Yet even officers who were not directly responding to eastern critics filled their letters, diaries, and books with defenses of army activities. Striving to present the military in a positive light, they insisted on its humanity, moral rectitude, and integrity. Some even pressed beyond a defensive posture to celebrate the army's efforts, which they believed went unheralded as the nation ignored the sacrifices that officers and enlisted men alike endured. All of this indicates that, at the very least, officers deeply cared how others—particularly wives, parents, children and friends—perceived their work and the officers themselves. It also suggests, however, that some were responding to internal doubts concerning the merits of their actions. In personal journals and letters to family members, they often revealed their more intimate feelings and thoughts about the special ethical concerns of fighting Indians.

These men were not, therefore, robots directed from Washington. They wrestled with the moral dimensions of their actions, and a significant number revealed personal misgivings about their participation in the Indian wars—particularly those who viewed whites as largely responsible for inciting frontier conflicts in the first place. Their situation presented a universal problem for soldiers, who are compelled by their role as military men to implement policies and fight bloody wars that make few allowances for personal ethical considerations.

Some handled the situation by presenting their participation in professional military terms and accepting their duty as disagreeable but necessary. They believed that the human circumstance thrust on men many wretched responsibilities and gruesome tasks. Given the dark side of human nature, warfare and bloodshed were inescapable. Unable to alter this fact, their duty required only that they, as soldiers, do their job well. It was in this spirit that Lieutenant Edward Steptoe explained to his younger brother, then enrolled at West Point, that "So long as Governments will affront each other & fall out, wars must continue, that is, until the 'Lion & Lamb lie down together.' . . . The profession of arms I hold to be as honorable in a moral or Christian view as any whatever—only act well your role in it."[28]

Denying that feasible alternatives to the use of force on the frontier existed, another officer maintained in his memoir that every generation had its share of people who "decry the strong arm of the sword and advocate tribunes of arbitration; but such advocacy will never prevail; and such peaceful tribune will ever be the iridescent dream of the imagination." On a somewhat less eloquent note, Lieutenant Colonel George A. Forsyth found hunting Indians to be "terribly rough work" and "wiping them out . . . after they had refused to surrender . . . a most dangerous, grisly, gruesome, and revolting task," yet one "imposed by military necessity."[29]

These men found relief in emphasizing their soldierly duty to follow orders regardless of the nature of those orders. This allowed them to avoid moral responsibility for the warfare by claiming that they did not formulate Indian policy or declare war on Indians; they simply followed the course devised by others. Many years after his frontier service, Frank Baldwin, who had reached the rank of brigadier general before his retirement in 1902, wrote to a young man who was recovering from a World War I wound. Baldwin explained that from the moment a cadet entered West Point or an enlisted man joined his regiment, he was taught two important things: the "honour of the service and the necessity of always and under all circumstances doing his duty." "Bear in mind," Baldwin went on, "that patience and perfect obedience to every order is a sure indication of a model and high-toned soldier." The old Indian campaigner had never expressed much consternation over the Indian wars, yet his letter provides an insight into a military mentality that no doubt soothed some of his more introspective colleagues. Lieutenant Colonel Eugene Carr confessed to his sister that "it looks hard to see such suffering" as that he witnessed among the Indians at Camp Grant in Arizona Territory in 1873, but he found comfort in stating, "I have tried to do my duty here, and have, I think, performed some service useful to the country."[30]

Perhaps the most thoughtful, and tortured, statement of this point of view came in Lieutenant Edward Steptoe's letter to his brother. Steptoe, who later saw service in the trans-Mississippi West, wrote this letter during his service in the Seminole War of 1842:

> The profession of arms, my dear William, is one of the most honorable & distinguished that you could enter. . . . The *motives* of our rulers we have no way of finding out, nor should we make *obedience* dependent upon our knowledge of their motives. If the Government declares a war however unjust, its citizens are as much bound, individually, to help its prosecution, as to continue *allegiance* to that government after it passes iniquitous laws, exterminating the Indians or sanctioning slavery, or partitioning Poland, or any laws on record that are condemned by mankind. Governments are responsible, not we—if they do injustice they must answer, not we. The Bible only enjoins upon Soldiers as individuals to abstain from cruelty. . . . [A]gainst them as a *body* it says nothing.

Steptoe added: "These remarks I make mostly for Pa's eyes being not sure that he regards me as much better than a national murderer."[31]

Steptoe and others harbored doubts about the morality of Indian wars but sidestepped personal ethical responsibilities by blaming civilian governments and policymakers. As human beings, these men could empathize with Indians. As military men, they did not question orders. Though they felt sympathy for Indians, in the end their actions contributed to the effort to dispossess Indians of their land and violently change their lives. Several spoke out on behalf of particular tribes—Crook on the Poncas and the Chiricahua Apaches, for example.[32] But for the most part, loyalty to national goals and military duty won out over moral scruples. At the same time, officers like Steptoe were not unmoved by the ethical dilemma they faced as instruments of a policy over which, they claimed, they had no control.

These sentiments came from contemporary personal writings. Officers who *published* accounts of their frontier military careers often turned in another direction when justifying their part in "the Indian drama," presenting the conflict in the familiar terms of an heroic effort to ensure civilization's triumph over savagery. "Since the establishment of our government," Colonel Richard Irving Dodge proclaimed, "the army has been the bulwark of civilization; the rock on which the forces of barbarism were shattered and expended, . . . giving a continent to civilization and rendering possible an immigration unequalled in the history of the world."[33] Many insisted that it was not necessary to apologize for the dispossession of Indians' lands because the land had to be reclaimed from savages and made into farms for civilized men and women.

Missing from almost all officers' accounts, however, is the term "manifest destiny" and any reference to a "providential mission." Such phrases apparently did not capture their attention or become part of their everyday vocabulary. Albert K. Weinberg defined manifest destiny as the dogma that "America's incorporation of all adjacent lands was the virtually inevitable fulfillment of a moral mission delegated to the nation by Providence itself." While many officers may have agreed with this justification of expansionism, they simply did not use its language in their writings. Here and there an individual would use the word "providence" but not in relation to the conquest of Indians. As Lewis O. Saum pointed out about nineteenth-century Americans: "In the writings of the common man, the providential emphasis is on the personal and the immediate, not on the national and the historical."[34] The same holds true for army officers.

Nor did they rely on religious arguments to defend their actions. As a group, officers were not particularly religious. Certainly, some were committed members of a church. Others were interested in religious issues but were not church members. But for many, religion was simply not important. The army as an institution was partly responsible for this. In 1874 only thirty of three hundred military stations had chaplains. Further, army regulations required inspections and reviews on Sundays, making it difficult for officers to observe the sabbath. Yet the non-religious character of at least West Point–educated officers was evident earlier in their careers. One scholar found that all references to spiritual matters, particularly compulsory Sunday chapel, in West Point cadets' letters and diaries were derogatory and that the waves of religious enthusiasm that swept other segments of the population in the nineteenth century made no impact on the corps of cadets.[35]

Rather than adopting the language of manifest destiny or religious doctrine, officers' justifications, particularly in post–Civil War statements, reflected a belief in the idea of progress and a familiarity with the naturalist mood of their time. They believed in a world of constant change, assuming that such change was for the betterment of all mankind and that it followed a linear rather than cyclical pattern, which they called progress. In addition, they accepted an evolutionary view of progress whereby human history ascended from simple, primitive cultures to complex, sophisticated ones such as their own. Although few officers referred to Lewis Henry Morgan's work, many would have shared his view that savagery, barbarism, and civilization represented "an ascending order of complexity," as historian Stow Persons explained it, "and that races must pass through them in the same successive order if they were to advance at all."[36] Some races, lacking the capacity for improvement, even ceased to advance beyond certain stages.

Army officers disagreed on the issue of the Indians' capacity for improvement, but all agreed that their own culture, with its advanced technology, represented the highest state of man's development to date and that it would inevitably replace barbarism in the American West. They assumed that the law of evolution had a coercive power over nature and society, leaving little room for human freedom or ability to alter the process. In a naturalistic world of evolutionary social development, where death and suffering inevitably led to progression, army officers could find solace for their misgivings about their role in that bloodletting and pain. As Persons put it, "for the practical man it meant that what is, is right because what is, is what has to be." Though some regretted modern civilization's industrialism and commercialism, and though some longed for the freedom from restraint that primitive societies seemed to offer men from more mechanistic, controlled societies, army men ultimately concluded that the forces of progress and evolution determined their path and offered no alternatives. Moreover, most of these men embraced the nation's enthusiasm for the material possibilities of rich western lands and for the industrial revolution that made it possible to exploit them.[37]

As early as 1866, William B. Hazen pronounced that Indians were in the "way of the evolutions of progress." In an 1875 speech before the British Association for the Advancement of Science, retired Colonel Henry B. Carrington confirmed that Indians were "in the iron grip of the advancing empire" and would be "hurled aside in its progress" unless they accepted civilization and Christianity. In his memoir, General Nelson Miles claimed that the onward march of Anglo-American civilization on the western frontier was irresistible: "no human hand could stay that rolling tide of progress." With little apparent hesitation he asserted, "As a result of the military occupation of the Indian country came the first dawn of peace and a change from primitive, barbaric life to civilization." But it was Lieutenant Colonel George Forsyth who provided the classic statement of this view, seasoned with a sprinkling of Darwinian language. In acknowledging that "the Indian has been wronged, and deeply wronged, by bad white men," he wrote, "it must always be borne in mind that, cruel as the aphorism is, 'the survival of the fittest' is a truism that cannot be ignored nor gainsaid and barbarism must necessarily give way before advancing civilization."[38]

Retired brigadier general William Henry Bisbee also emphasized the inevitability of civilization's advance, although with less apparent confidence than Forsyth or Miles. In his autobiography, not published until 1931, he attempted to absolve himself and his fellow officers of personal responsibility in the conquest by picturing officers as pawns in the hands of historical forces beyond their control: "Why decry civilized action unfair as it may have been against the 'poor Indian' in the Prairie years? How could the red condition continue. . . . We were forced to consider the inevitable advance of civilization regardless of the feelings of either white men or Indians." In a perfect statement of army officer ambivalence, Bisbee observed that "[c]onsidering the circumstances and the result as it stands today, the outcome should justify the methods, weak and wicked as they were." He rather lamely concluded, "My only answer could be, we did it for civilization."[39]

To army wives as well, it was not only appropriate that Anglo-American civilization advance across the continent, it was inevitable. Grace Paulding, whose husband taught her about Indian customs, found that "they came to be real people to me," and she began to "see their difficulties and perplexities, caught, as they were in our civilization which was encroaching on the lands they had always considered their own." Yet she left her reader with the impression that nothing could be done to alter the situation. She probably would have agreed with Margaret Carrington that the new order had no place for "the bold warrior" who could only fight his way "through to the final home in the Spirit Land."[40]

Most army men and women, then, found some means of reconciling their actions with their doubts about Indian policy and their ambivalence about Indians. Officers did not resign their commissions over opposition to the government's treatment of Indians. To demand resignation as the true test of officers' sincerity in sympathizing with Indians or criticizing their countrymen, however, is unfair. The army was their career and their life. Moreover, as Steptoe demonstrated, the idea of a soldier's resigning because he disagreed with policy would have seemed bizarre. As professional military men, the officers' solemn duty was to follow orders, not to question them. Public duty prevailed over private conscience. Finally, all of these army officers shared their society's fundamental belief in the superiority of Anglo-American culture, although cracks in that confidence are visible. Consequently, their ethical qualms focused on the means, not the ends, of Indian policy, for the ends were not only appropriate but inevitable, being the natural working out of evolutionary progress.

Only one officer rejected the fundamental assumption of American civilization's superiority. But he came to this position long after his service in the Indian wars and at a time when the nation's intellectuals were discarding naturalist conceptions of social evolution, progress, and hierarchical civilizations. A reluctant soldier from the outset, Lieutenant C.E.S. Wood attended West Point at his father's command, and he demonstrated a special sensitivity to Indians while in uniform. Chief Joseph's surrender speech, some believe, was embellished by this poetically inclined lieutenant, who transcribed the translation during the actual surrender. Eventually Wood resigned from the army, became a lawyer, moved to Portland, Oregon, fathered some children, flirted with radical politics, and counted Emma Goldman and Lincoln Steffens among his friends. Having enjoyed a lucrative law practice, in his old age Wood turned his attention to his first love—poetry. Occasionally he dealt with themes of conquest, war, and civilization's right to rule. In a 1906 poem, written to "celebrate the glorious victory of Gen. Leonard Wood, who exterminated in the Island of Jolo [in the Philippines] six hundred Moros, men, women and children, who defended themselves in the crater of a mountain peak," Wood attacked the army and its role as the bearer of civilization to the uncivilized.

Six hundred Moros slain!—Good!
Caught in the crater's cup they lie,

Staring into the unresponsive sky,
Fathers, mothers, babes, the whole barbarian brood.
In this hollow of the highest peak,
Between the palm fringed earth and arching blue.
The rocks are crimson from the precious dew
Which slowly out from baby breasts did leak.
They fought, they would not quietly submit
Unto the rule of those who crossed the seas
To carry Christ and right to such as these,
The White Man's right to rule. Is there a doubt of it?[41]

In his 1915 poem, "The Poet in the Desert," Wood returned to this theme and brought it home, revealing profound doubts about his civilization's claim to supremacy:

I have lain out with the brown men
And know they are favored.
Nature whispered to them her secrets,
But passed me by.

I sprawled flat in the bunch-grass, a target
For the just bullets of my brown brothers betrayed.
I was a soldier, and, at command,
Had gone out to kill and be killed.

We swept like fire over the smoke-browned tee-pees;
Their conical tops peering above the willow.
We frightened the air with crackle of rifles,
Women's shrieks, children's screams,
Shrill yells of savages;
Curses of Christians.
The rifles chuckled continually.
A poor people who asked nothing but freedom,
Butchered in the dark.[42]

In rejecting the army's presumed role as the bearer of civilization to the uncivilized, C.E.S. Wood was not typical of Indian-fighting officers. He was, if anything, ahead of his time—anticipating attitudes more in line with modern cultural anthropologists than with those of his army compatriots. But though perhaps more outspoken and given to doubt than most, he was not alone in wrestling with the troubling moral implications of the Indian wars. A significant number of officers searched for ways to explain their participation in the westward expansion of an aggressive, even avaricious, nation, and they did not always resolve the conflict between professional duty and personal conscience. Concerned that parents and others viewed them as "national murderers" they could not always veil the troubled ambivalence of statements such as, "My only answer could be, we did it for civilization."

7 / Indian Warfare

*The Indians were brave and desperate fighters, and a foe
which could develop the real manhood of the frontier
soldier.*   —WILLIAM T. PARKER

In determined pursuit of the Nez Perce during the summer of
1877, Lieutenant C.E.S. Wood, many years before he penned the
poetry that closed the previous chapter, settled down to scribble
his thoughts in a small field journal. Reflections on battlefield
dangers and even mortality plagued the handsome, introspective lieutenant. He confessed: "fearing the field, peculiar ner-
vous feeling of going to death, shrinking from the expose. most
desire to be out of the expedition—Old soldiers the same way."
Several days later, after burying the army dead at White Bird
Canyon ("horrible stench, arms and cheeks gone, bellies swol-
len, blackened faces") he described the special tensions of war,
in which soldiers had to accept such gruesome sights and in
which, on the eve of yet another battle, they had to prepare for
their own possible end by composing last messages for families,
wives, and sweethearts.

When the fighting began again, Wood's mood changed: "All
thoughts of the future vanishing, only want a crack at an Indian
and feel no disposition to show any quarter." Yet again for Wood,
this angry outburst represented only a passing urge. Several
weeks later the young officer was more generous, entertain-
ing thoughts "on the Indian as a human being. A man and a
brother."[1]

It is one thing to reflect on causes and justifications of Indian
wars in relative safety. It is another to find the enemy (whatever
the justice of his reasons) shooting at you. In that context, more
immediate concerns—survival, for example—seem of greatest
importance. Given the fact that officers' lives were at stake, fear
and anger are understandable reactions. At the same time, given
their willingness to expose their countrymen's culpability in

inciting the Indian wars, did these men express other thoughts and feelings about the warfare and about their Indian enemies? How representative were Wood's battlefield meditations and changes of mood? How did wives feel about their husbands' participation in the Indian wars? Did their attitudes shift with the circumstances too? Finally, what assessments did officers make of Indians' military prowess?

Unfortunately, some men wrote little or nothing about their Indian-fighting experiences. Whether these individuals thought about such matters we shall never know. It may not have occurred to them to ponder these concerns, being less inclined, perhaps, than later generations to analyze the self or dwell on individual feelings.[2] Others may have found it too difficult to recreate on paper the emotional and psychological side of Indian campaigning, while still others probably never felt compelled to muse at any length on these subjects, accepting their soldierly duty as an unpleasant but inevitable aspect of the human condition.

Fortunately, some did reflect on the actual fighting. Letters from the field could elicit chilling responses to killing Indians when officers, unlike C.E.S. Wood, appeared unmoved by the violence and death. Self-interest often seemed paramount in many of these cases. The men naturally preferred to survive. In describing an engagement in the Nez Perce War to his wife, for example, Lieutenant C. A. Woodruff explained that seventy-five to a hundred Indians had died. "We killed them right and left," he wrote. "Hurlburt of 'K' killed the Indian that shot [Lieutenant James] Bradley, Jacobs killed three, Renn two, Harding & Woodbridge one each. I didn't get a chance to kill any of them. I was carrying orders." Flushed with anger and anxiety during the fight, Woodruff told his wife, "I began to fear I should never see you again." Revealing an aspect of his own battlefield psychology, he added, "I got my two revolvers, said my prayers, thought of you and Bertie and determined to kill a few Indians before I died. I didn't know how much I loved you until I thought we would never see each other again."[3]

One of the best descriptions of this response to battle came from the pen of Edmund Hardcastle in a letter written to his aunt from the Mexican War. It is reasonable to assume that soldiers in the Indian wars experienced similar reactions. He explained that during a fight,

> Every man has his duties to perform. And with the mind thus occupied he is debarred from reflection & he soon becomes so animated with the excitement, that all around him tends to produce, that anything else save the destruction of the foe, is forgotten. T'is strange but too true that man's feelings can be made such as to rejoice in the blood of his fellow man. But this is but one of the necessary consequences flowing from a state of war; and it must not continue, but increase, so long as such a state exists.[4]

More than one officer thought beyond survival to prospects of earning distinction in the Indian wars and consequent public accolades (although not necessarily promotion). In the nineteenth-century American army, promotion came through seniority rather than merit. Valor on the battlefield could be rewarded with brevet, or honorary, rank, but even that did not apply to Indian warfare until 1890, when Congress finally invited brevet nominations for Indian engagements. Also in 1890, congressional reform made physical and professional examinations part of the promotion process for ranks through major. But through most of the nineteenth century, notable battle conduct did not lead to promotion.[5]

The limited effect that battlefield exploits would have on advancement did not, however, diminish individual officers' hopes for distinction. Sometimes men hoped to demonstrate their abilities only to themselves. At other times they yearned for more public recognition. In anticipation of a battle with the "Utahs" in 1855, Assistant Surgeon DeWitt Clinton Peters informed his father that he was feeling ambivalent about the prospects. For one thing, "extracting bullets and shooting them are two different things as far as public renown is concerned." But even more important, this officer claimed, was his "inward monitor." He would be happy if he conducted his role to the best of his ability. "[T]hat I may be allowed to go to the full of my ambition and that in the end I may live with an unstained and honest name is my wish and prayer."[6]

Throughout the Indian wars, other military men revealed similar concerns about proving their mettle. Lieutenant John Bourke understood that many younger officers enthusiastically anticipated the spring 1876 Sioux and Cheyenne campaign "partly from the hope of distinction that may be gained." But such hopes were not for junior officers alone. Later that year Lieutenant Colonel Richard Irving Dodge filled his journal with thoughts of personal success. At one point during the savagely cold Powder River Expedition, General George Crook, Colonel Ranald Mackenzie, and Dodge considered halting the campaign because, after Mackenzie's men destroyed Dull Knife's Cheyenne village, they had not located any more Indians, and rations were running low. "I said that I would probably gain more by a successful campaign than either of them," Dodge confided to his journal, "and that my disposition was to stick as long as there was a chance." But his colleagues argued that there remained little likelihood of engaging the Cheyenne in battle, so Dodge reluctantly agreed to conclude the expedition and put aside his hopes for distinction in battle.[7] Upon returning to the garrison, Dodge received a letter from his parents, expressing hope that he would distinguish himself, although not at the cost of his health or his life. Dodge found comfort in their concern:

> It did me a world of good and reconciled me somewhat to going home without any special glory. The world applauds success— while success is an accident that may come to the stupid and energetic, as well as to the brightest and hardest worker. The world applauds the success, but conscience approves him who does his work to the best of his ability whether he be successful or not. Neither myself nor my Command have done anything brilliant, but we have done our very best and had our luck put us in a fight, we would have made a name for ourselves—or I am mightily mistaken. That's all![8]

While Dodge consoled himself in this fashion, Lieutenant Frank Baldwin hoped for more public attention and applause. He reported to his wife while encamped on the Washita River in 1874 that Nelson Miles seemed pleased with his safe return from a scouting mission, and "as I killed the first Indian on the expedition I of course was the hero." This kind of success had its drawbacks, however, for he also noted that "the Cav. officers act very much annoyed at it and I can see that they are jellous as they can be." Several months later he boasted that with 125 men and some artillery he would "have a fine chance to fight and gain a victory which [would] add new laurels" to his name. It was not until five years later, however, that Baldwin received a captaincy, and thirty years passed before he received the Congressional Medal of Honor for distinguished and gallant service against Indians in Texas. This was a rare honor, particularly for a soldier in the Indian wars. In another case, Second Lieutenant Stephen Mills told his mother in an 1882 letter from Arizona Territory that upon breaking out from their reservation, some Warm Springs Indians had been practically exterminated. His command pursued them into Mexico, where some Mexicans "finished the job." Mills exuberantly reported, "It's the best piece of Indian work that has been done in the south west for many years and I think we have a right to feel proud of it." He was later honored with a brevet rank of first lieutenant for his efforts.[9]

Sometimes officers worried less about laurels than about the consequences of failure. One man remembered that while escorting the Yakima leader Owhi to Fort Walla Walla after the 1856 Battle of Four Lakes in Washington Territory, the Indian attempted to escape. This first lieutenant, only several years out of West Point, followed in swift pursuit, revolver in hand and "angry because I feared he might escape and that would end my military career." Finally he discharged three bullets into Owhi, who somehow remained seated on his pony. Having exhausted all the charges in his weapon, the furious officer ordered his sergeant to shoot Owhi yet again, which he did.[10]

In wartime it was quite common and natural for these men to think about personal concerns such as survival and career advancement. Officers' wives' attitudes were affected by personal concerns too, particularly their husbands' well-being. When war broke out, these women perceived Indians first as the enemy, and considerations of Indian humanity faded, at least temporarily. They expressed hatred toward Indians when they felt threatened by them or when they believed their husbands' lives were in danger. Frances Carrington, in other respects fairly sympathetic toward Indians, admitted some satisfaction when Colonel Henry Carrington fired three howitzers into the midst of a group of Sioux and Cheyenne men outside Fort Phil Kearny. Under the stress of a besieged garrison, she was understandably less inclined to consider the Indians' point of view.[11]

An outbreak could even bring talk of extermination. Teresa Viele concluded that extermination was the only remedy when her boat attracted Comanche fire on the Rio Grande. Similarly, Emily Fitzgerald, upon receiving word of Custer's defeat at the Little Big Horn, wrote to her mother from Fort Lapwai in Idaho Territory:

> Did you ever hear anything more terrible than the massacre of poor Custer and his command. . . . War is dreadful anyway, but an Indian war is worst of all. They respect no code of warfare, flags of truce, wounded—nothing is respected! It is like fighting to exterminate wild animals, horrible beasts! Don't let anybody talk of peace until the Indians are taught a lesson and, if not exterminated, so weakened they will never molest and butcher again.

Once the Nez Perce War began, Emily wrote home, "Oh, how I hate them. I wish they could be exterminated, but without bloodshed among our soldiers," and "I wish all the Indians in the country will have trouble until they are exterminated." Concern for her husband's safety prompted Emily's great distress and harsh words. She had witnessed the grim results of the early battles and asked her family, "Can you imagine how terrible it is for us women at Lapwai with all this horrible Indian war around us, and with these . . . women who have lost their husbands, constantly before our eyes, and we not knowing who will be the next sufferer."[12]

The anxieties of an Indian war elicited a somewhat different response from Alice Baldwin. First she railed against the limitations of her sex in a letter to her husband, Frank:

> It is so easy for you to *tell* me to not be so discouraged & blue & to not feel uneasy but with you how different from me. *You* are living a life *fraught* with peril & excitement . . . you are living

the *Life you love*—that's everything and besides all this you are a Man! Now look at me—I am a *woman* with all the love & anxiety of a wife for the man she loves. I have no stirring scenes to pass thro—there are no eventful episodes in *my* existence. I am not living the life *I* love. All I have to do are a few paltry insignificant duties to perform & that makes up my daily life.

A month later she turned her frustrations elsewhere. "You call this duty imposed on you a *compliment*," she wrote to her husband. "Maybe it is but it seems to me as if [General Nelson] Miles was making you do all the drudgery of the whole command. . . . I wish Miles was dead or something." Mrs. Baldwin's exasperation is compelling because it is so human, so understandable. Most other wives, however, placed the blame for their husband's absence or vulnerability on Indians rather than their government or their spouse's commanders. Far more typical was Caroline Frey Winne's reaction to the Bannock War: "I hate the sight of an Indian ever since this news came," or Sarah Ovenshine's comment on the Sioux: "The wretches, how can they be ranked among human beings."[13]

Beyond the personal concerns, their repeated exposure to death and brutality on the frontier also influenced army people's attitudes regarding the Indian-killing business. In his memoirs, Lieutenant Britton Davis referred to "the callousness with which the white man had come to regard the taking of the red man's life. Exasperated, our senses blunted by Indian atrocities, we hunted them and killed them as we hunted and killed wolves." Davis admitted that he was similarly unfeeling until he lived with some Apaches for a time, with no companionship except that of the Indians. It was only then, he claimed, that "the feeling that there could be no possible ground upon which we could meet as man to man passed away."[14]

It was not always necessary for an officer to live with Indians in order to empathize with them, however. A significant number demonstrated anger with Indian enemies during a war, followed by great sympathy for the same Indians when the fighting ended. Army wives did the same. After battle, it was not unusual for military people to reflect upon Indians as men—if not as "brothers," as C.E.S. Wood had put it. One officer described the Modoc, during hostilities, as perpetrators of atrocities, but once the leaders were captured and held for trial, he depicted them as victims, writing, "it was a sickening sight to see those six vanquished savages . . . arraigned for ceremonious trial before the cultivated, uniformed victors against whom they had waged such desperate and unequal war." In their defeat, this officer acknowledged, the Modocs suffered from wrongs that entitled them to sympathy and help.[15]

During the Rogue River War, Lieutenant E.O.C. Ord took pride in a successful skirmish against the enemy wherein, he informed his wife, "we killed their principal chief." Yet he also told her, "I never lose sight of what is right and just—and even think how *little* harm I can do the poor wretches I have to fight so as, at the same time, to produce peace." And Lieutenant Charles Gatewood, who witnessed Geronimo's surrender in 1886, wrote his wife that the Apaches were being shipped without families to Florida as punishment for leaving their reservation. "I really felt sorry for [them]," he confessed, "for I know how it is to yearn after one's family. . . . [W]ouldn't *I* prance around lively if they moved you off to Florida."[16]

At least one officer openly criticized his superior's wartime actions. Terribly disturbed at the sight of a battlefield littered with bodies during the Gila Expedition of 1857, Lieutenant John Van Deusen Du Bois called the event a massacre and agonized in his journal, "I could not avoid asking myself why we had killed these poor harmless savages. It is not pretended that they ever did any harm to us." Further, he damned the order by his commanding officer, Colonel Benjamin Bonneville, to execute a captive, "a fine looking Indian brave" who was shot "like a dog" by a Pueblo scout. "May God grant," Du Bois declared in his journal, "that Indian fighting may never make me a brute or harden me so that I can act the coward in this way. Humanity, honor, a soldier's pride, every feeling of good in me was & is shocked by this one act." Expressing his outrage to fellow officers, he found, "thank God, that but one officer presumes to defend it."[17]

Once the hostilities had ended and the threat had passed, officers' wives also expressed sympathy for their former enemies. They acknowledged the Indians' point of view and expressed understanding, if not respect, for their resistance to white advances into their country. Emily Fitzgerald pitied the Nez Perce prisoners of war, especially those separated from their families. Of the Bannock prisoners, Mrs. Winne wrote, "We all felt a great deal of sympathy for them." Teresa Viele declared, "I cannot refrain from some feelings of sympathy for a people, who are driven from their rightful possessions, and can see, in their ignorance, many excuses for their tiger-like ferocity and bitter hatred of those who they feel have wronged them so sorely."[18]

Even women who lost husbands in Indian fights could muster some sympathy for the enemy's situation. Katherine Gibson, whose husband died in the Battle of the Little Big Horn, remembered hearing Elizabeth Custer talk about the Battle of the Washita. Mrs. Gibson explained that "it confused my sense of justice. Doubtless the white men were right, but were the Indians entirely wrong? After all, these broad prairies had belonged to them." Frances Carrington, widow of Lieutenant George Grummond, who perished in the Fetterman disaster, wrote years later, "It had become apparent to any sensible observer that the Indians of that country would fight to the death for home and native land, with spirit akin to that of the American soldier of our early history, and who could say that their spirit was not commendable and to be respected."[19]

If a good number of army people respected the Indian resisters' spirit, did they also commend their military techniques? What assessments did army officers make of Indians as fighters? Several things made evaluating Indians' martial abilities difficult for the officers. First, the Indians relied on unconventional, guerrilla techniques. They engaged in decoy and ambush methods or raiding rather than meeting troops on an open field of battle. A few officers would argue, as a consequence, that Indians did not practice true war but mere violence. Because some Indians preferred to fight only when the odds favored their side, they might evade army troops rather than fight them. Was that wisdom or cowardice? Further, Indians' taboos and rituals regarding warfare were foreign to the Anglo-American soldier. In some cases, Indians saw plunder and combat honors, as well as the defense of their home, as reasonable motivations for making war. Their goals in a war, then, could differ from those of officers trained to fight European—or as they saw it, civilized—enemies. In the end, army men found it nearly impossible to approve of any of the Indians' fighting practices that differed from their own.[20]

Yet, while much separated officer from Indian, much also joined them. They appreciated fellow fighters. They admired certain martial skills wherever they found them, whether within their own ranks or those of the enemy. They applauded those aspects of the Indians' tactics that approximated their own. In fact, in acknowledging many Indians' accurate marksmanship, able horsemanship, and courage, officers seemed to stress their advantages in battle.

Of course, officer accolades for Indians' military prowess could be self-serving. They might explain, for instance, army defeats. Conversely, a successful campaign against a formidable foe rather than a weak one could enhance a soldier's reputation back home. It could heighten the glory of victory. A worthy adversary not only meant more status but perhaps also psychological comfort to those who perceived Indians as both primitive and preyed upon by white settlers. In addition, by stressing the Indians' fighting skills, military men could reinforce their appeals to congressmen and other policymakers that the army should retain its role in Indian affairs and that well-funded professional troops, rather than volunteers, were essential for effective control of the western tribes.

In expressing their admiration for Indian military prowess, then, officers certainly revealed a degree of defensiveness, sparked perhaps by eastern criticism of army policy or even by their own consciences. Self-interest was also a factor. But to dismiss their praise of warriors as mere psychological or political manipulation would be a disservice to officers and Indians alike. The frequency and spirit with which officers reported Indians' talents, along with the Indians' impressive successes in resisting federal forces, suggest that a fair amount of praise was sincerely offered and justly deserved.

Further, in discussing Indian advantages in warfare, the officers attempted to be somewhat objective. To be sure, some officers' positive assessments of Indians in battle inevitably reflected the noble-savage motif reinforced by romantic expectations. A handful offered images of Plains tribes' "barbaric magnificence" in battlefield array or resorted to heroic imagery in depicting an individual Indian's courage under fire.[21] Such resort to the noble-savage idea, however, was rare in army evaluations. The majority of men who praised Indian fighters approached the issue with more practical considerations in mind, befitting their role as military professionals. They spoke of Indian access to modern weapons and skill in using them. They mentioned horsemanship, an ability to travel quickly and without cumbersome pack trains, and knowledge of terrain. In other words, they tried to evaluate Indian abilities in objective military terms. None of them succeeded, of course, in obtaining complete objectivity. They continued to use value-laden terms such as "savage," "fiendish," "crafty," and "ferocious," but they also communicated substantial respect for Indian fighters—a respect that stemmed from practical considerations rather than from romanticized notions of Indians and Indian warfare.

Officers most frequently cited splendid horsemanship as an Indian strength, even outright advantage, in battle. They recounted wondrous tales of Indians (usually Plains Indians) who clung to the sides of their horses, shooting their rifles under the animals' necks while whirling across open and difficult country. One man claimed that a Comanche could ride his horse full speed and easily snatch a hat, a bow or an arrow from the ground. Another maintained that the Nez Perce trained their horses to obey verbal commands. And a good number pronounced Indians "the best skirmishers in the world" or "the best cavalry soldiers on earth." Interestingly, officers did not note that Indians were relative newcomers to the horse. Oblivious to tribal histories, they could not know how truly impressive such mastery of mounted warfare was, having been developed in a matter of only a few generations. Instead, they tended to emphasize that Indian men grew up with horses, while many army recruits knew nothing of them.[22]

Officers lauded Indians' precise marksmanship with the rifle, as well as with the bow and arrow, although here their testimony is more suspect. General George Crook, for example, maintained a healthy respect for Pacific Coast tribesmen who, at sixty yards, could shoot an arrow through an enemy's body so that the point protruded out the other side. Similarly, John Gibbon explained that during the Nez Perce War, with almost every crack of a Nez Perce rifle a member of his command fell.[23]

At the same time that the men praised Indian marksmanship, they complained that army recruits were much less skilled with weapons. One grumbled that the Seventh Cavalry's soldiers could not hit a barn door, much less an Indian, at three hundred yards, while the enemy, often experienced hunters, did not fire unless they had "a fair prospect of hitting something." Beyond that, another believed that Indians were brought up with the knowledge and use of arms from childhood and were perfectly comfortable using them in warfare. Therefore, "knowing from past experience how important they are for [their] preservation, [they take] much better care of them than does the white soldier out of garrison."[24]

A number of officers also insisted that Indians had access to weapons equal to or better than those supplied to their troops. In a letter penned not long after his 1858 defeat in what became eastern Washington, Colonel Edward J. Steptoe explained that the army musketoons were no match for the enemies' rifles and Hudson's Bay muskets. The latter had a greater range than the army's mountain howitzer. Several decades later, Lieutenant Frank Baldwin fumed about unscrupulous frontier traders who sold guns to Indians, stating in 1874 that "today the wild indians are armed as well as our soldiers were in 1872 and so slight is the difference between their arms & those now in the hands of troops that we may say as well as the U.S. troops of today."[25]

Did Indian foes really enjoy access to weapons as good as those issued to the soldiers? And did they truly demonstrate greater skill with their rifles? After the Civil War the army witnessed the most significant advances in weaponry. Breech-loading rifles and metal cartridges made for easier loading, faster firing, and greater velocity and accuracy than the muzzle loaders of Steptoe's day. But when soldiers received better arms, so too did some Indians (although not all). Indian enemies received enough repeating rifles—obtained, as Baldwin asserted, through trade—to warrant the officers' comments.[26]

It is also true that the army was quite lax in its official encouragement of marksmanship both before and after the Civil War. The army allotted ten rounds per man for practice each month (which many soldiers never received). There was an overall indifference to training for the range. In 1877 many units still did not conduct regular target practice, with E.O.C. Ord's Department of California the sole exception. There, at least, Ord had instituted weekly target practice in 1869 and demanded periodic progress reports. By 1880 the rest of the army had begun to show more interest in marksmanship and had instituted regular practice.[27]

This does not necessarily mean, of course, that Indians were better marksmen. Lieutenant DeWitt Clinton Peters may have been the most honest when he informed his father in 1855 that in a close encounter with a "Utah," neither man was particularly adept at handling his weapon. When the Indian's arrow passed between Peters and his horse, the officer "let go my revolver at him until its five barrels were expended and being excited I then threw the pistol at him (in hopes I suppose now of giving him a black eye, for that I find is the best way I can fight)." The Indian shot three arrows at the lieutenant before both retired. Apparently, due to mutually poor marksmanship, neither was the worse for wear, with the possible exception of bruised pride. Allowing for individual as well as tribal differences on this matter, one could not say categorically that Indian men were better marksmen than the soldiers they fought.[28]

Nevertheless, officers certainly argued that army weaknesses enhanced Indian strengths. The problem, these men maintained, was not with the officers but with the enlisted men. Some argued that Indian men were not only more adept with weapons but also, by being inured to hunger, pain, and fatigue from cradle to grave, they learned military skills early in life.

The cavalry soldier, on the other hand, was recruited for a period of only five years, with the army seemingly recruiting any apparently able-bodied man whether or not he had ever ridden a horse. That the enlisted cavalryman could "still contend with the Indian on anything like equal terms," according to Colonel Richard Irving Dodge, "is his highest commendation, for the Indian is his superior in every soldierlike quality, except subordination to discipline, and indomitable courage."[29]

Bourke, too, lamented the poor training of army recruits in the art of Indian fighting. Several weeks after the Custer defeat, Bourke wrote in his diary that the news "made every lip quiver and every cheek blanch with terror and dismay." He also complained that the "men are so occupied with the extraneous duties of building posts and cantonments, no time is left for learning military evolutions. They are all willing and brave enough, but are deficient in experience and military intelligence." Later in life, while reminiscing about the Apache campaigns, Bourke argued that to be successful the army either had to find Indians to fight Indians or train the civilized soldier "down as closely as possible to the level of the savage." For no matter how intelligent or brave a white soldier was, it took training and time to teach him how to care for himself, "in the face of so subtle an enemy as the Apache." Unfortunately, he added, the army recruited "very inferior material" from urban slums and generally accepted anybody whose weight, height, and measurements met official requirements.[30]

To make matters worse, officers emphasized, the government scattered military posts across the vast West, thus fragmenting its forces into garrisons that were too small for effective offensive action. It was certainly the case that the basic strategy, at least until the 1890s, was to disperse army troops throughout the region. Their presence alone was expected to pacify the Indians. But insufficient numbers of soldiers hindered rapid, forceful replies to trouble. When an Indian war broke out, the army would concentrate enough troops for a temporary defense. Overall, it was not a satisfactory approach. As Robert Utley put it, "the dispersed garrisons were too few and too weak to present

an effective defense." On the other hand, "the offensive expedi-
tions, formed only by weakening the defenses, took too long to
assemble and proceeded under handicaps that too often negated
their effectiveness for defense."[31]

To further confound the army efforts, officers contended,
Indians only fought when they outnumbered their enemy. If fortune turned against them on a battlefield, they dispersed in various directions to evade the army. As a result, some officers expressed their frustration at trying to bring them to battle in the
first place, noting in letters and journals that *finding* Indians to
engage in combat was the most difficult challenge of frontier
warfare. They spent more time tracking these people than
fighting them. Most viewed this tendency to flight as strategy
rather than cowardice, although Lieutenant Thomas Sweeny reported to his family in 1855 that the Indians near Fort Pierre
had gone off to the Black Hills, "where they generally fly on the
approach of danger." Comparing scouting to the process of flush-
ing out one's quarry, Lieutenant William H. Beck noted that
"this hunting squads of Indians by detail is almost like trying to
catch wild spring turkeys in the tall grass. Once in a while one
catches one, but it is an occurrence so rare that he feels like
laughing the whole summer about it, but not like trying for
another."[32]

The Plains Indians' nomadic life, army men argued, particularly helped them to elude federal troops. They traveled free of
baggage, wagons and pack trains, using the land itself as their
commissariat. As Robert G. Carter explained it, like "all nomadic races . . . they carried their homes and all that was necessary to furnish their bases of supply with them. With immense
herds of buffalo always all about them or nearby, they were foot
loose and independent."[33]

Because of their mobility, officers maintained, Indian enemies
possessed the additional advantages of choosing when and
where to engage troops, resorting to tactics of decoy and ambush, and generally taking the offensive. Through the use of
small scouting and hunting parties, George Price explained,
Plains tribes such as the Sioux and Cheyenne were "almost

invariably enabled to choose their own time and place of combat, or avoid it altogether if they desired to do so." Others marveled at the Indians' ability to hide along creek and river banks or in ravines before springing upon their unsuspecting prey. Their "faculty to disappear is beyond one's belief," General Grenville Dodge claimed, and in "skulking . . . they are adept."[34]

Only a few officers suggested that the moral force of defending home and family against white intruders provided Indian enemies with an added edge in their wars against Anglo-Americans. Given the predominance of this theme in officer accounts of the causes of Indian wars, its relative absence in the context of Indian warfare is striking. Perhaps the officers' inability to place themselves in the role of an aggressor or to blame themselves provides a partial explanation. In other cases, officers may have presumed that nomadic Plains people, for example, lacked any attachment to place. Yet Captain Frederick Benteen did admit that although Sioux and Cheyenne fighters outnumbered white troopers at the Battle of the Little Big Horn, and although those Indians proved themselves "powerful good shots," he added that in protecting "their hearths and homes . . . they were fighting for all the good God gives anyone to fight for." James Fry, adjutant general of the Division of the Pacific in the post–Civil War years, somewhat ambiguously noted that the "deep wrongs" to which whites subjected Indians increased "in about the same ratio as [their] power to avenge them." Fry remained vague about which whites had committed these deep wrongs.[35]

Finally, in analyzing Indians' strengths in warfare against the U.S. Army, most officers did acknowledge their foe's courage, although not always in especially flattering terms. Richard Irving Dodge, for example, put it this way:

> No man possesses more of that quality of brute courage which impels the smallest and most insignificant animal to fight to the death when cornered. . . . No man can more gallantly dash into danger when his reward in honors, scalps or plunder, appears sure and immediate. No man can take more chances when acting under the influence of superstition in risking his life to carry off unscalped his dead and wounded comrades.

What distinguished civilized courage from savage courage, according to Dodge, was a concept of moral virtue—courage for the sake of principle and out of a sense of duty without expectation of reward. Enlisted men presumably operated under the influence of such moral qualities; Indians did not. Others, however, more generously praised Indian bravery. One officer admitted that the cruelty of Indian warfare deserved the civilized world's censure but added that "the courage with which they fought against the irresistible march of civilization will always command the admiration of the soldiers who conquered them."[36]

Beyond generalizations about Indians as fighters, army officers identified certain tribes as particularly brave and skillful. The Nez Perce, Sioux, Cheyenne, and Apache received the most frequent citations for extraordinary ability and heroism on the battlefield. Not surprisingly, these tribes accumulated an impressive record of successes against the army. The Nez Perce, of course, were among officers' favorite tribes anyway. But when war broke out between the nontreaty Nez Perce and the United States, officers continued to express their admiration for these people even though they had become enemies. Army surgeon John Fitzgerald, for example, lauded the greatly outnumbered Nez Perce in a letter to his wife, adding, "I am actually beginning to admire their bravery and endurance in the face of so many well equipped enemies." And Colonel Nelson Miles, marveling at the Nez Perce's success in defeating or evading three thousand troops, told his wife that the "whole Nez Perce movement is unequaled in the history of Indian warfare."[37] Miles, of course, secured the Nez Perce surrender.

Other officers' respect for this tribe as a fighting force no doubt stemmed from the Indians' success against them. Colonel John Gibbon was defeated by the Nez Perce at Big Hole Basin. He remembered judging Nez Perce mock military maneuvers at Fort Shaw to be a ridiculous farce, concluding that they were far from a dangerous enemy. "Many of those looking on," he wrote, "had occasion afterwards to recall this reflection." Pitted against the Nez Perce's "superior marksmanship," Gibbon admitted that his troops "could not compete, for (it must be admitted), with

General John Gibbon, and other officers, expressed admiration for the Nez Perce leader Chief Joseph. (*Wyoming State Archives, Museums and Historical Department*)

very few exceptions, the command did not contain any such marksmen as the Nez Perces, drilled to the use of the rifle from childhood, showed themselves to be."[38]

But it was Apache fighters who received the greatest acclaim from officers. While they displayed the same martial skills exhibited by other tribes, officers also stressed the nature of the southwestern landscape and the Apaches' adaptation to the Arizona environment as factors that set this tribe apart from all the others as an impressive fighting force. Moreover, the Apaches compiled a series of successes against army troops, though white soldiers continually outnumbered them. As a result, some officers contended that it was only after the army engaged Apache scouts to fight other Apaches that troops conquered them.

Officers' attitudes toward Apache warriors were mixed. In their view, no Indian commanded more respect as an expert fighter, yet none was viewed as more savage. Typically, Bourke presented the Apache fighter this way:

> For centuries he has been pre-eminent over the more peaceful nations about him for courage, skill, and daring in war; cunning in deceiving and evading his enemies, ferocity in attack when skillfully-planned ambuscades have led an unwary foe into his clutches; cruelty and brutality to captives; patient endurance and fortitude under the greatest privations. . . . No Indian has more virtues and none has been more truly ferocious when aroused.

And Nelson Miles echoed Bourke's remarks, claiming that the Apache excelled in "activity, cunning, endurance, and cruelty."[39]

Clearly, respect for Apache fighting prowess did not necessarily translate into respect for the Apaches as human beings. In fact, officers often relied upon animal imagery to describe Apache warriors, arguing that it was their closeness to nature, their savagery, and their animal-like tendencies that limited their wants and allowed them to hold off military forces for long periods of time. While it was not unusual for nineteenth-century writers to assign animal imagery to Anglo-American frontiersmen, as well as others deemed to be particularly close to nature, the frequency and type of such allusions in the case of the Apaches seems particularly striking and, in the end, dehumanizing. Bourke depended heavily on animal metaphors and similes in describing the Apache at war. "No serpent can surpass him in cunning," he wrote, "he will dodge and twist and bend in all directions, boxing the compass, doubling like a fox, scattering his party the moment a piece of rocky ground is reached over which it would, under the best circumstances, be difficult to follow." If pursued, they "scattered like their own crested mountain quail," and they disguised themselves so thoroughly by rubbing their bodies with clay and sand that they remained undetected by whites as they moved along "as sinuously and as venomously as the rattler itself." According to Forsyth, Crook named the Apache the "tiger of the human species." Lieutenant Britton Davis claimed that if cornered, the Apache was "as desperate and dangerous as a wounded wolf." Nelson Miles said that in pursuing them, he "adopted the same methods used to capture wild horses."[40]

In acknowledging the Indian enemy's military talents and presumed advantages in warfare, most army officers intended to express respect for their adversaries and demonstrate to family, friends, and fellow citizens the rigors, challenges, and difficulties of frontier military service. They did not intend to proclaim overall Indian superiority. The majority of military men believed that the army would ultimately triumph despite disadvantages in numbers, horsemanship, mobility, marksmanship, and recruits. Offsetting these disadvantages, they argued, were the civilized soldier's superior intelligence and courage plus the army's more scientific military strategies, although, surprisingly, most officers remained reticent about technological advantages.

Colonel Luther Bradley demonstrated his confidence that the army would prevail when he wrote his fiancée in 1867 en route to Fort C. F. Smith. He was not in the least afraid of the Sioux, he said. In fact, the more he saw of them, the more convinced he became that his troops were superior "not only in education but in courage, capacity, & everything that goes to make man a fighting animal." Fort C. F. Smith was one of those remote Bozeman Trail posts that attracted the enmity of many Sioux, Cheyenne, and Arapaho people between 1866 and 1868 and thus served as the scene for numerous skirmishes and violent confrontations. In disparaging the Sioux as fighters, perhaps he hoped to calm his fiancée's fears about his presence in the hotly contested Powder River country. It is also possible, however, that Bradley was genuinely convinced that the Sioux posed no serious threat to the army, although he acknowledged that conquering them would involve some danger. Of the final outcome, Bradley seemed to have no doubt, and as to the fighting ability of the Sioux, he insisted that they were overrated. "I have no fears of their attacking me," he wrote, "they are a set of cowards, judged by the rules that apply to white men, & they dare not attack a large party, prepared to fight. They show themselves every day on the hills . . . but they take good care to keep out of the reach of our rifles."[41]

Others echoed Bradley's confidence in the white soldiers' ability to prevail. Such confidence seems to have been part bravado, part acknowledgment of the army's ultimate advantages in weaponry, technology, and manpower. In 1858 Captain E.O.C. Ord assured his wife in a letter from Fort Vancouver that "if . . . we can get a fight out of [the Indian enemy] there is not much doubt as to the result—our victory & a consequent acknowledgement of control by the troops." Similarly, Colonel Richard Irving Dodge observed in his journal in 1878 that in "a fight the Army will almost always beat the Indians." Nelson Miles admitted that Indians possessed certain skills and advantages, but he also believed that white soldiers could master these skills. His rationale was clearly racist: "Possessing more intelligence, the same art can be acquired with careful practice by white men with almost, if not quite, equal success," he reported in 1888. Lieutenant Robert Carter insisted that if the troops remained in the field long enough, with adequate supplies to feed men and horses, they could ultimately defeat their Indian enemies. The actual fighting, Carter believed, "was a mere bagatelle as compared to even any skirmish the writer ever saw in front of our battle lines during the Civil War."[42]

What officers failed to discuss about Indian fighting, however, can be as revealing as what they emphasized. Very few attempted, for instance, to describe Indian traditions or ceremonies associated with warfare, other than to dismiss them as superstition or one of the trials they had to endure in working with Indian scouts and allies. They would certainly not see these practices as providing the enemy any spiritual, let alone practical, advantage. They omitted notice of such Plains Indian practices as counting coup, the act of striking an enemy with a hand or stick to garner honor for bravery. In the infrequent attempts to explain warfare from within the social, cultural, and political context of a tribe, officers rarely demonstrated any understanding, let alone respect.

Colonel Trobriand did, however, acknowledge that many Indian groups had different concepts of the purpose of warfare or different standards of valor. He explained that to achieve the status of chief, for instance, Sioux men had to prove their military skills. But Sioux notions of bravery, he contended, did not "mean exposing themselves to danger for difficult or uncertain outcome." Instead, their exploits earned more praise if they could garner scalps, horses, and mules with the least possible risk. Upon returning home with such trophies, the warriors then acquired respect and the right to sit in the council. While not particularly impressed with these customs, Trobriand did add with irony that a warrior was "promoted by brevet as it is understood in our army, with this difference—he had to do something to get the said brevet, while with us, it is the least necessary condition."[43] Such efforts to comprehend Indian cultural or religious motivations, however, were exceedingly rare.

So too were discussions of the army's ultimate technological advantages in the form of breech-loading rifles, cannons, Gatling guns, Hotchkiss "mountain guns," steamboats, railroads, telegraph lines, and other products of a modern industrial nation. As early as 1855, Captain Granville Haller tried to impress upon tribes of the Columbia Plateau the folly of resisting the white man, who "makes all kinds of guns and knives, Powder, Bullets, and things which in war makes him strong, so that he can easily destroy his enemy."[44] Others probably made the same point in parlays with Indians, but few officers stressed the white man's technological advantages in their published accounts of the Indian wars.

The officers did discuss the Indians' amazement concerning these technological innovations, but they refrained from pointing out these weapons' ultimate power in warfare against Indians. Retired brigadier general Anson Mills remembered, in fact, that after demonstrating the wonders of the telegraph to the Shoshones at Fort Bridger in the years following the Civil War, they "used this knowledge in cutting down and burning the poles and destroying the wire to keep the whites from telling where they had been on mischief, and to prevent the soldiers from following." On the other hand, in 1883 General William T. Sherman admitted that the railroad accounted "fully for the peace and good order that now prevails throughout our country." Sherman recognized that the army was only one factor in the final conquest of the West's Indians. Federal troops were joined—often preceded—by miners, stockmen, farmers, and merchants. But in the end, if he had to choose one factor above all others that helped explain civilization's victory, Sherman concluded that it would be the railroad: "the *railroad* which used to follow in the rear now goes forward with the picket line in the great battle of civilization with barbarism, and has become the *greater* cause."[45]

The officers' reticence in pointing out the power of technology in part reflected a desire to discourage the impression that the army was brutalizing a technologically backward people. Such ideas could serve as ammunition for those who accused the military of cruelty to Indians, or they could undermine the heroic image of frontier service. It is also quite possible that officers simply took these technological advantages for granted and assumed that their readers would too. In a few instances, however, army officers clearly admired Indian *defiance* of technology and mechanized fighting forces, arguing in effect that Indians were superior fighters because, as one put it, they "will not brook the restraints which, under our notions of discipline, change men into machines." Another glorified the Indian fighter's supposed freedom and independence compared to "the machinery and formalities of much that is called civilized life."[46] Such comments, of course, reflected individual discontent with certain aspects of their own culture's industrialization or their profession's transformation of men into presumably efficient units of destruction. But none could deny the tangible benefits technology brought to the war effort on the frontier.

In their assessment of Indians' fighting skills, officers presented their most consistently favorable images of Indian men. Nevertheless, by stressing Indian strengths, even advantages, in warfare, their accounts might strike modern readers as somewhat defensive and less than completely forthright. To a degree, this is accurate. The advantage in manpower, gunpowder, and technology obviously rested with the United States Army, and the officers must have understood this. Their principal handicap in fighting Indians was one of mobility, of bringing the enemy to battle. But if they succeeded in finding and fighting Indians, their greater numbers, firepower, organization, and discipline usually brought success.[47] Further, by the 1880s the railroads had made it easier to consolidate troops for quickly prepared offensives. Officers preferred, however, to understate these strengths and to stress the troopers' supposedly superior intelligence and bravery as the crucial factor in their ability inevitably to prevail over their Indian enemies.

Further, officers praised those Indian modes of warfare that paralleled their own, thus acknowledging similarities, perhaps even ties of a sort. But they did not understand, let alone admire or respect, practices that were alien to their ways. In other words, officers valued the Indians' way of fighting only to the extent that it resembled Euro-American techniques. Their accounts provide little information about the dynamics of Indian warfare from within the cultural, political, social, or military context of tribes or bands. They seemed content to disparage Indian practices such as ceremonial preparations for warfare without attempting to understand or explain them. This proved to be the case not only with Indians who were enemies but also with Indians who were allies, auxiliaries, and scouts working in conjunction with the army to defeat their common foe.

8 /   The Indian Scout as Ally

*Unless savage should be pitted against savage, the white
man would be outwitted, exhausted, circumvented, possibly
ambuscaded and destroyed.* —CAPTAIN JOHN BOURKE

It was so hot during the summer of 1886 that army rifle barrels
defied the touch. Leonard Wood, a medical officer, was among
those soldiers in Mexico's Sierra Madre Mountains pursuing
Geronimo and his followers, who had fled the San Carlos Reservation. Wood, who later distinguished himself as the army chief
of staff and governor-general of the Philippines, would lose
thirty pounds during the summer's work for this was no bugles-
and-guidons campaign. Instead, it would entail the slow, torturous tracking of an intrepid enemy, one who knew the Mexican
mountains better than Wood and his white compatriots. General Nelson Miles understood this too, so San Carlos and White
Mountain Apache scouts joined the soldiers on the campaign.
For the most part, these scouts did their job. "Our Indians
did some wonderful tracking," Wood noted in his campaign
diary, "keeping the trail for miles, when it seemed to be all
washed out."

But things were not always peaceable with the Indian allies.
A little over a month after observing how wonderfully the
Apache scouts tracked, Wood noticed that upon leaving a town
for camp, some of the Indian scouts in the rear of the column
were drunk. He soon learned that these men wanted to go off
and kill some Mexicans. Since he had hunted with them a good
deal, they invited him to join in the drunken sport. Finally Wood
was able to pull away, reach camp, and give the alarm. Another
officer and several sober scouts returned with him to the inebri-
ated Apaches and eventually brought them all into the army
camp. Several, whom Wood described as especially drunk and
dangerous, had to be tied up until the crisis passed. In the meantime, some of the scouts were loading their guns and pointing

them toward whites or into the air. The sober scouts used the butts of their weapons to down the drunken ones. "The result," according to Wood, "was a rather damaged looking lot of drunks" and "a rather lively day." Fortunately, no one was killed. The summer's work eventually ended in August, when two Chiricahua scouts joined the group and led Lieutenant Charles Gatewood to Geronimo's Mexican camp, where the three men persuaded the Apaches to surrender.[1]

Army officers who commanded or traveled with Indian scouts and auxiliaries had a unique opportunity to learn about Indians. After all, they shared immediate wartime interests and experienced prolonged daily contact. A few officers took advantage of these opportunities. Most did not. Rather, like Leonard Wood, they maintained their distance, wrote little about the scouts, and evidently learned little about native cultures. It is noteworthy that Wood's lengthiest passage about the Apache scouts presents them in a negative, even violent, light.

But officers' views of Indian scouts, as with so many other matters involving Indians and the Indian wars, defy simple summaries. While they relied on Indian scouts, a number doubted the wisdom of doing so, for they distrusted the scouts' motivations and loyalty to the United States. At the same time, officers frequently admitted that these scouts were invaluable to the war effort, particularly in tracking the enemy, and they admired the scouts' martial zeal. Further, the relationship between the Indian scouts and army personnel demanded a special effort to communicate and to share military goals. This meant an acknowledgment, if not an appreciation, of distinctive values and even worldviews. The overall result was guarded respect and limited understanding and communication. Officers were too close to scouts to present them as perfect, yet too distant and ethnocentric to see them as equals. Mostly they saw the scouts as not only different but deficient.

As Thomas Dunlay has pointed out, the use of Indian scouts and allies had a long tradition in the New World, beginning with Cortez's use of the Aztecs' enemies to conquer Mexico. The United States Army demonstrated a less systematic use of Indian allies than the Spanish, but government troops had relied on them, nonetheless, since the American Revolution. So by 1848 it was almost a foregone conclusion that the army would form Indian alliances in the trans-Mississippi West. Usually these relationships were haphazard. Although an 1866 act of Congress allowed the official enlistment of Indian scouts on a regular basis, officers often continued to opt for less formal arrangements.[2]

The use of Indian scouts and auxiliary troops certainly engendered debate within army ranks. A few believed that Indians should scout but not engage in combat. Some feared that the use of talented Indian fighters could undermine white troopers' morale if the Indians outfought their supposedly superior allies. Some thought Indians incapable of sentiments such as loyalty or trust. But surprisingly few carefully pondered, or at least wrote about, Indian scouts' motivations for joining with the army in its wars against other Indians, or in some cases, against members of their own tribe. Of those who did consider this issue, a typical explanation was that Indian men became scouts to provide an outlet for their savage love of warfare. General John M. Schofield, for instance, claimed that the War Department had decided to incorporate Indian scouts into the army in order to provide a legitimate means by which Indian warriors could realize their "irrepressible love of military life." In this way, ambitious young men moved "from the ranks of more or less probable savage enemies to the ranks of friends and practically civilized allies." He also argued that the scouting experience would provide a transitional period for young Indian men as they changed "from the life and character of savage warriors to those of civilized husbandmen, under the system of allotments in severalty." It is interesting to note that Schofield had no personal experience in Indian warfare or contact with Indian scouts.[3]

Officers with frontier experience came closer to understanding Indians' motivations for allying with the army. Lieutenant Colonel W. H. Carter noted that tribal animosities supplied the army with some scouts in Arizona, but he also noted, in less objective terms, that when these scouts were used against their own people, they operated "with the unerring instincts of the bloodhound, and . . . killed them as remorselessly as they would have done their white enemies." It was, he claimed, only the presence of civilized soldiers that spared women and children from the scouts' hands. Savagery got the better of them and came before all other impulses, including those of family attachment. "Their savage natures may be comprehended," Carter claimed, "when it is known that in one instance a scout, having learned that his father had been proclaimed an outlaw, went into the mountains and killed him, hoping to secure a reward."[4]

George Crook, one of the most vocal and consistent advocates of enlisting Indian scouts, demonstrated a greater comprehension of actual scout motivations when he spoke to the Indians who were with his Powder River Expedition in November 1876. Addressing the issue of self-interest, Crook informed them that their options were peace with white men or war and consequent annihilation. By joining forces with the conqueror rather than resisting him, they would spare their own people further death and devastation. With the acceptance of American law, he promised, they would find not tyranny but tranquility. Finally, he told them, they would be well paid.[5]

But most officers did not see beyond the scouts' presumed mercenary self-interest or savage love of warfare. They rarely considered motivations such as the dynamics of intertribal warfare and tribal factionalism, or the desire to gain the American government's favor and thus secure tangible rewards for their people. To have recognized these factors would have meant acknowledging rational, politically sophisticated motivations among a people the officers persistently deemed to be savage. In addition, an understanding of these incentives would have required some comprehension of tribal customs—something that eluded most officers. Finally, beyond policy considerations, some Indian men gained other gratifications through scouting, including wealth (especially horses), prestige, and temporary release from "the painful process of enforced acculturation" on reservations.[6] Officers, however, failed to note these inducements.

Indifferent as they might be to the scouts' actual motivations, officers did not fail to accord Indian allies their share of praise

This Yuma-Apache was one of many Indian men who served the army as a scout. (*American Heritage Center, University of Wyoming*)

in battle. While Schofield argued that the Indian men benefited from the scouting experience by becoming "practically civilized," most officers recognized that the real benefit of this relationship accrued to the army. Indian scouts knew the terrain, possessed greater experience in fighting Indians, and could communicate more effectively with "hostiles"—especially if they were of the same tribe. They provided, in other words, many practical advantages for army troops.

One of the first officers to understand the scouts' value and encourage their use in the trans-Mississippi West was Captain Randolph Marcy. While exploring the source of the Red River in 1852, Marcy hired Delaware guides. He found them exceedingly astute at reading trails and tracks—abilities that he believed were intuitive and confined solely to Indians. At least, Marcy said, he had never seen a white man who could judge such matters as effectively. "A few such men as the Delawares," he reported, "attached to each company of troops upon the Indian frontier would, by their knowledge of Indian character and habits, and their wonderful powers of judging of country, following tracks . . . (which soldiers cannot be taught), enable us to operate to much better advantage against the prairie tribes." He concluded that his Indian guides were "intelligent, brave, reliable, and in every respect well qualified to fill their position."[7]

Early on, military men also realized that Indian scouts could prove valuable in combat situations. Major J. G. Trimble, who had been with the disastrous expedition led by Major Edward Steptoe in Washington Territory in 1856, believed that had it not been for the "faithful Nez Perce guides . . . it is probable the entire command would have been destroyed." Beyond guiding and guarding the defeated troops during their retreat, Nez Perce men and women treated the wounded and cooked salmon for the famished soldiers.[8]

Others who followed Marcy and Trimble in the postbellum period also readily acknowledged Indian scouts' talents. Lieutenant Colonel O. L. Hein claimed (inaccurately) that Crook had inaugurated the policy of enlisting friendly Indians into service against the Apaches. He more accurately added that "they proved to be of invaluable assistance, as they were acquainted with the location of the haunts of the hostiles, and were familiar with their mode of warfare." Crook himself argued that without the aid of his Chiricahua scouts, his operations against the Apaches of Arizona would have failed. In fact, he stated, "without reserve or qualification of any nature, . . . these Chiricahua scouts, under Chiefs Chatto, Noche, and others, did most excellent service, and were of more value in hunting down and compelling the surrender of the renegades, than all other troops engaged in operations against them." Crook denied rumors that these scouts were disloyal, spiriting weapons, supplies, and other assistance to the "renegade" Apaches. He claimed that the scouts were responsible for every successful encounter with the Apache enemy and that by nature and training they were better qualified than anyone else for fighting in the mountains of Arizona and Mexico.[9]

Crook's faith in Apache scouts, in fact, led to the final breakdown of the friendship he had forged with Philip Sheridan at West Point many years before. By 1886 Sheridan had come to the conclusion that Indian scouts were not trustworthy. This sentiment was partly due to the one episode in the trans-Mississippi West in which Indian scouts turned against U.S. troops—at Cibicu Creek in Arizona Territory in 1881. Crook's belief in the value of Apache scouts was not shaken by this incident, and he enlisted Chiricahuas to help him bring in Geronimo in 1886. Sheridan did not approve. When Crook secured Geronimo's surrender in March, President Grover Cleveland, acting under Sheridan's influence, refused to accept anything short of an unconditional surrender. Meanwhile, Geronimo again slipped away into Mexico. At this point, a disgusted and frustrated Crook requested that he be relieved of his command, and Sheridan immediately saw to it. He replaced Crook with Nelson Miles, who did not rely on Chiricahua scouts (until near the end of the campaign), although he did employ Apache scouts from other bands. When Geronimo finally surrendered in August, all of the Chiricahua Apaches, including those who had served as scouts for the army, were removed to Florida. Crook was outraged at this treatment of his former scouts, and until he died in 1890, he continued to campaign for the return of the Chiricahuas to Arizona. As Paul Hutton put it, Crook "never forgave Sheridan, and their long but stormy relationship came to a sad close."[10]

Crook's regard for his Indian scouts evidently went beyond respect for their fighting ability. According to Lieutenant Colonel Richard Irving Dodge, Crook preferred the scouts' company to that of his own officers during the 1876 Powder River Expedition. Grousing that Crook allowed his Indian scouts to appropriate all the choice camping spots so that "his Indians wash[ed] the entrails of the beeves in the stream from which his troops [had] to drink below," Dodge also complained that Crook "scarcely treats [Ranald] McKenzie and I decently, but he will spend hours chatting pleasantly with an Indian or a dirty scout."[11] Obviously, in Dodge's mind such close interaction between Crook and his Indian assistants was not appropriate behavior for an officer. Nor did Crook's apparent preference for the scouts' society over that of the officers please him.

If other officers did not share Crook's desire to socialize with Indian scouts, they often did share his opinion that scouts proved superior to white troops in fighting. Even former enemies who later joined ranks with the army received accolades, although some officers remained doubtful about their trustworthiness. During the Nez Perce War, Lieutenant Hugh Scott commanded thirty-five Northern Cheyenne scouts—men who had only recently surrendered to the army. While some of his colleagues warned Scott about their capacity for treachery, Scott dismissed these fears. Instead, he trusted them, calling them

> keen, athletic, young men [who were] tall and lean and brave . . . real specimens of manhood more than any body of men I have ever seen before or since. They were perfectly adapted to their environment, and knew just what to do in every emergency and when to do it, without any confusion or lost motion.
>
> Their poise and dignity were superb; no royal person ever had more assured manners. I watched their every movement and learned lessons from them that later saved my life many times on the prairie.[12]

Other military men initially had reservations about the scouts' soldierly abilities but found their qualms to be unjustified. These men demonstrated a willingness to reject those racial stereotypes that their experiences did not bear out. Retired colonel Richard Pratt remembered commanding twenty-five Caddo and Wichita scouts in 1867 and admitted his surprise at their intelligence, common sense, and level of civilization. He had believed that they were little better than "atrocious aborigines." Instead, he found that they had "manly bearing and fine physiques." Moreover, he used this experience to augment his assimilationist point of view, claiming that they had enlisted to perform the highest function of citizenship, being willing to give their lives in the line of duty. Therefore, they should be freed from their reservation prisons and be made citizens with the full guarantee of constitutional rights.[13]

To say that officers praised the capabilities of Indian scouts and recognized the importance of their service is not to say that they overlooked their supposed savagery. In fact, in some cases military men attributed the scouts' success to their savagery, which, they argued, would have been unrestrained without the officers' influence. "Crook recognized," Bourke wrote, "that a white man's strength and sagacity were no match for the cunning of savages who had been running about in these hills and mountains since childhood. . . . [U]nless savage should be pitted against savage, the white man would be outwitted, exhausted, circumvented, possibly ambuscaded and destroyed." What made the Apache an ideal scout, according to Bourke, were his animal-like attributes, including "vision as keen as a hawk's" and "tread as untiring and as stealthy as the panther's."[14]

Occasionally, officers openly chafed at the scouts' tactics in warfare and doubted the wisdom of a presumably civilized people allying with savages. One man reported that in December 1876 General Nelson Miles became furious when some Crow allies killed five Sioux who were attempting to surrender under a flag of truce. Upset with their violation of his military code, he ordered the Crows disarmed, and they promptly left. The Sioux dead included an Oglala named Sitting Bull (not the more famous Hunkpapa but a leader of a peace faction from

Crazy Horse's village). Miles seized the Crows' horses and other personal property and sent them to the Sioux in the hope of reopening negotiations. But in the short term, at least, nothing came of this.[15]

On a related, though less bloody, issue, Eugene Carr opposed the enlistment of Indian scouts because he was ethically opposed to their practice of fighting for plunder. In 1869, Carr with the Fifth Cavalry and some Pawnee scouts attacked Tall Bull's Sioux village on the south fork of the Platte River. After the battle, Carr concluded that the property of the village should be returned to the owners, if possible, or sold and the proceeds given to the United States Treasury. But the scouts claimed that they had been promised the plunder, and Carr submitted.[16]

In spite of their reservations about some scouts' wartime practices, the majority of officers who worked with Indian scouts concluded that their contributions made them worthwhile allies. To some degree, shared interests, including survival itself, could bring the officers and scouts together in a cooperative working relationship. Occasionally an officer did indicate an interest in his scouts' culture. Lieutenant William Philo Clark, for example, wrote a book called *The Indian Sign Language*, and his interest in the Northern Cheyenne undoubtedly benefited his working relationship with them.[17] Yet for the officers as a whole, a seemingly insurmountable cultural gap remained, a gap nearly all officers recognized. They valued the scouts' martial abilities, but they did not understand, admire, or respect their cultures, religions, and lifeways. Indeed, the scouts' traditions, customs, and behavior often frustrated, annoyed, and puzzled them, for most officers never overcame their ethnocentrism in observing and evaluating them. Their baleful assessments of scouts' ways most often reflected the officers' almost perturbed state of mind in working with Indians. It was, it seems, vexatious to work with men of different cultures.

Further, while they sometimes depended on Indian allies for safety, a good number of officers continued to consider it folly to rely on Indian loyalty. Operating on assumptions about Indian character and expectations about racial solidarity, soldiers confessed fears that the native allies would lead them into ambush.

To officers, American expansion posed a very serious threat to Indian life, and they expected all Indians to understand that and act accordingly.

Suspicions, doubts, and misunderstandings were evidently mutual, and scouts, too, recognized the problems that cultural differences posed to alliances. While recruiting Crow scouts in 1876, one officer reported that several Crow leaders had told John Gibbon that whites and Indians had very different methods of warfare and that neither understood that of the other. Therefore, the Crow had decided that while their hearts were good toward the white man, they should remain separate and make war in their own way. Another said that he often talked with the Crow scouts who eventually joined Gibbon's forces about "the mysteries and advantages of our prolonged movements and combined operations of different columns" but that his explanations merely perplexed the Crow, who preferred their own "simple methods of a dash in and out with a single force."[18]

For the most part, however, officers tended to record their own doubts and anxieties rather than those of their Indian allies. Presumably, wartime partnerships could have eroded these suspicions and misunderstandings, for during campaigns army officers often observed Indian scouts and their cultural practices at close range. Yet few availed themselves of the opportunity for more than a cursory look, and they usually interpreted the customs and manners they observed in highly subjective ways. Thus, while Lieutenant John Bigelow explained that his Apache scouts' war dances served the same purpose that military balls and champagne suppers did for their "civilized guardians," he treated them with condescension and dismissed them as savage ceremonies. In contrast, Captain John Bourke's great interest in Indian cultures, languages, and religious observances led him to associate as much as possible with Indian scouts. "Nearly all the talk I had with anybody was with them," he wrote, "and the result was the enrichment of note-books with references to aboriginal customs in war and peace which probably could not have been obtained under circumstances of greater advantage." According to Lee Clark Mitchell, Bourke's later work conveyed "extreme sensitivity, especially for Hopi efforts to defend the

integrity of their sacred institutions." Mitchell identified
Bourke as one of the nineteenth-century observers who challenged conventional assumptions about tribal life and who consequently represented an increased tolerance that over time developed into cultural relativism.[19] But while he was a soldier
pursuing the Sioux and Cheyenne in 1876, Bourke did not record Indian customs with the objectivity readers expect of twentieth-century observers. Looking into a Crow or Shoshone tipi
was, he maintained, like "peeping through the key-hole of
Hell," for the swarthy, naked Indians' moaning and chanting
took on the character of "an abominable incantation." On
another occasion, while he demonstrated a sense of humor
about a fellow officer, he did so at the expense of the Shoshone
scouts:

> One bright night we were awakened by the special energy of the
> chorus; I asked the interpreter for an explanation, he answered
> that the *Indians* were singing to the moon. While we were talk-
> ing, I heard the deep earnest tones of a voice in prayer—it was
> *Major Randall*, praying for rain. The thought struck me that if
> the chanting of the Shoshones was efficacious enough to turn
> such a sinner as Jake Randall to prayer it was highly commend-
> able and from that time on, in face of bitter prejudice and cynical
> criticism, I constituted myself the champion of the Shoshone
> songsters.[20]

To be sure, language problems compounded misunderstandings. According to Richard Irving Dodge, when Sharp Nose, an
Arapaho, made a speech during the Powder River Expedition,
his words were translated into Sioux and English. Then the English version was translated into all the other languages of the
Indians present. "In such a Babel of language," Dodge marveled,
"it is only a wonder how any one could understand." Lieutenant
Frank Baldwin experienced his own communication difficulties
with Delaware scouts at the Battle of the Adobe Walls. Ordering
them to start in advance of white troops as skirmishers, they
did so only after much "persuasion and driving." They hesitated, Baldwin believed, not out of cowardice but because they
did not understand his orders.[21]

The greatest difficulty for the officers, however, was their profound suspicion of Indian friendship and loyalty. During an 1857 Gila expedition, Lieutenant John Van Deusen Du Bois remarked that soldiers saw no signs of the enemy, but the native guides did. None of the white men, however, would trust the scouts. Moreover, Du Bois found that the scouts "comprise[d] as scoundrelly a set of cowards as ever betrayed Indians." Similarly, Lieutenant James Bradley found in 1876 that his fellow officers, who doubted his Crow scouts' loyalty and competence, often dismissed the intelligence they gathered.[22] Ultimately, the officers could not shake their fundamental distrust of all Indians, whether friend or foe, although the intensity of such feelings varied depending on the individual officer and the circumstances under which officer and scouts operated. Some officers merely perpetuated stereotypes based on ideas of Indian treachery. Others expected Indian people to demonstrate, in the end, an allegiance to race.

Lieutenant James Bradley, charged with commanding those Crow scouts who joined Colonel John Gibbon's Montana Column during the Sioux campaign of 1876, most neatly demonstrated many officers' ambivalent, perplexed feelings about Indian scouts on such issues as trust, communication, and mutual understanding. His campaign journal provides an illuminating commentary on officer-scout relations, and it is worth a close look. Bradley, an Ohioan and a Civil War veteran, was, according to one historian, the "most enterprising and effective intelligence officer in the field that summer," yet his accomplishments, including his reports of immense Sioux villages on the Tongue River in May 1876, "were often ignored or spurned by Gibbon."[23] If heeded, his intelligence might have saved Custer's command and meant a successful campaign rather than a disastrous one, from the army's point of view."

Bradley's delightful journal exudes a spirit of adventure and a sense of history. He expressed an initial satisfaction with the scouting assignment and, to a certain extent, took advantage of his position to learn something about the Crows' origins and culture. Resting for several days at abandoned Fort F. D. Pease, for example, he queried tribal elders about Crow history and recorded their responses concerning the tribe's migration from the southeast as well as their stories of warfare with the Sioux and Cheyenne. Bradley's version of Crow history has been rejected by more recent investigators, but his curiosity about the scouts' heritage is certainly noteworthy. Interestingly, Bradley did not make the connection between these historic animosities and the Crows' willingness to scout for the army in 1876, although he acknowledged that it was "their best policy" to remain friends with whites. He attributed their friendship and cooperation to a story the elders told him. The Crows explained to him that the Spirits created a number of tribes, including white people. The white people were nearest the spirits and "after they had shaken hands, the spirit said so as to be heard by everyone: 'All people are dear to us, but the white people are dearest of all; we command you always to live at peace with the white people.'" Bradley added, "surely this injunction of what they take to be divine authority has been better obeyed by the Crows than are behests from the same high source by their brethren of the white-skin."[24]

Bradley, however, was bewildered by and frustrated with the Crow scouts and was suspicious of their character. He identified several problems in working with Indian scouts. First, they did not have formal military training and were not accustomed to obeying orders. He found it difficult to impress upon them that, from the army's perspective, their acts of enlistment meant they would follow their commander's directions and refrain from "that free skurrying to and fro over the country to which they have been accustomed." Bradley admitted that when they applied themselves, the Crows were excellent scouts, but he also complained that, if indulged, "they would be mere camp loafers." He also complained of communication problems with the scouts. Early in the expedition, when he found himself caught without an interpreter, Bradley concluded that the Crows were deliberately taking advantage of his inability to give them orders in order to fall behind the main column rather than remain in advance. Later, rejoicing at the arrival of his interpreter, he expressed his hope that hereafter he would "have the best of these slippery Crows."

Further, the lieutenant, who survived the Sioux campaign only to die in the Nez Perce War the following year, believed that the Crows distrusted whites, doubted their promises, and lacked respect for their fighting ability. "Nor," Bradley added, "did we get through this campaign without unfortunately affording some further grounds for their distrust." The Crow leaders were reluctant to help the expedition in the first place because of fundamental differences in military technique. The Crows, they explained, moved swiftly, but white warriors moved slowly, laden with pack trains and long columns of troopers. They also feared that in the midst of battle, white soldiers would not be able to distinguish Crow from Sioux and would unwittingly kill their friends. The twenty-three Crow men who finally joined the Montana Column insisted that Bradley and Gibbon swear to believe everything the Crow scouts told them and do all they asked. This was "rather a preposterous proposition," he observed, yet both officers took the oath.[25] Needless to say, they did not keep it.

Bradley acknowledged that part of the Crows' reluctance to follow orders stemmed from doubts about the officers' judgments in the field. On May 16, 1876, a little more than a month before Custer's fateful encounter with an immense Indian camp on the Little Big Horn, Bradley's scouting detachment found a large Sioux village on the Tongue River, and Bradley wanted to take a closer look to determine its size. The Crows violently opposed the plan, as they were certain it would result in discovery and destruction. Bradley added that "it was evident that they sincerely believed that no white man had the address necessary to the successful management of such an enterprise." The next day when an expedition against the Sioux village was canceled because of difficulties in getting men and horses across a stream, the Crows, according to their commander, were "inclined to look upon it as a device to conceal our cowardice." But Bradley lacked confidence in the Crow as well. He would not allow them to approach the village alone for fear their "horse-stealing proclivities would get the better of them" and that "in their effort to possess themselves of a few Sioux ponies, they would be liable to bring the whole village down upon us."[26]

Bradley's confidence in his scouts' judgment had been shaken a week earlier during a night march to look for signs of Sioux. The Crow detachment found a band of buffalo, and before Bradley could halt their charge, the Indians raced into the herd and fired their weapons. Bradley noted ruefully that the "carelessness of these fellows at times is simply amazing. One would think that the Indian's life of constant danger would make caution and precaution so much his habit that he would never lay them aside, but it is quite otherwise." In fact, Lieutenant Bradley maintained, he was on constant guard to prevent them from "some foolish or foolhardy thing that could have destroyed them all."[27]

Bradley was also ambivalent about the Crows' military skills. Early in the campaign, the Crows mistook one of their own hunting parties for some Sioux, leaving him with "impaired confidence" in their judgment. On another occasion, Bradley believed that the Crow scouts deliberately selected a bad route to tire him, waste time, and encourage him to abandon an assault on a Sioux camp. Finally, he reported, "I halted the column and gave them a severe lecture. I was satisfied from their replies that I had not misjudged them, and assured them that we would go to Tongue River if it took a month." He thought that the problem partially stemmed from the Crows' doubts about their white allies' ability to defeat the Sioux. But as the Montana Column approached the Little Big Horn River in the early summer of 1876, Bradley also concluded that the Crow were "mortally afraid of the Sioux."[28]

Yet he never considered them cowards. When a party of Sioux made off with all the scouts' horses, several of the scouts mounted, followed their enemy's trail, charged a Sioux camp, and reclaimed several of the stolen animals. Bradley admitted that he was impressed with their perseverance and courage. For the most part, he found that the Crows were willing to fight, and he believed they would do so bravely. But he also believed that within their hearts the greatest number were resolved to let the white soldiers do most of the fighting while they gathered in enemy ponies.[29]

Profound cultural differences between officers and Indians, then, clearly undermined mutual understanding and trust. But occasionally these men exhibited some feeling, even compassion, for each other, although few real friendships formed between white soldiers and Indian allies. Bourke, for example, wrote in June 1876 that the Crows were "soon on terms of easy familiarity with our soldiers, some of whom can talk a few words of *Crow* and others a little of the *'sign language.'*" But later he noted that the scouts chose white friends rather carefully, most energetically seeking associations with men such as Lieutenant Charles Rockwell, the commissary, who controlled the coffee and sugar supplies. Similarly, Captain Charles King said that the soldiers had no difficulty in making friends with Crow scouts, especially if they had plug tobacco to serve as a medium of introduction. As he remembered it, "if you give one Indian a piece as big as a postage-stamp, the whole tribe will come in to claim acquaintance." Several years later, Lieutenant William Carey Brown wrote his mother that during the Bannock War, Cayuse scouts entertained the military men, giving them a war song and dance practically every night. But he also described these Cayuse men as "laughing & jabbering as happy as black birds in a cornfield." Some of Crook's officers joined a scout war dance at the close of an Apache campaign in 1873, but this was at the indirect suggestion of their commander.[30]

Nonetheless, officers seemed prepared to accept individual scouts' affections, attentions, and accolades, which suggests that at least some military men cared what scouts thought of them. In 1882, Lieutenant Stephen Mills informed his mother that Loco, a White Mountain Apache scout, had taken him under his special care, treating him "very much as a small child he was bound to protect." Moreover, to the officer's pleasure, Loco paid Mills a great compliment, pronouncing that he knew more about scouting and hunting than any other officer Loco had ever known. Richard Irving Dodge also delighted in compliments from Indian allies. Anglo-American scout Frank North informed Dodge that the Pawnee were prepared to provide him any service, and Dodge noted in his 1876 diary, "I have several times noticed that they look at me very intently and pleasantly as I ride past them on the march, but have always supposed it only the recognition of my being the Big Chief of the 'walk a heaps.' Frank's story puts a different construction on it and a more gratifying one." But scouts did not always pursue friendships with whites, especially if a particular Indian man did not feel they merited regard. Charles King claimed that one warrior dropped him after he learned that King had never killed a Sioux.[31]

Certainly, shared experiences of campaign deprivations and battlefield traumas could bring some officers and Indian scouts together. During the 1872 Apache campaign, Bourke remembered that in the midst of the battle, a little boy ran out and stood between the two lines of fire. A scout, Nantaje, rushed forward, grabbed the infant, and brought him back unhurt to the army line. The emotion of such a daring deed at least momentarily dissolved racial and cultural distinctions. "Our men suspended their firing," Bourke wrote, "to cheer Nantaje and welcome the new arrival."[32]

Further, when a campaign ended, some officers and Indians separated with emotional farewells. "Our parting with them," Bourke said about the Shoshone scouts with the November 1876 Powder River expedition, "was such as would take place between brothers bound together by the ties of dangers conquered and elements defied together"—a rather different experience from that of the previous summer, when Lieutenant Bradley's Crow scouts, after learning of Custer's fate, abruptly left government service and hurried to their homes at the Crow agency. Less romantically, William Carey Brown claimed that upon leaving his Cayuse scouts, "it must be confessed that they showed as much feeling as white people would under similar circumstances."[33]

An examination of officers' accounts alone makes it more difficult to determine the scouts' assessments of army officers. Bearing in mind that officers may have been projecting their own attitudes onto the Indian scouts, the white men's accounts do suggest that the scouts returned officers' doubts and misgivings about their temporary allies. If individuals such as Lieutenant Bradley can be believed, at any rate, the Crows were uncertain about the officers' military abilities and courage and remained convinced that their own modes of warfare were far superior to those of the United States Army. Distrust, bewilderment, and misunderstanding were apparently mutual, and in this the army men and the Indians shared more than most officers, and perhaps most scouts, realized.

Conclusion

"Legends," Robert M. Utley once observed, "are far more influential in shaping our attitudes and beliefs than the complex, contradictory, and ambiguous truth."[1] The power of legend and stereotype prevails not only in Anglo-American attitudes toward Indians but also in many Americans' attitudes toward the frontier army officers who fought them. Legends aside, it should now be clear that these men were neither unconscionable exterminationists nor civilization's heroic saviors. Rather, they were complex, contradictory, and ambiguous human beings, caught in a morally difficult and often terribly bloody struggle for control of a continent. Some of them, to be sure, apparently did not concern themselves with the ethical aspects of their work. They did their jobs and thought or wrote little about it. But others deplored the abuses heaped upon native people by unsavory and unscrupulous frontiersmen and corrupt or inept government officials. A significant number struggled with the morality of fighting Indians to serve the purposes of greedy Americans. Some of them revealed hearts in conflict with their actions.

Further, it should also be clear that when it came to matters of Indians, Indian policy, and the morality of the Indian wars, they demonstrated an irrepressible individuality. In the nineteenth-century West, there was no monolithic military mind with respect to any of these concerns. Instead, officers and their wives offered a spectrum of opinions, attitudes, temperaments, and levels of sophistication. It was only on certain fundamental assumptions about savagery and civilization, the army's supposedly irreproachable conduct on the frontier, and the military's presumed special qualifications to manage Indian affairs that they found unanimity.

Unfortunately, an analysis of the differences among the officers' views yields no neat formulas or patterns that explain them. Women proved to be neither more nor less sympathetic to Indians than men. Staff officers appeared neither more nor less sympathetic than line officers. The same held true for other possible divisions, such as high rank versus low, northern background versus southern, western background versus eastern, religious outlook versus nonreligious, or native-born versus foreign-born. These categories offer handy distinctions, but they prove inadequate in explaining individual points of view. The explanation for differences must be more complicated. The only apparent keys to differing perceptions of Indians were the nebulous, even unmanageable, ones of individual personality, temperament, and circumstance. In addition, the specific tribe under an officer's scrutiny and the amount of time he spent with that tribe could also affect an individual's perceptions.

Moreover, military men and women maintained this diversity of opinion throughout the last half of the nineteenth century, with little noticeable alteration in the questions they raised or the concepts, ideas, and language they employed to answer them. No marked shifts in the nature of the debate about Indians occurred within the ranks of the officer corps after the Civil War, for example, or in the later decades of the century as the army closed in on the last of the reservation resisters, or as the precepts of social Darwinism became more prominent in the national debate over social and racial issues. To be sure, individual officers experienced change over time. Some men, such as Pope and Hazen, became more sympathetic to Indians as they experienced disillusionment with white frontiersmen or as they developed greater respect for Indian people. Others, such as Lieutenant George Templeton, became less sympathetic as they discovered that most Indians could not live up to their Cooper-inspired expectations of noble grandeur. As a group, however, they did not alter their opinions dramatically from the middle of the century to its end.

In this respect, the army people reflected the larger society's experiences and attitudes. In the nineteenth century, Anglo-Americans sustained consistent perceptions of Indians that remained substantially unchallenged until well into the twentieth century. While the officers' functions in the West set them apart from other groups, and while they perceived themselves as distinct, isolated, and sometimes in opposition to both eastern humanitarians and western frontiersmen, these men and their wives for the most part embraced their culture's ideas about Indians. Some—Miles and Crook, for example—tried to mitigate the effects of policy on particular groups of Indians, but none took issue with the ultimate goals of policy or seriously challenged the assumptions about civilization and savagery that served as the intellectual underpinning of that policy.[2] As a result, their similarities to the so-called eastern humanitarians or reformers in their overall attitudes toward Indians and Indian policy seem more impressive than their differences. The major debate between the two groups focused on who should administer the policy rather than on the assumptions, direction, and goals of the policy itself.

On the other hand, though they perceived themselves as civilization's guardians, the officers understood that the pioneer did not always represent a model of gentility. He could be brutal, crude, and grasping. Consequently, army officers sometimes felt compelled to protect Indians from whites, not because they wanted to preserve Indian ways of life, but because they hoped to save them for civilization. They guarded civilization, then, not only from savages, but from the white world's own baser elements, who, if left unchecked, would wipe out the Indians. In their expressions of sympathy, even empathy, for American Indians, in their troubled efforts to justify their personal involvement in the Indian wars, and in their occasional attempts to explain Indians' behavior on the basis of their native cultures and traditions, officers presented what could be considered remarkably modern ideas.

They saw merits in both nature and civilization. If the military men and women viewed Indian warfare as an inevitable aspect of progress, they did not delight in that prospect. They expressed some compassion for the people whose cultures they saw as doomed. They identified what they saw as native virtues and expressed misgivings about the presumed passing away of the Indian. They revealed some soul-searching, some hesitance, about the future of modern America. In this respect, the views of army officers and officers' wives support Lee Clark Mitchell's contention that "Our nineteenth-century predecessors swaggered with less thoughtless confidence than the historical record suggests, and we need to . . . recognize that they could be nearly as troubled as we are."[3] Too often we have presented the "humanitarian" assimilationists and the "racist" Indian haters as the sum total of nineteenth-century white attitudes toward Indians, in an effort perhaps to separate ourselves from them. But such a view fails to consider the various shades of grey in between those points of black and white, gradations so well represented by army officers and their wives.

Notes

INTRODUCTION

1. Some historians have written articles on this topic. They include Thomas C. Leonard, "Red, White and the Army Blue: Empathy and Anger in the American West," *American Quarterly* 26 (May 1974): 176–190; idem, "The Reluctant Conquerors: How the Generals Viewed the Indians," *American Heritage* 27 (August 1976): 34–41; William B. Skelton, "Army Officers' Attitudes Toward Indians, 1830–1860," *Pacific Northwest Quarterly* 67 (July 1976): 113–124; Richard N. Ellis, "The Humanitarian Generals," *Western Historical Quarterly* 3 (April 1972): 169–178. See also Edward M. Coffman, *The Old Army: A Portrait of the American Army in Peacetime, 1784–1898* (New York: Oxford University Press, 1986), 34–35, 73–78, 254–261.

2. Paul Andrew Hutton, "From Little Bighorn to Little Big Man: The Changing Image of a Western Hero," *Western Historical Quarterly* 7 (January 1976): 19–45.

3. Coffman, *Old Army*, 103, 276.

4. Recent efforts to analyze women's experiences in the West, in contrast to men's, include Glenda Riley, *Women and Indians on the Frontier, 1825–1915* (Albuquerque: University of New Mexico Press, 1984); John Mack Faragher, *Women and Men on the Overland Trail* (New Haven: Yale University Press, 1979); Julie Roy Jeffrey, *Frontier Women: The Trans-Mississippi West, 1840–1880* (New York: Hill and Wang, 1979); and Lillian Schlissel, *Women's Diaries of the Westward Journey* (New York: Schocken Books, 1982).

5. James L. Morrison, "The United States Military Academy, 1833–1866: Years of Progress and Turmoil" (Ph.D. diss., Columbia University, 1971), 292–293.

6. An additional comment on the subject of rank is in order. The officers usually referred to themselves and to one another by brevet, or honorary, rank. In the pages that follow, however, officers are identified by their actual rank at the time they wrote the letter

or memoir that is quoted. George Armstrong Custer's Civil War exploits, for example, brought him the rank of brevet major general, and he and his wife, Elizabeth, used that title in their publications. However, when he wrote *My Life on the Plains*, Custer's actual rank was lieutenant colonel, and it is by that rank that he is identified here.

7. Robert F. Berkhofer, *The White Man's Indian: Images of the American Indian from Columbus to the Present* (New York: Alfred A. Knopf, 1978), 26.

8. Prucha is quoted in James P. Tate, ed., *The American Military on the Frontier: Proceedings of the 7th Military History Symposium, United States Air Force Academy* (Washington, D.C.: Office of Air Force History, 1978), 176. See also B. Franklin Cooling, "Military History: A Blending of Old and New," *OAH Newsletter*, February 1984, 14–15.

9. Roy Harvey Pearce, *Savagism and Civilization: A Study of the Indian and the American Mind* (Baltimore: Johns Hopkins Press, 1967), v.

CHAPTER 1. OFFICERS AS OBSERVERS

1. Louis L. Simonin, *The Rocky Mountain West in 1867*, translated by Wilson O. Clough (Lincoln: University of Nebraska Press, 1966), 71–72.

2. Quoted in Richard N. Ellis, *General Pope and U.S. Indian Policy* (Albuquerque: University of New Mexico Press, 1970), 239.

3. Robert M. Utley, *The Contribution of the Frontier to the American Military Tradition*, The Harmon Memorial Lectures in Military History, no. 19 (Colorado Springs, Colo.: United States Air Force Academy, 1977), 3.

4. Edward M. Coffman, *The Old Army: A Portrait of the American Army in Peacetime, 1784–1898* (New York: Oxford University Press, 1986), 66–67. See also Robert M. Utley, *Frontiersmen in Blue: The United States Army and the Indian, 1848–1865* (New York: Macmillan Publishing Co., 1967), 35; Marcus Cunliffe, *Soldiers and Civilians: The Martial Spirit in America, 1775–1865* (Boston: Little, Brown and Co., 1968), 141; James L. Morrison, Jr., "The United States Military Academy, 1833–1866: Years of Progress and Turmoil" (Ph.D. diss., Columbia University, 1971), 290. Morrison argues that the notion that West Point was pro-Southern is mostly mythical, noting that "the defection rate of Southern West Pointers was noticeably lower than that of other agencies of the federal government or of northern civilian colleges."

5. Robert M. Utley, *Frontier Regulars: The United States Army and the Indian, 1866–1891* (New York: Macmillan Publishing Co., 1973), 18; Coffman, *Old Army*, 219, 222–223.

6. Patricia Y. Stallard, *Glittering Misery: Dependents of the Indian Fighting Army* (Fort Collins, Colo.: Old Army Press, 1978), 15–52; Sandra L. Myres, "Romance and Reality on the American Frontier: Views of Army Wives," *Western Historical Quarterly* 13 (October 1982): 409–427; and Coffman, *Old Army*, 287–327.

7. Paul Andrew Hutton, *Phil Sheridan and His Army* (Lincoln: University of Nebraska Press, 1985), 169, 173–175; Coffman, *Old Army*, 247; Utley, *Frontiersmen in Blue*, 29–31.

8. James Parker to brother, October 7, 1876, James Parker Papers, United States Military Academy, West Point, New York.

9. DeWitt Clinton Peters to sister, December 20, 1854, July 15, 1856, DeWitt Clinton Peters Papers, Bancroft Library, Berkeley, California.

10. Quoted in Hutton, *Phil Sheridan*, 143. One officer presented his version of the ideal this way: "Stalwart of build, splendidly erect, neat in person, temperate in habits, and low of voice save when upon drill. Apt to be sparing of speech, and as a general thing not given to discussion or argument. Tenacious of his own opinion, but always willing to listen to those who disagree with him, and with a thorough respect for all legally constituted authority, as well as a decent respect for his own position and himself. Considerate of his inferiors and unquestionably obedient to his superiors in rank. Thoughtful over orders, but always promptly obedient to the tenor." Brigadier General George A. Forsyth, *The Story of the Soldier* (New York: Brampton Society, 1908), 2:374.

11. Robert C. Kemble, *The Image of the Army Officer in America: Background for Current Views* (Westport, Conn.: Greenwood Press, 1973), 82, 101. See also Thomas L. Haskell, *The Emergence of Professional Social Science: The American Social Science Association and the Nineteenth-Century Crisis of Authority* (Urbana: University of Illinois Press, 1977), 65, 19.

12. James W. Steele, *Frontier Army Sketches* (Chicago: Jansen, McClurg and Co., 1883), 4–5. For other examples of similar statements, see William Henry Bisbee, *Through Four American Wars* (Boston: Meador Publishing Co., 1931), 62; Parmenus T. Turnley, *Reminiscences of Parmenus Taylor Turnley, From the Cradle to Three Score and Ten* (Chicago: Donohue and Henneberry, 1892), 286; R. H. McKay, *Little Pills: An Army Story, Being Some Experiences of a United States Army Medical Officer on the Frontier*

Nearly a Half Century Ago (Pittsburg, Kan.: Pittsburg Headlight, 1918), 8.

13. Quoted in Coffman, *Old Army*, 215.

14. Ibid., 103.

15. Quoted in Cunliffe, *Soldiers and Civilians*, 103.

16. See Desmond Morton, "Comparison of U.S./Canadian Military Experience on the Frontier," in James P. Tate, ed., *The American Military on the Frontier: Proceedings of the 7th Military History Symposium, United States Air Force Academy* (Washington, D.C.: Office of Air Force History, 1978), 127–130; Richard N. Ellis, "The Political Role of the Military on the Frontier," in Tate, *American Military*, 75–76; Walter Scott Dillard, "The United States Military Academy, 1865–1900: The Uncertain Years" (Ph.D. diss., University of Washington, 1972), 13–14; Utley, *Frontiersmen in Blue*, 10–19; Utley, *Frontier Regulars*, 12–18; Kemble, *Image of the Army Officer*, 127–130; and Coffman, *Old Army*, 38, 103, 254, 401–402.

One would err in drawing broad general conclusions about Americans' images of the military. They defy any neatly drawn patterns. There was no consensus in either the East or the West. Military men were both respected and held in contempt, admired and distrusted. Not surprisingly, these attitudes reflected social tensions of the times, with sectional and national, genteel and democratic, conservative and politically progressive tensions manifested in attitudes toward military men. "The soldier's image," according to Kemble, "has been as many faceted as the American mind itself." One could add as many faceted as the soldiers themselves. See Kemble, *Image of the Army Officer*, 197.

17. Carter, *From Yorktown to Santiago*, 1, 16–17. This profound sense of national ingratitude remained for years after the close of the Indian wars. During World War I, William T. Parker, an enlisted man who became a doctor, bitterly remarked on how few people understood that veterans of the Indian wars had also faced "perils, and privations and constant nerve strain," yet they had never been duly honored for their part in the birth of a mighty empire. Asserting that no Civil War battle ever called forth more military courage and fortitude than an Indian campaign, Parker complained, "War is hell, but Indian war is 'hell boiled down!' It is surprising that when the National Government, or State, or municipal authorities endeavor to honor veterans, *the Indian war veteran is seldom, if ever, honored, or even recognized.*" William Thornton Parker, *Personal Experiences Among Our North American Indians, From 1867 to 1885* (Northampton, Mass., 1913), 19, 5. The last statement came

from the 1918 edition's "Supplement," n.p.

18. Utley, *Contribution of the Frontier*, 4.

19. Morrison, "United States Military Academy," 165; Dillard, "United States Military Academy," 283; and Rodney Glisan, *Journal of Army Life* (San Francisco: A. L. Bancroft and Co., 1874), 237.

20. H. H. McConnell, *Five Years a Cavalryman; or, Sketches of Regular Army Life on the Texas Frontier, Twenty Odd Years Ago* (Jacksboro, Tex.: J. N. Rogers and Co., 1889), 219.

21. Joseph Agonito, "The Art of Plains Indian Warfare," *Order of the Indian Wars Journal* 1 (Winter 1980): 1.

22. Robert F. Berkhofer, Jr., *The White Man's Indian: Images of the American Indian from Columbus to the Present* (New York: Alfred A. Knopf, 1978), 26–27; Brian W. Dippie, *The Vanishing American: White Attitudes and U.S. Policy* (Middletown, Conn.: Wesleyan University Press, 1982), xi. For other studies of Euro-Americans' attitudes toward Indians, see Roy Harvey Pearce, *Savagism and Civilization: A Study of the Indian and the American Mind* (Baltimore: Johns Hopkins Press, 1967); Richard Drinnon, *Facing West: The Metaphysics of Indian-Hating and Empire-Building* (Minneapolis: University of Minnesota Press, 1980); Richard Slotkin, *Regeneration Through Violence: The Mythology of the American Frontier* (Middletown, Conn.: Wesleyan University Press, 1973); idem, *The Fatal Environment: The Myth of the Frontier in the Age of Industrialization, 1800–1890* (New York: Atheneum, 1985); Frederick W. Turner, *Beyond Geography: The Western Spirit Against the Wilderness* (New York: Viking Press, 1980); William Stedman, *Shadows of the Indian: Stereotypes in American Culture* (Norman: University of Oklahoma Press, 1982); Lewis O. Saum, *The Fur Trader and the Indian* (Seattle: University of Washington Press, 1965); Robert F. Berkhofer, Jr., *Salvation and the Savage: An Analysis of Protestant Missions and the American Indian Response, 1787–1862* (Lexington: University of Kentucky Press, 1965); Glenda Riley, *Women and Indians on the Frontier, 1825–1915* (Albuquerque: University of New Mexico Press, 1984); and Sandra L. Myres, *Westering Women and the Frontier Experience, 1800–1915* (Albuquerque: University of New Mexico Press, 1982), 48–49, 64–66.

CHAPTER 2. INDIAN CHARACTER

1. George Armstrong Custer, *My Life on the Plains; or, Personal Experiences with Indians* (Norman: University of Oklahoma Press, 1976), 13, 19.

2. Ibid., 13. In marked contrast to the majority of officers who invoked Cooper's images, General Oliver O. Howard found that Cooper had ameliorated Howard's own family-instilled prejudices about Indians. As he related the process in his autobiography, his grandfather, an old Indian fighter himself, had regaled the young Howard with stories of wild and savage Indians—"worse than Tories"—who spared neither woman nor child. "It took," Howard reminisced, "the broadening influence of years and the stories of William Penn, and of Pocahontas, besides the persuasive charm of James Fenimore Cooper's novels, to allay my strong prejudice and show me the equal or greater sinfulness of the Anglo-Saxon." See *My Life and Experiences Among Our Hostile Indians* (New York: De Capo Press, 1972), 45.

3. Robert M. Utley, ed., *Life in Custer's Cavalry: Diaries and Letters of Albert and Jennie Barnitz, 1867–1868* (New Haven: Yale University Press, 1977), 55; Martha Summerhayes, *Vanished Arizona: Recollections of the Army Life of a New England Woman* (Tucson: Arizona Silhouettes, 1960), 51. This book was reprinted by the University of Nebraska Press in 1979. Practically every army officer's wife expressed some fear of Indians. For other examples, see Frances M. A. Roe, *Army Letters From an Officer's Wife* (New York: D. Appleton and Co., 1909), 57, 64–65; Frances Carrington, *My Army Life and the Fort Phil Kearny Massacre* (Philadelphia: J. B. Lippincott Co., 1911), 30, 86; Elizabeth B. Custer, *"Boots and Saddles"; or, Life in Dakota with General Custer* (Norman: University of Oklahoma Press, 1961), 4, 58–59, 67; Anna Page Russell Maus, "Old Army Days: Reminiscences of the Wife of an Army Surgeon," Haustead-Maus Family Papers, United States Army Military History Institute, Carlisle Barracks, Pennsylvania; Caroline Frey Winne to Ludlow, January 22, 1875, May 25, 1879, Caroline Frey Winne Papers, New-York Historical Society Library, New York; and Josephine Clifford, *"Another Juanita" and Other Stories* (Buffalo: Charles Wells Moulton, 1893), 33, 37–43, 103; and idem, *Overland Tales* (Philadelphia: Claxton, Remsen and Haffelfinger, 1877), 306–308.

4. Robert C. Carriker and Eleanor R. Carriker, eds., *An Army Wife on the Frontier: The Memoirs of Alice Blackwood Baldwin, 1867–1877* (Salt Lake City: Tanner Trust Fund, 1975), 67. For an equally plucky response to an Indian attack, see Sandra L. Myres, ed., *Cavalry Wife: The Diary of Eveline M. Alexander, 1866–1867* (College Station: Texas A & M University Press, 1977), 92–93.

5. Roy Harvey Pearce, *Savagism and Civilization: A Study of the Indian and the American Mind* (Baltimore: Johns Hopkins

Press, 1967), 58. See also Dawn Lander Gherman, "From Parlour to Tepee: The White Squaw on the American Frontier" (Ph.D. diss., University of Massachusetts, 1975), 12; Lydia Spencer Lane, *I Married a Soldier; or, Old Days in the Old Army* (Albuquerque: Horn and Wallace Publishers, 1964), 73–74. Elizabeth Custer is quoted in Marguerite Merington, ed., *The Custer Story: The Life and Intimate Letters of General George A. Custer and His Wife Elizabeth* (New York: Devin-Adair Co., 1950), 284; Ray Mattison, ed., "An Army Wife on the Upper Missouri: The Diary of Sarah E. Canfield, 1866–1868," *North Dakota History* 20 (October 1953): 217.

6. William B. Skelton, "Army Officers' Attitudes Toward Indians, 1830–1860," *Pacific Northwest Quarterly* 67 (July 1976): 113.

7. J. Lee Humfreville, *Twenty Years Among Our Hostile Indians* (New York: Hunter and Co., 1903), xii. Few officers argued that Indians were savage because they were not Christian. One who did, however, was Captain Randolph C. Marcy; see his *Border Reminiscences* (New York: Harper and Brothers, 1872), 38.

8. Dodge, *Our Wild Indians*, 56. Dodge also argued that Plains Indians were "habitually and universally the happiest people I ever saw. They thoroughly enjoy the present, make no worry over the possibilities of the future and 'never cry over spilt milk.' It may be argued that their apparent happiness is only insensibility, the happiness of the mere animal, whose animal desires are satisfied. It may be so. The Indian is proud, sensitive, quick-tempered, easily wounded, easily excited, but though utterly unforgiving, he never broods. This, in my opinion, is the whole secret of his happiness" (p. 248).

9. Hugh Lenox Scott, *Some Memories of a Soldier* (New York: Century Co., 1928), 116. For a similar comment, see Major General A. W. Greely, *Reminiscences of Adventure and Service: A Record of Sixty-Five Years* (New York: Charles Scribner's Sons, 1927), 62.

10. Lucille M. Kane, ed., *Military Life in Dakota* (St. Paul: Alvord Memorial Commission, 1951), 231.

11. Humfreville, *Twenty Years*, xii–xiii. Some, of course, depicted Indians as thoroughly savage both before and after contact with whites. For examples, see Captain R. G. Carter, *On the Border with Mackenzie; or, Winning West Texas From the Comanches* (New York: Antiquarian Press, 1961), 278–279, 282; General Philip H. Sheridan, *Personal Memoirs* (New York: Charles L. Webster and Co., 1888), 1:106–108. For examples of army wives who emphasized the negative aspects of "Indian character," see Roe, *Army Letters*, 64–65, 359; Emily Fitzgerald's letters collected in Abe

Laufe, ed., *An Army Doctor's Wife on the Frontier: Letters From Alaska and the Far West, 1874–1878* (Pittsburgh: University of Pittsburgh Press, 1962), 119–121, 249, 259; and Caroline Frey Winne to her father, March 1, 1875, and to Ludlow, July 29, October 9, 1879, Caroline Frey Winne Papers, New-York Historical Society Library.

12. Dodge, *Our Wild Indians*, 41–42, 533–534.

13. Captain John Bourke, *On the Border With Crook* (New York: Charles Scribner's Sons, 1891), 114–115.

14. Crook is quoted in Thomas C. Leonard, "The Reluctant Conquerors: How the Generals Viewed the Indians," *American Heritage* 27 (August 1976): 37. In his autobiography, Crook was a bit less complimentary toward Indian character, writing, "It is an easy matter for anyone to see the salient points of Indian character, namely that they are filthy, odoriferous, treacherous, ungrateful, pitiless, cruel and lazy. But it is the fewest who ever get beyond this, and see his other side, which, I must admit, is small, and almost latent." See General George Crook, *His Autobiography*, edited by Martin F. Schmitt (Norman: University of Oklahoma Press, 1960), 69.

15. Howard, *My Life and Experiences*, 549, 433.

16. Nelson Miles, *Personal Recollections and Observations* (Chicago: Werner Co., 1896), 88; idem, *Serving the Republic: Memoirs of the Civil and Military Life of Nelson A. Miles* (New York: Harper and Brothers, 1911), 114, 188.

17. Captain E. L. Huggins, *Winona: A Dakota Legend and Other Poems* (New York: G. P. Putnam's Sons, 1890), 3, 4.

18. Skelton, "Army Officers' Attitudes," 114.

CHAPTER 3. TRIBES AND CHIEFS

1. Ada Adams Vogdes journal, July 2, July 28, August 23, November 5, 1868; April 27, July 14, 1870, Huntington Library, San Marino, California. All quotations are taken from the original manuscript. Portions of this journal appeared in Donald K. Adams, ed., "The Journal of Ada A. Vogdes," *Montana: The Magazine of Western History* 13 (Summer 1963): 2–17.

2. William Thornton Parker, *Personal Experiences Among Our North American Indians, From 1867 to 1885* (Northampton, Mass., 1913), 72, 33–34; Colonel Richard Irving Dodge, *Our Wild Indians: Thirty-Three Years' Personal Experience Among the Red Men of the Great West* (Hartford, Conn.: A. D. Worthington and Co., 1883), 53.

3. Erasmus Darwin Keyes, *Fifty Years' Observation of Men and Events, Civil and Military* (New York: Charles Scribner's Sons,

Sons, 1884), 131; Benjamin Grierson, "Notes on Indians," dated February 22, 1869, Fort Gibson, Indian Territory, Benjamin Grierson Papers, Newberry Library, Chicago; and Captain R. G. Carter, *On the Border With Mackenzie; or, Winning West Texas from the Comanches* (New York: Antiquarian Press, 1961), 367. See also Eveline Alexander's comments in Sandra Myres, ed., *Cavalry Wife: The Diary of Eveline M. Alexander, 1866–1867* (College Station, Tex.; Texas A & M University Press, 1977), 42, 44.

4. Carter, *On the Border*, 366–367.

5. Dodge, *Our Wild Indians*, 53.

6. Lieutenant Lawrence Kip, *Army Life on the Pacific: A Journal of the Expedition Against the Northern Indians, the Tribes of the Coeur d'Alenes, Spokans, and Pelouzes, in the Summer of 1858* (New York: Redfield, 1859), 33–34.

7. Lieutenant George Templeton diary, December 10, 19, 1866, and April 10, 1867, Newberry Library, Chicago.

8. Nelson A. Miles, *Serving the Republic: Memoirs of the Civil and Military Life of Nelson A. Miles* (New York: Harper and Brothers, 1911), 171, 181. Sounding a rare negative note on the Nez Perce, Captain John Kress, chief ordnance officer of the Department of the Columbia, remarked that with the commencement of the 1877 war, the Nez Perce "mounted their ponies and started vigorously on the war-path, in their usual murderous style." Kress, *Autobiography* (n.p., 1929), 47. This book is available in the Northwest Collection, University of Washington Library, Seattle.

9. Oliver O. Howard, *Nez Perce Joseph* (Boston: Lee and Shepard, 1881), iii, 14. Howard made similar distinctions among the Puget Sound tribes between those who adopted Anglo-American ways and those who "adhered tenaciously to old Indian customs." See O. O. Howard, *My Life and Experiences Among Our Hostile Indians* (New York: De Capo Press, 1972), 301–302.

10. James W. Steele, *Frontier Army Sketches* (Chicago: Jansen, McClurg and Co., 1883), 184–185. See also Lieutenant David Sloane Stanley, "Diary of an Expedition . . . from Fort Smith, Arkansas, . . . to San Diego, 1853–1854," entry for September 17, 1853, typescript, Huntington Library; Bernard James Byrne, *A Frontier Army Surgeon: Life in Colorado in the Eighties* (New York: Exposition Press, 1962), 17; R. H. McKay, *Little Pills: An Army Story, Being Some Experiences of a United States Army Medical Officer on the Frontier Nearly a Half Century Ago* (Pittsburg, Kan.: Pittsburg Headlight, 1918), 19.

11. Major General George A. McCall, *Letters From the Frontiers, Written During a Period of Thirty Years' Service in the Army of the*

United States (Philadelphia: J. B. Lippincott and Co., 1868), 498–499; Myres, *Cavalry Wife*, 105; and Martha Summerhayes, *Vanished Arizona: Recollections of the Army Life of a New England Woman* (Tucson: Arizona Silhouettes, 1960), 205. See also Alexander's comments on the Hopi; Myres, *Cavalry Wife*, 109–110.

12. Steele, *Frontier Army Sketches*, 183, 186.

13. George P. Hammond, ed., *Campaigns in the West, 1856–1861: The Journal and Letters of Colonel John Van Deusen Du Bois* (Tucson: Arizona Pioneers Historical Society, 1949), 121; McCall, *Letters From the Frontiers*, 502, 512. Officers' wives exhibited similar ambivalence about the Navajos. Alice Baldwin did not completely trust the Navajos she met at Fort Wingate in New Mexico Territory in 1867 and 1868. Yet she found them fond of music and would play the organ for Navajo visitors to her home. See Robert C. Carriker and Eleanor R. Carriker, eds., *An Army Wife on the Frontier: The Memoirs of Alice Blackwood Baldwin, 1867–1877* (Salt Lake City: Tanner Trust Fund, 1975), 78–79. See also Myres, *Cavalry Wife*, 116–119, for Evy Alexander on the Navajos and pp. 30–31 for her positive comments on the Pima and Maricopa; also, Mrs. Orsemus Boyd, *Cavalry Life in Tent and Field* (New York: J. Selwin Tait, 1894), 155; and Maria Brace Kimball, *My Eighty Years* (Boston: By the author, 1936), 32.

14. John G. Bourke, *The Snake-Dance of the Moquis of Arizona* (New York: Charles Scribner's Sons, 1884), 63; Byrne, *Frontier Army Surgeon*, 29.

15. John Bourke diary, October 13, 15, 1874, Denver Public Library; Bourke, *On the Border*, 114, 124. Of course, not all officers admired the Apache. Upon visiting Fort Apache in 1886, Nelson Miles reported that the Chiricahua and Warm Springs Apaches were "dissipated" and that much of their earnings went for "tiswin" drunks. He claimed that bloody riots were not unusual and that "indolent and vicious young men and boys were just the material to furnish warriors for the future." See Nelson Miles, *Annual Report . . . Department of Arizona, 1886*, copy in Henry Lawton Collection, Newberry Library. George A. Forsyth stressed the Apaches' supposed worst qualities but explained that the Spaniards' and Mexicans' attempts to enslave them over two hundred years had developed these qualities in them. See Forsyth, *The Story of the Soldier* (New York: Brampton Society, 1908), 2:267–268. For more on Bourke's attitude toward the Hopi, see Joseph C. Porter, *Paper Medicine Man: John Gregory Bourke and His American West* (Norman: University of Oklahoma Press, 1986), 95–111.

16. Joseph Sladen to Mrs. Alice Crane, October 26, 1896, United

States Army Military History Institute, Carlisle Barracks, Pennsylvania. Other officers also expressed disgust at physical contact with Indians. Granville O. Haller attended a council with some Shoshone and confided in his diary that he was "obliged to take a seat among the Indians, much to my disgust as I was sure of getting fleas on me and was not disappointed"; Haller diary, July 16, 1855, Granville O. Haller Papers, Suzzallo Library, University of Washington, Seattle.

17. Kip, *Army Life*, 20; and Granville O. Haller to unknown, July 31, 1855, in Correspondence From Headquarters During Winnass Expedition, 1855, Granville O. Haller Papers.

18. George Armstrong Custer, *My Life on the Plains; or, Personal Experiences with Indians* (Norman: University of Oklahoma Press, 1976), 20, 22.

19. Lee Clark Mitchell, *Witnesses to a Vanishing America: The Nineteenth Century Response* (Princeton: Princeton University Press, 1981), xiii–xiv.

20. Miles, *Serving the Republic*, 113–114. See also Thomas C. Leonard, "Red, White and the Army Blue: Empathy and Anger in the American West," *American Quarterly* 26 (May 1974): 184.

21. Howard, *My Life*, 459, 463; Bradley's comments appear in Edgar I. Stewart, ed., *The March of the Montana Column: A Prelude to the Custer Disaster* (Norman: University of Oklahoma Press, 1961), 113. For other remarks on the Sioux, see Maria Brace Kimball, *A Soldier-Doctor of Our Army: James P. Kimball* (Boston: Houghton Mifflin Co., 1917), 40; Anson Mills, *My Story* (Washington, D.C.: By the author, 1918), 406; James H. Bradley, "History of the Sioux," *Contributions to the Historical Society of Montana* 9 (1923): 124–125; Templeton diary, September 13, 1866, Newberry Library; and Langdon Sully, *No Tears for the General: The Life of Alfred Sully, 1821–1879* (Palo Alto, Calif.: American West Publishing Co., 1974), 192, 194.

Officers' attitudes toward particular Plains tribes are described in a number of works. On the Blackfoot, see Lieutenant James H. Bradley, "Characteristics, Habits and Customs of the Blackfeet Indians," *Contributions to the Historical Society of Montana* 9 (1923): 270; and Kip, *Army Life*, 33. On the Kiowa, see C. C. Augur Letterbook, 1872–1875, Newberry Library; and Stanley, "Diary of an Expedition," September 9, 1853, Huntington Library. On the Arapahoe, see Captain Henry Alvord to Benjamin Grierson, February 2, 1869, in Grierson Papers, Newberry Library; and Colonel R. I. Dodge diary, March 25, 1879, Dodge Papers, Newberry Library. On the Utes, see General James F. Rusling, *Across America; or, The*

Great West and the Pacific Coast (New York: Sheldon and Co., 1874), 116, 118, 134. On the Kickapoo, see Marcy, *Thirty Years*, 93. On the Otoes, see William E. Waters, *Life Among the Mormons, and a March to Their Zion* (New York: Moorhead, Simpson and Bond, 1868), 8. On the Comanches, see Randolph Marcy, *Adventure on the Red River*, 161; Teresa Viele, *"Following the Drum": A Glimpse of Frontier Life* (New York: Rudd and Carleton, 1859), 190–191, 123–124; and Myres, *Cavalry Wife*, 63–65.

22. Robert M. Utley, ed., *Life in Custer's Cavalry: Diaries and Letters of Albert and Jennie Barnitz, 1867–1868* (New Haven: Yale University Press, 1977), 114–115; Charles King, *Campaigning With Crook and Stories of Army Life* (New York: Harper and Brothers, 1890), 33.

23. Paul Andrew Hutton, *Phil Sheridan and His Army* (Lincoln: University of Nebraska Press, 1985), 334.

24. Hugh Scott to his mother, November 23, 1877, Hugh Lenox Scott Papers, Library of Congress. Others who especially liked the Cheyenne included Richard I. Dodge (see his diary for April 14, 1879, Dodge Papers, Newberry Library) and James Parker (see Parker to his mother, October 13, 1878, James Parker Papers, United States Military Academy Library, West Point, New York).

25. Rusling, *Across America*, 360–361; Bourke, *On the Border*, 65.

26. Edward K. Eckert and Nicholas J. Amato, eds., *Ten Years in the Saddle: The Memoir of William Woods Averell* (San Rafael, Calif.: Presidio Press, 1978), 129.

27. Lucille M. Kane, ed., *Military Life in Dakota* (St. Paul: Alvord Memorial Commission, 1951), 249–250.

28. Erasmus Darwin Keyes, *From West Point to California* (Oakland, Calif.: Biobooks, 1950), 15–18.

29. Eckert and Amato, *Ten Years*, 212, 213–214; Rodney Glisan, *Journal of Army Life* (San Francisco: A. L. Bancroft and Co., 1874), 364, 427. John Van Deusen Du Bois heralded a young man who surrendered during the 1857 Gila Expedition as "a noble specimen of humanity, tall and formed like an Apollo"; Hammond, *Campaigns in the West*, 31. Lieutenant Thomas W. Sweeny described Santiago, a Yuma leader, as "a perfect Hercules in stature"; Arthur Woodward, ed., *Journal of Lt. Thomas W. Sweeny, 1849–1853* (Los Angeles: Westernlore Press, 1956), 64. Averell, however, was the only officer to suggest any resemblance between an Indian and Jesus Christ. Upon learning that a Navajo had murdered a negro slave, the army officials demanded the murderer. According to Averell, the tribe killed and brought in an innocent young man to appease

the Anglo-Americans, delivering the body to Averell's post. Averell, who inspected the dead body, claimed that this young Navajo was sacrificed to save his people from the punishment of war, and he added that the "recumbent figure with the loin covering the long hair and the suggestion of blood, surrounded with sinister Hebraic faces, brought to my mind a quick unspeakable hint of a similar scene which has been recalled by the Christian world on every Good Friday throughout eighteen centuries." See Eckert and Amato, *Ten Years in the Saddle,* 172.

30. Ellen McGowan Biddle, *Reminiscences of a Soldier's Wife* (Philadelphia: J. B. Lippincott Co., 1907), 182.

31. Summerhayes, *Vanished Arizona,* 179–180, 124–125.

32. Ione Bradley, "Recollections of Army Life," Luther P. Bradley Papers, United States Army Military History Institute; Ray Mattison, ed., "An Army Wife on the Upper Missouri: The Diary of Sarah E. Canfield, 1866–1868," *North Dakota History* 20 (October 1953): 204; Summerhayes, *Vanished Arizona,* 64, 73–74; Frances M. A. Roe, *Army Letters From an Officer's Wife* (New York: D. Appleton and Co., 1909), 107; Abe Laufe, ed., *An Army Doctor's Wife on the Frontier: Letters from Alaska and the Far West, 1874–1878* (Pittsburgh: University of Pittsburgh Press, 1962), 204. See also Elizabeth B. Custer, *"Boots and Saddles"; or, Life in Dakota with General Custer* (Norman: University of Oklahoma Press, 1961), 186, 188. For a discussion of Anglo women who married Indian men, see Glenda Riley, *Women and Indians on the Frontier, 1825–1915* (Albuquerque: University of New Mexico Press, 1984), 181–184.

33. John G. Bourke diary, February 3, 1873, Denver Public Library; Howard, *My Life,* 205.

34. Joseph Sladen to Mrs. Alice Crane, October 26, 1896, United States Army Military History Institute. Sladen provided a warm account not only of Cochise but also of his nephew, Chie. Chie joined Sladen's party, believing that he could help find Cochise and open communications. Sladen described him as "a handsome young fellow, about twenty years of age, bright and full of fun and as keen and accomplished in an Indian craft as any wild Apache could possibly be. He had a wife, a young baby, both of which he was loth to leave."

35. Arthur Woodward, ed., *On the Bloody Trail of Geronimo* (Los Angeles: Westernlore Press, 1958), xxiii–xxiv. Henry Lawton thought of ways to destroy Geronimo before the latter's surrender, but after Geronimo did surrender, the army officer presented him in a more affectionate light. See Henry Lawton to his wife, July 16, August 26, 1886, Henry Ware Lawton Papers, Library of Congress.

36. See C.E.S. Wood letter to Moorfield Story, May 27, 1895, reprinted in *Oregon Inn-Side News* (Nov./Dec. 1947), and undated, untitled news article by Wood, both in Scrapbook, C.E.S. Wood Papers, Huntington Library; Erskine Wood, *Life of Charles Erskine Scott Wood* (Portland, Ore.: By the author, 1978), 14–23, 110–118; Howard, *Nez Perce Joseph*, 29. For other examples, see Miles on Chief Joseph's surrender: "Chief Joseph surrendered like a man. He is a very superior Indian . . . in intelligence and ability, and a fine looking, mild mannered man"; Virginia W. Johnson, *The Unregimented General: A Biography of Nelson A. Miles* (Boston: Houghton Mifflin Co., 1962), 207. See also Miles, *Serving the Republic*, 181. There are inevitable exceptions to any of these rules. Several officers' accounts of the Kiowa leader Satanta smack of the romantic detachment noted above in accounts of less famous Indians. See Carter, *On the Border*, 136; and McKay, *Little Pills*, 51.

37. Mills, *My Story*, 158.

38. William T. Corbusier, *Verde to San Carlos: Recollections of a Famous Army Surgeon and His Observant Family on the Western Frontier, 1869–1886* (Tucson: Dale Stuart King, 1968), 194; Merrill J. Mattes, ed., *Indians, Infants and Infantry: Andrew and Elizabeth Burt on the Frontier* (Denver: Old West Publishing Co., 1960), 84–85; Summerhayes, *Vanished Arizona*, 179–180. Caroline Frey Winne also thought that Washakie resembled Henry Ward Beecher; see Caroline Frey Winne to Ludlow, May 25, 1879, Caroline Frey Winne Papers, New-York Historical Society Library, New York.

39. Miles is quoted in Johnson, *The Unregimented General*, 118; Kane, ed., *Military Life*, 289; O. O. Howard, *Famous Indian Chiefs I Have Known* (New York: Century Company, 1908), 311–312; Anna Maus, "Old Army Days," Haustead-Maus Family Papers, United States Army Military History Institute. See also Heistand, "Army Scraps," 120–127.

40. Joseph Sladen to Mrs. Alice Crane, October 26, 1896, United States Army Military History Institute.

41. Kip, *Army Life*, 104–105.

42. Keyes, *Fifty Years' Observation*, 279, 281.

43. Ibid., 257, 258.

44. Luther Bradley to Ione Bradley, September 5, 9, 1877, Luther P. Bradley Papers, United States Army Military History Institute.

CHAPTER 4. INDIAN WOMEN

1. John Bourke, *The Snake-Dance of the Moquis of Arizona* (New York: Charles Scribner's Sons, 1884), 45, 46. Lieutenant James

Bradley also remarked on the Indians' affection between the sexes, noting the kisses and embraces Blackfoot warriors received from female relatives, which they did not "disdain to receive"; Bradley, "Characteristics, Habits and Customs of the Blackfeet Indians," *Contributions to the Historical Society of Montana* 9 (1923): 270. See also Nelson Miles's comments quoted in Virginia W. Johnson, *The Unregimented General: A Biography of Nelson A. Miles* (Boston: Houghton Mifflin Co., 1962), 166–167.

2. Rayna Green, "The Pocahontas Perplex: The Image of Indian Women in American Culture," *Massachusetts Review* 26 (Autumn 1975): 703–704, 713. See also Alison Bernstein, "Outgrowing Pocahontas: Toward a New History of American Indian Women," *Minority Notes* 2 (Spring/Summer 1981): 3–4.

3. Lieutenant C. A. Woodward, "Journal of an Expedition to Wichita Mountains from June 1 to July 13, 1863," Benjamin Grierson Papers, Newberry Library, Chicago; General James F. Rusling, *Across America; or, The Great West and the Pacific Coast* (New York: Sheldon and Co., 1874), 116.

4. James W. Steele, *Frontier Army Sketches* (Chicago: Jansen, McClurg and Co., 1883), 84. For similar comments, see John Turner to unknown, July 7, 1856, United States Army Military History Institute, Carlisle Barracks, Pennsylvania; William E. Waters, *Life Among the Mormons, and a March to Their Zion* (New York: Moorhead, Simpson and Bond, 1868), 206–207; Randolph Marcy, *Thirty Years of Army Life on the Frontier* (New York: Harper and Brothers, 1866), 25, 28–29, 31; idem, *Adventure on the Red River: Report on the Exploration of the Headwaters of the Red River by Captain Randolph P. Marcy and Captain G. B. McClellan*, edited by Grant Foreman (Norman: University of Oklahoma Press, 1937), 157, 166–167; Colonel Richard Irving Dodge, *Our Wild Indians: Thirty-Three Years' Personal Experience Among the Red Men of the Great West* (Hartford, Conn.: A. D. Worthington and Co., 1883), 193, 198, 204, 205; Rodney Glisan, *Journal of Army Life* (San Francisco: A. L. Bancroft and Co., 1874), 247; Captain R. G. Carter, *On the Border With Mackenzie; or, Winning West Texas From the Comanches* (New York: Antiquarian Press, 1961), 286; Rusling, *Across America*, 134; George Templeton diary, July 8, 1866, Newberry Library; Lieutenant C. A. Woodward, "Journal of an Expedition," June 19, 1863, Newberry Library; and Eli Huggins to his sister, November 6, 1880, Huggins Papers, Bancroft Library, Berkeley, California.

5. Ellen McGowan Biddle, *Reminiscences of a Soldier's Wife* (Philadelphia: J. B. Lippincott Co., 1907), 116 (Biddle found Pima women "very ugly" also; *Reminiscences*, 198); Teresa Viele, "*Fol-*

lowing the Drum": A Glimpse of Frontier Life (New York: Rudd and Carleton, 1859), 203. See also Elizabeth Custer, *Following the Guidon: Into the Indian Wars With General Custer and the Seventh Cavalry* (Norman: University of Oklahoma Press, 1966), 87; Ada Adams Vogdes diary, February 24, 1871, Huntington Library, San Marino, California. For an exception, see Martha Summerhayes, *Vanished Arizona: Recollections of the Army Life of a New England Woman* (Tucson: Arizona Silhouettes, 1960), 32, 64–65. Summerhayes allowed that some of the younger women among the Apaches were attractive, but she was horrified that some of the "older squaws" were disfigured by the practice of slitting the noses of those "who were unfaithful to their lords." To Summerhayes this reflected "the cruel and revengeful nature of the Apache."

6. Frances M. A. Roe, *Army Letters From an Officer's Wife* (New York: D. Appleton and Co., 1909), 91; Elizabeth Custer, *Following the Guidon*, 90, 92.

7. Brigadier General Richard W. Johnson, *A Soldier's Reminiscences in Peace and War* (Philadelphia: J. B. Lippincott Co., 1886), 144. For similar comments, see Dodge, *Our Wild Indians*, 345–346; and Marcy, *Adventure on the Red River*, 166–167.

8. Britton Davis, *The Truth About Geronimo* (New Haven: Yale University Press, 1929), 72.

9. Dodge, *Our Wild Indians*, 204–205; Brackett, "Fort Bridger," undated typescript, Colorado Historical Society, Denver, 11.

10. Joseph Sladen to Mrs. Alice Crane, October 26, 1896, United States Army Military History Institute; Marcy, *Adventure on the Red River*, 156.

11. Edward K. Eckert and Nicholas J. Amato, eds., *Ten Years in the Saddle: The Memoir of William Woods Averell* (San Rafael, Calif.: Presidio Press, 1978), 154–155; Bourke, *Snake-Dance*, 259.

12. Steele, *Frontier Army Sketches*, 188–189, 192. James Parker made no comment about Indian women's rights, but he wrote a favorable review of Kiowa women's good housekeeping and presented a generally positive view of these women and their work; see Parker to Lizzie, October 12, 1876, James Parker Papers, United States Military Academy, West Point, New York. Colonel Henry Heistand also compared Indian women with women's rights advocates; see "The Indian Woman," pp. 24–25, Henry O. S. Heistand Papers, United States Military Academy.

13. Marcy, *Thirty Years*, 88–89. Heistand's view of Indian women's powers was more circumscribed. In his unpublished manuscript "The Indian Woman," he maintained that Indians were

polygamous in theory, "but the women do not as a rule take kindly to the institution and while most of the men would prefer a plurality of wives their powers of [illegible] are sufficient to preserve a peaceful household; therefore one wife is usually sold or discarded before a second is installed" (p. 45).

14. Dodge, *Our Wild Indians*, 215. See also General George Armstrong Custer, *My Life on the Plains; or, Personal Experiences with Indians* (Norman: University of Oklahoma Press, 1976), 284.

15. Lucille M. Kane, ed., *Military Life in Dakota* (St. Paul: Alvord Memorial Commission, 1951), 85. For another view of the issue of premarital chastity, see Captain E. L. Huggins, *Winona: A Dakota Legend and Other Poems* (New York: G. P. Putnam's Sons, 1890), 3–40.

16. Merrill J. Mattes, ed., *Indians, Infants and Infantry: Andrew and Elizabeth Burt on the Frontier* (Denver: Old West Publishing Co., 1960), 88–89; Elizabeth Custer, *Following the Guidon*, 98, 86; William T. Corbusier, *Verde to San Carlos: Recollections of a Famous Army Surgeon and His Observant Family on the Western Frontier, 1869–1886* (Tucson: Dale Stuart King, 1968), 93. For other examples, see Ray Mattison, ed., "An Army Wife on the Upper Missouri: The Diary of Sarah E. Canfield, 1866–1868," *North Dakota History* 20 (October 1953): 202; Mary Katherine Jackson English, "Army Girl: Experiences on the Frontier," *The Westerners Brand Book* (Denver, Colo., 1949), 3:48–49; and Mary Heistand, "Scraps from an Army Woman's Diary," p. 49, Heistand Papers, Bancroft Library.

17. For a recent attempt to present the reality of some Indian women's lives, see Patricia Albers and Beatrice Medicine, eds., *The Hidden Half: Studies of Plains Indian Women* (Washington, D.C.: University Press of America, 1983); Marla N. Powers, *Oglala Women: Myth, Ritual and Reality* (Chicago: University of Chicago Press, 1986).

18. Julie Roy Jeffrey, *Frontier Women: The Trans-Mississippi West, 1840–1880* (New York: Hill and Wang, 1979), 6.

19. Kane, *Military Life in Dakota*, 146.

20. William T. Parker, *Personal Experiences Among Our North American Indians From 1867 to 1885* (Northampton, Mass., 1913), 101, 103. Less confident than Parker and Trobriand that the "Indian way" was preferable, Lieutenant James H. Bradley agreed that Blackfoot women had relatively easy childbirths. He knew Blackfoot women who resumed work within a day, and sometimes within hours, of their baby's birth, although most rested a week in camp to

regain their strength. Bradley believed, however, that early resumption of work brought on premature aging and accounted for what he considered to be their miserable and haggard appearance. See Bradley, "Characteristics," 274.

21. Lydia Spencer Lane, *I Married a Soldier; or, Old Days in the Old Army* (Albuquerque: Horn and Wallace Publishers, 1964), 67; Katherine Gibson Fougera, *With Custer's Cavalry* (Caldwell, Idaho: Caxton Printers, 1942), 282.

22. Summerhayes, *Vanished Arizona*, 100–101.

23. Quoted in Robert M. Utley, ed., *Battlefield and Classroom: Four Decades With the American Indian, 1867–1904* (New Haven: Yale University Press, 1964), 37–38.

24. For a sampling of officers' comments on this issue, see Dodge, *Our Wild Indians*, 466; and John Fitzgerald as quoted in Abe Laufe, ed., *An Army Doctor's Wife on the Frontier, Letters From Alaska and the Far West, 1874–1878* (Pittsburgh: University of Pittsburgh Press, 1962), 304. On reformers' attitudes toward Indian policy and the military's role in Indian affairs, see Robert W. Mardock, *The Reformers and the American Indian* (Columbia: University of Missouri Press, 1971); Frances Paul Prucha, *American Indian Policy in Crisis: Christian Reformers and the Indian, 1865–1900* (Norman: University of Oklahoma Press, 1976).

25. Carter, *On the Border*, 287. See also John G. Bourke, *An Apache Campaign in the Sierra Madre: An Account of the Expedition in Pursuit of Hostile Chiricahua Apaches in the Spring of 1883* (New York: Charles Scribner's Sons, 1886), 90–91.

26. Henry O. S. Heistand, "Indian Woman," 35; George P. Hammond, ed., *Campaigns in the West, 1856–1861: The Journal and Letters of Colonel John Van Deusen Du Bois* (Tucson: Arizona Pioneers Historical Society, 1949), 30; Joseph Sladen to Mrs. Crane, October 26, 1896, United States Army Military History Institute; Davis, *Truth About Geronimo*, 26.

27. Walter S. Schuyler, "Notes of a Scout From Camp Verde to McDowell and Return, Dec. 1, 1873—Jan. 26, 1874," entry for December 14, 1873, and Walter S. Schuyler to George Washington Schuyler, September 29, 1872, both in Walter Scribner Schuyler Papers, Huntington Library. In a letter to his father, Assistant Surgeon DeWitt Clinton Peters explained that a Ute woman had told them she had killed her own child and niece rather than have them captured by the army—and that others did the same; DeWitt Clinton Peters to his father, April 5, 1855, DeWitt Clinton Peters Papers, Bancroft Library.

28. John G. Bourke diary, December 26, 1872, microfilm, Denver Public Library; Fitzgerald is quoted in Laufe, *An Army Doctor's Wife*, 304.

29. Robert M. Utley, *Frontiersmen in Blue: The United States Army and the Indian, 1848–1865* (New York: Macmillan Publishing Co., 1967), 345–346; Paul Andrew Hutton, *Phil Sheridan and His Army* (Lincoln: University of Nebraska Press, 1985), 17, 71, 100. Robert Wooster maintains that the use of total war against Indian enemies predates the Civil War. He also says that the doctrine of total war did not win the full approval of officers in spite of the influence of advocates such as Sheridan and Sherman. See Wooster, *The Military and United States Indian Policy, 1865–1903* (New Haven: Yale University Press, 1988), 141–143.

30. Thompson is quoted in Theodore F. Rodenbough, *From Everglade to Cañon With the Second Dragoons* (New York: D. Van Nostrand, 1875), 403.

31. Quoted in Laufe, *An Army Doctor's Wife*, 350.

32. John G. Bourke diary, September 9, 1876, Denver Public Library; King, *Campaigning With Crook*, 121–122; and Anson Mills, *My Story* (Washington, D.C.: By the author, 1918), 171–172.

33. The information about Ogarita is from a letter from Alice Margaret Knight to author, June 25, 1980. Mrs. Knight is S.B.M. Young's granddaughter. Unfortunately, Young's personal papers contain no references to Ogarita. Brigadier General L. W. Colby adopted a three- or four-month-old infant found lying next to her dead mother at Wounded Knee. She was wrapped in a blanket and had a buckskin cap decorated with a beaded American flag upon her head. Colby named her "Marguerite," although the Sioux women called her "Lost Bird" or "Child of the Battlefield." See Marion F. Briggs and Sarah D. McAnulty, *The Ghost Dance Tragedy at Wounded Knee: A Visual Presentation* (Washington, D.C.: Smithsonian Institution, 1977), 26. For information on C.E.S. Wood's kindness to an old woman during the Bannock War, see Wood, "Private Journal," 22.

34. Patricia Albers, "Introduction: New Perspectives on Plains Indian Women," in Albers and Medicine, *Hidden Half*, 3.

35. James Parker to Lizzie, October 12, 1876, James Parker Papers, United States Military Academy.

36. Elizabeth Custer, *Following the Guidon*, 98, 99. She also noted that "brown mothers were just as susceptible to flattery concerning their babies as white women are" (p. 90).

37. Robert C. Carriker and Eleanor R. Carriker, eds., *An Army*

Wife on the Frontier: The Memoirs of Alice Blackwood Baldwin, 1867–1877 (Salt Lake City: Tanner Trust Fund, 1975), 79, 99–100.

38. Biddle, *Reminiscences*, 116. On the matter of Indians' curiosity about officers' wives, see also Elizabeth Custer, *Following the Guidon*, 88. When Sarah Canfield visited an Indian village outside Fort Berthold, she created quite a sensation among the children. As she wandered through the camp, Canfield realized, "*I* was a curiosity to them for they often ran in front of us and peering into my face which was somewhat hidden by my sunbonnet, then dodge back laughing and chattering as though it was great fun." See Mattison, "An Army Wife," 204.

39. Elizabeth Custer, *Following the Guidon*, 89, 95; Frances C. Carrington, *My Army Life and the Fort Phil Kearny Massacre* (Philadelphia: J. B. Lippincott Co., 1911), 58; Anna Maus, "Old Army Days," Haustead-Maus Family Papers, United States Army Military History Institute; Mary Allen to Carleton Allen, October 1, 1872, typescript, Colonel Harvey Abner Allen and Mary Allen Papers, San Juan Island National Historic Site, Friday Harbor, San Juan Island, Washington.

40. Parmenus T. Turnley, *Reminiscences of Parmenus Taylor Turnley, From the Cradle to Three Score and Ten* (Chicago: Donohue and Henneberry, 1892), 169; Mrs. Orsemus Boyd, *Cavalry Life in Tent and Field* (New York: J. Selwin Tait, 1894), 70–71, 156.

41. Corbusier, *Verde to San Carlos*, 211. The boy died within several months of enrolling at the school. For other examples of army people who took in Indian children as household help and expressed concern for their future, see Sandra L. Myres, "Evy Alexander: The Colonel's Lady at McDowell," *Montana: The Magazine of Western History* 24 (Summer 1974): 31–32; Mary Heistand, "Scraps," 56–63; and English, "Army Girl," 141–142.

42. Almira Russell Hancock, *Reminiscences of Winfield Scott Hancock* (New York: Charles L. Webster and Co., 1887), 119.

43. Sylvia Van Kirk, *Many Tender Ties: Women in Fur-Trade Society, 1670–1870* (Norman: University of Oklahoma Press, 1983), 4–7. See also Jennifer S. H. Brown, *Strangers in Blood: Fur Trade Company Families in Indian Country* (Vancouver: University of British Columbia Press, 1980).

44. See Patricia Y. Stallard, *Glittering Misery: Dependents of the Indian Fighting Army* (Fort Collins, Colo.: Old Army Press, 1978), 69–70.

45. Anne Butler, "Military Myopia: Prostitution on the Frontier," *Prologue* 13 (Winter 1981): 241. Also, see her book *Daughters*

of Joy, Sisters of Misery: Prostitutes in the American West, 1865–90 (Urbana: University of Illinois Press, 1985), 122–149.

46. Quoted in Hutton, *Phil Sheridan*, 74, 389. See also Green, "Pocahontas Perplex," 713.

47. Frederick W. Benteen to Theodore Goldin, February 14, 17, 1886, typescript in Ayer Collection, Newberry Library; Hutton, *Phil Sheridan*, 389.

48. Lieutenant E.O.C. Ord to Molly Ord, July 4, 1858, E.O.C. Ord Papers, Stanford University Library, Palo Alto, California.

49. Luther Bradley to Ione Dewey, July 10, 1867, Luther P. Bradley Papers, United States Army Military History Institute; Robert M. Utley, ed., *Life in Custer's Cavalry: Diaries and Letters of Albert and Jennie Barnitz, 1867–1868* (New Haven: Yale University Press, 1977), 110, 111. Martha Summerhayes acknowledged flirtations between young lieutenants and attractive Apache women but concluded that the Indian women seemed to prefer men of their own race; Summerhayes, *Vanished Arizona*, 65.

50. Marcy, *Thirty Years*, 57.

51. James Parker to R. Wayne Parker, October 7, 1876, James Parker Papers, United States Military Academy.

52. William Parker, *Personal Experiences*, 105; Dodge, *Our Wild Indians*, 205. For comments on the value of chastity among particular Indian tribes, see, on Apaches, Oliver Otis Howard, *My Life and Experiences Among Our Hostile Indians* (New York: De Capo Press, 1972), 214; on the Hopi, Bourke, *Snake-Dance*, 248; and on the Crows, Henry Heistand, "The Indian Woman," 15.

53. Hammond, *Campaigns in the West*, 26, 28.

54. Marcy, *Thirty Years*, 49–50.

55. Davis, *Truth About Geronimo*, 72–73.

56. See Stephen Perry Jocelyn, *Mostly Alkali* (Caldwell, Idaho: Caxton Printers, 1953), 86; Joseph C. Porter, *Paper Medicine Man: John Gregory Bourke and His American West* (Norman: University of Oklahoma Press, 1986), 114.

57. Howard, *My Life*, 525–526; Dodge, *Our Wild Indians*, 603.

58. General Charles King, *An Apache Princess: A Tale of the Indian Frontier* (New York: Hobart Co., 1903), 16–17, 282.

59. Arthur Woodward, ed., *Journal of Lt. Thomas W. Sweeny, 1849–1853* (Los Angeles: Westernlore Press, 1956), 68, 127–128.

60. Eckert and Amato, *My Ten Years*, 205.

61. Hutton, *Phil Sheridan*, 10, 376; Colonel Richard Irving Dodge noticed that Sheridan easily kissed two Indian girls who welcomed him with songs and speeches at the Colville Indian Reservation.

"Color is no object to him," Dodge explained. See Richard Irving Dodge diary, August 7, 1883, Dodge Papers, Newberry Library.

62. Custer, *My Life on the Plains*, 282.

CHAPTER 5. THOUGHTS ON INDIAN POLICY

1. Quoted in Gary L. Roberts, "Condition of the Tribes, 1865: The Report of General McCook," *Montana: The Magazine of Western History* 24 (January 1974): 23.

2. Robert M. Utley, *The Indian Frontier of the American West, 1846–1890* (Albuquerque: University of New Mexico Press, 1984), 63.

3. Brigadier General Richard W. Johnson, *A Soldier's Reminiscences in Peace and War* (Philadelphia: J. B. Lippincott Co., 1886), 49. Gibbon's article is reprinted in E. A. Brininstool, *Troopers With Custer: Historic Incidents of the Battle of the Little Big Horn* (Harrisburg, Pa.: Stackpole Co., 1952), 334–336. General William T. Sherman published a defense of civilian agents, however. "I have personally met a great number of these who are generally kind, honest and well meaning people," he wrote in his introduction to Richard Irving Dodge's *Our Wild Indians: Thirty-Three Years' Personal Experience Among the Red Men of the Great West* (Hartford, Conn.: A. D. Worthington and Co., 1883), xxxvi–xxxvii. For negative comments on the Indian Ring, see William Thornton Parker, *Personal Experiences Among Our North American Indians, From 1867 to 1885* (Northampton, Mass., 1913), 145; Captain S.B.M. Young to General A. L. Pearson, December 1, 1880, S.B.M. Young Papers, United States Army Military History Institute, Carlisle Barracks, Pennsylvania; George Crook to Walter S. Schuyler, November 9, 1874, Walter Scribner Schuyler Papers, Huntington Library, San Marino, California; Rodney Glisan, *Journal of Army Life* (San Francisco: A. L. Bancroft and Co., 1874), 434; Benjamin Grierson to Alice Grierson, August 1, 1880, Benjamin Grierson Papers, Newberry Library, Chicago; Parmenus T. Turnley, *Reminiscences of Parmenus Taylor Turnley, From the Cradle to Three Score and Ten* (Chicago: Donohue and Henneberry, 1892), 172, 173; Bernard J. Byrne, *A Frontier Army Surgeon: Life in Colorado in the Eighties* (New York: Exposition Press, 1962), 30; Rachel Sherman Thorndike, ed., *The Sherman Letters: Correspondence Between General and Senator Sherman from 1837 to 1891* (New York: Charles Scribner's Sons, 1894), 344; Lucille M. Kane, ed., *Military Life in Dakota* (St. Paul: Alvord Memorial Commission, 1951), 157; and Richard Irving Dodge diary, June 12, 22, 1875, Richard Irving Dodge Papers, Newberry Library.

4. Frank Baldwin, "Adobe Walls Journal," undated, George Baird Papers, Kansas State Historical Society, Topeka. For biographical information on Baldwin, see Robert C. Carriker, "Frank D. Baldwin," in Paul Andrew Hutton, ed., *Soldiers West: Biographies from the Military Frontier* (Lincoln: University of Nebraska Press, 1987), 228–242. For similar comments on Indian agents, see General James F. Rusling, *Across America; or, The Great West and the Pacific Coast* (New York: Sheldon and Co., 1874), 412.

5. John G. Bourke, *An Apache Campaign in the Sierra Madre: An Account of the Expedition in Pursuit of the Hostile Chiricahua Apaches in the Spring of 1883* (New York: Charles Scribner's Sons, 1886), 4–5.

6. John Bourke diary, May 12, 1876, microfilm, Denver Public Library. The original Bourke diaries are deposited at the United States Military Academy, West Point, New York.

7. Dodge, *Our Wild Indians*, 94.

8. Francis Paul Prucha, *American Indian Policy in Crisis: Christian Reformers and the Indian, 1865–1900* (Norman: University of Oklahoma Press, 1976), 77, 90; Robert Winston Mardock, *The Reformers and the American Indian* (Columbia: University of Missouri Press, 1971), 146–148. For more examples of officers who argued in favor of military control of Indian affairs, see Sherman in *Reports of Inspection Made in the Summer of 1877 by Generals P. H. Sheridan and W. T. Sherman of Country North of the Union Pacific Railroad* (Washington, D.C.: GPO, 1878), 48; Johnson, *Soldier's Reminiscences*, 142; and Hugh Lenox Scott, *Some Memories of a Soldier* (New York: Century Co., 1928), 135. For John Bigelow's unique argument that Indian policy should be a local question rather than a federal one, see Arthur Woodward, *On the Bloody Trail of Geronimo* (Los Angeles: Westernlore Press, 1958), 4.

9. See John G. Bourke diary, May 12, 1876, microfilm, Denver Public Library; Parker, *Personal Experiences*, 149; and Philippe Regis de Trobriand, as quoted in Kane, *Military Life*, 157.

10. Frank Baldwin diary, August 19, 1874, Frank Baldwin Papers, Huntington Library; Bourke diary, May 12, 1876, Denver Public Library; see also Richmond L. Clow, "William S. Harney," in Hutton, *Soldiers West*, 51.

11. Sherman, *Reports of Inspection*, 48; Captain R. G. Carter, *On the Border With Mackenzie; or, Winning West Texas From the Comanches* (New York: Antiquarian Press, 1961), 369. See also Nelson Miles, *Serving the Republic: Memoirs of the Civil and Military Life of Nelson A. Miles* (New York: Harper and Brothers Publishers, 1911), 203; and C. C. Augur to unknown, April 18, 1876, in Letter-

book, C. C. Augur Papers, Newberry Library.

12. James W. Steele, *Frontier Army Sketches* (Chicago: Jansen, McClurg and Co., 1883), 104.

13. Granville O. Haller, "The Indian War of 1855–56 in Washington and Oregon," Granville O. Haller Papers, Suzzallo Library, University of Washington, Seattle; Walter S. Schuyler to G. W. Schuyler, June 26, 1874, in Walter Scribner Schuyler Papers, Huntington Library.

14. Parker, *Personal Experiences*, 48; see also Brigadier General John Wool, quoted in U.S. Congress, House, *Correspondence Between the Late Secretary of War and General Wool*, 35th Cong., 1st sess., H. Doc. 88 (Washington, D.C.: GPO, 1857–58), 4; Randolph Marcy, *Thirty Years of Army Life on the Frontier* (New York: Harper and Brothers, 1866), 38–39; Oliver O. Howard, *My Life and Experiences Among Our Hostile Indians* (New York: De Capo Press, 1972), 251; O. O. Howard, *Nez Perce Joseph* (Boston: Lee and Shepard, Publishers, 1881), 55–56; D. H. Stanley to Major J. H. Hearn, January 23, 1870, Robert M. Patterson Papers, Denver Public Library; Rusling, *Across America*, 412–413; and Marvin E. Krocker, "William B. Hazen," in Hutton, *Soldiers West*, 197. As late as 1913, Hugh Scott, who was quite sympathetic to Indians, was also arguing the necessity of force; Hugh Scott to Lindley M. Garrison, December 2, 1913, Hugh Lenox Scott, 4879 ACP 1876, RG 94, National Archives, Washington, D.C. See also Scott, *Some Memories*, 156–157.

15. General Philip H. Sheridan, *Personal Memoirs* (New York: Charles L. Webster and Co., 1888), 2:286, 291; Philip Sheridan to Colonel Benjamin Grierson, February 23, 1869, Benjamin Grierson Papers, Newberry Library. For a good discussion of Sheridan's views on Indian policy, see Paul Andrew Hutton, *Phil Sheridan and His Army* (Lincoln: University of Nebraska Press, 1985), 10, 17, 180–185.

16. Quoted in U.S. Congress, Senate, *Indian Operations on the Plains*, 50th Cong., 1st sess., S. Doc. 33 (Washington: GPO, 1888), 4, 39. Interestingly, one of Carrington's contemporaries, Lieutenant Colonel Luther Bradley, who was stationed at the equally dangerous Ft. C. F. Smith, later tempered his faith in a forceful approach to Indians; see Luther Bradley to Ione Dewey, May 25, 1867; Luther Bradley to H. S. Nichols, July 12, 1867; and Luther Bradley to Ione Dewey, September 5, 1867, Luther P. Bradley Papers, United States Army Military History Institute.

17. Sheridan, *Personal Memoirs*, 1:119–120.

18. William T. Sherman to Benjamin Grierson, June 12, 23, 1871,

Benjamin Grierson Papers, Newberry Library.

19. Arthur Woodward, ed., *Journal of Lt. Thomas W. Sweeny, 1849–1853* (Los Angeles: Westernlore Press, 1956), 55–58.

20. Walter S. Schuyler to George Schuyler, July 6, 1873, Walter Scribner Schuyler Papers, Huntington Library.

21. For recent biographies of Grierson, see William H. Leckie and Shirley A. Leckie, *Unlikely Warriors: General Benjamin H. Grierson and His Family* (Norman: University of Oklahoma Press, 1984); and Bruce Dinges, "Benjamin H. Grierson," in Hutton, *Soldiers West*, 157–176. Dinges states that there is no evidence to support the story that Grierson was afraid of horses (p. 173).

22. Benjamin Grierson to Alice Grierson, April 7, 1869; and Benjamin Grierson to John Grierson, February 25, 1870, Benjamin Grierson Papers, Newberry Library.

23. Hutton, *Phil Sheridan*, 230–231. For an extended discussion of Grierson and the Peace Policy, see Leckie and Leckie, *Unlikely Warriors*, 142–210.

24. Benjamin Grierson to Lawrie Tatum, September 30, 1869; and Benjamin Grierson to Felix Brunot, November 22, 1872, Benjamin Grierson Papers, Newberry Library.

25. Hutton, *Phil Sheridan*, 227–261; Leckie and Leckie, *Unlikely Warriors*, 171–210.

26. Lieutenant Henry E. Alvord to Benjamin Grierson, May 16, 1869, and October 16, 1870, Benjamin Grierson Papers, Newberry Library.

27. General George Crook, *His Autobiography*, edited by Martin F. Schmitt (Norman: University of Oklahoma Press, 1960), xvi.

28. Robert M. Utley, *Frontier Regulars: The United States Army and the Indian, 1866–1891* (New York: Macmillan Publishing Co., 1973), 52; Henry B. Carrington, *The Indian Question* (Boston: Charles H. Whiting, Publisher, 1884), 12.

29. Richard Pratt is quoted in Robert M. Utley, ed., *Battlefield and Classroom: Four Decades With the American Indian, 1867–1904* (New Haven: Yale University Press, 1964), 169; Marcy, *Thirty Years*, 62, 66. See also Miles, *Serving the Republic*, 197–200; and Parker, *Personal Experiences*, 85–86. Several officers pointed to the Spanish success with acculturation. See Alfred Sully's view as presented in Langdon Sully, *No Tears for the General: The Life of Alfred Sully, 1821–1879* (Palo Alto, Calif.: American West Publishing Co., 1974), 75; John G. Bourke, "The Laws of Spain in Their Application to the American Indians," *American Anthropologist* 7 (April 1894): 194–195.

30. Benjamin Grierson to Alice Grierson, April 12, 1880, Benja-

min Grierson Papers, Newberry Library. For other examples of this point of view, see Edgar I. Stewart, ed., *The March of the Montana Column: A Prelude to the Custer Disaster* (Norman: University of Oklahoma Press, 1961), 87; Richard Irving Dodge diary, November 28, 1876, Dodge Papers, Newberry Library.

31. August V. Kautz, *Annual Report . . . Department of Arizona, 1876–77*, 11–12, copy in Graff Collection, Newberry Library.

32. Utley, *Battlefield and Classroom*, 33, 100, 213–214, 311–312, 266. George Crook disagreed that Indians' and blacks' positions were analogous. In an 1883 report, he indicated that the Apache "cannot be governed or protected by the same methods that have proved so successful in the management of the freedman of the south" because he did not speak English and had never been "domesticated." Therefore, Indians must be segregated "until they learn the ways of the whites and until mutual interests spring up between them." See Crook, *Annual Report . . . Department of Arizona, 1883*, 13, Graff Collection, Newberry Library.

33. George Crook, *Resume of Operations Against Apache Indians, 1882–1886*, 4, copy in Graff Collection, Newberry Library; Bates is quoted in Rodenbough, *From Everglade*, 394. See also Carrington, "Indian Question," preface, n.p.

34. Miles, *Serving the Republic*, 203, 204.

35. Glisan, *Journal*, 430; Dodge, *Our Wild Indians*, 50–51, 66–67, 407.

36. Grierson, *Annual Report, 1888*, 6; Crook, *Annual Report, 1883*, 11. Pope agreed with the idea behind allotment—that Indians should become property owners—but he recognized that not all Indians were equally prepared for this and that not all reservations were suitable for agriculture; see Richard N. Ellis, *General Pope and U.S. Indian Policy* (Albuquerque: University of New Mexico Press, 1970), 234. Bourke agreed that they had "to be living in well-watered, fertile lands in order to become 'agronomical.'" He, too, favored allotment, although he believed that the lands in severalty should not be alienable for fifty years. See Bourke diary, December 18, 1876, Denver Public Library.

37. Woodward, *On the Bloody Trail*, 121.

CHAPTER 6. EXPLANATIONS OF THE INDIAN WARS

1. Ethan Allen Hitchcock, *Fifty Years in Camp and Field* (New York: G. P. Putnam's Sons, 1909), 395, 125.

2. Granville O. Haller diary, November 13, 1855, and "The Indian War of 1855–6 in Washington and Oregon," both in Gran-

ville O. Haller Papers, Suzzallo Library, University of Washington, Seattle.

3. Oliver O. Howard, *Nez Perce Joseph* (Boston: Lee and Shepard, Publishers, 1881), 32–33, 478; Arrell Morgan Gibson, *The American Indian: Prehistory to the Present* (Lexington, Mass.: D. C. Heath and Co., 1980), 473–474. See also Christopher L. Miller, *Prophetic Worlds: Indians and Whites on the Columbia Plateau* (New Brunswick, N.J.: Rutgers University Press, 1985).

4. For other examples of officers who shared Howard's belief that a handful of troublemakers or superstitious medicine men moved larger numbers to pursue all-out war, see William Paulding, "A Few Words on My Army Life From 1874 to 1913," William and Grace Paulding Papers, United States Army Military History Institute; and Colonel Benjamin Grierson to General William T. Sherman, September 5, 1871, Benjamin Grierson Papers, Newberry Library. Grierson did not consistently blame Indians for the warfare, however, as the discussion on policy demonstrated.

Sometimes officers recognized factions within a tribal group and also understood that those who favored peace sometimes suffered the same horrific consequences of an army attack as those who preferred violent resistance. Then, in reaction to the onslaught of criticism of the military, army officers would hasten to justify their actions and protect the military by repeating oversimplifications. For Sheridan's position on the Piegan case as an example, see Paul Andrew Hutton, *Phil Sheridan and His Army* (Lincoln: University of Nebraska Press, 1985), 186–200.

5. Lucille M. Kane, ed., *Military Life in Dakota* (St. Paul: Alvord Memorial Commission, 1951), 265. See also Nelson Miles on Sitting Bull and the "hostile element" among the Sioux in *Serving the Republic*, 237. On Red Cloud's limited powers, see Christopher C. Augur to Brevet Major General E. D. Townsend, May 28, 1870, Letterbook, Box 4, C. C. Augur Papers, Newberry Library.

6. Carter, *On the Border*, 159, xix, 253. Another man, again reflecting officer sensitivity to army critics, wrote that in Texas and New Mexico, wrong existed on both sides, but he asserted, "I am personally far from believing the Indians themselves to be saints . . . and that all the fault is on the side of the white people." He had witnessed "too much of their cruelty to believe that." Yet, he added, "at the same time, I think they were sometimes—not often—imposed upon." They remained, however, "predatory bands of savages" and, in the end, cavalry regiments were forced to fight them "by the circumstances of the country." Demonstrating a fundamental ambivalence about all this, he concluded, "I think no one now

doubts its having been a wise measure." See Albert G. Brackett, *History of the United States Cavalry* (New York: Harper and Brothers, Publishers, 1865), 127, 140–141.

7. Captain John Bourke, *On the Border With Crook* (New York: Charles Scribner's Sons, 1891), 104.

8. General Philip H. Sheridan, *Personal Memoirs* (New York: Charles L. Webster and Co., 1888), 1:89; Rodney Glisan, *Journal of Army Life* (San Francisco: A. L. Bancroft and Co., 1874), 317. General George Crook also believed that Indians deserved some consideration in their supposed propensity to savage violence because of fundamental flaws in their primitive character. Reflecting on the death of General E. S. Canby and several other Peace Commissioners during the Modoc War, Crook noted in a diary, "However deplorable the massacre of Gen. Canby & the Peace Commissioners is, we should remember that it was done by a people who can no more help being treacherous than they can help their coming into this world. Treachery is as much their nature as it is the nature of a rattlesnake to bite when angry. Therefore the Modocs were not so much to blame for this massacre as were the persons responsible for these Commissioners being placed in the Indians' power." See "Modocs," George Crook journal, February 10, 11, 1873, George W. Crook-L.W.V. Kennon Papers, United States Army Military History Institute.

9. Quoted in Langdon Sully, *No Tears for the General: The Life of Alfred Sully, 1821–1879* (Palo Alto, Calif.: American West Publishing Co., 1974), 99–100. Lieutenant E.O.C. Ord found the Rogue River Indians "infested with vermin, incorrigibly addicted to vice and the gratification of savage passions," but he also said that "the volunteers who are trying to drive them from this, their country are not much better—not as brave—with a worse cause"; E.O.C. Ord to Molly Ord, May 9, 1856, E.O.C. Ord Papers, Stanford University Library, Palo Alto, California. Fourteen years later, Ord continued to place much of the blame for frontier conflict on white frontiersmen; see draft copy of the annual report of the headquarters of the Department of California, September 23, 1869, Bancroft Library.

10. James Parker to his mother, January 26, 1878, James Parker Papers, U.S. Military Academy Library, West Point.

11. Major-General John Sedgwick, *Correspondence of John Sedgwick, Major-General* (Carl Stoeckel, 1903), 2:24. For other comments on miners, see Kane, *Military Life*, 277; Anson Mills, *My Story* (Washington, D.C.: By the author, 1918), 156; Army Surgeon James Kimball's remarks as quoted in Maria Brace Kimball, *A*

Soldier-Doctor of Our Army: James P. Kimball (Boston and New York: Houghton Mifflin Co., 1917), 143; Glisan, *Journal*, 317; Haller, "Genesis of Indian Dissatisfaction and Hostilities," n.p., and "The Indian War of 1855–6," pt. 2, p. 2, both in the Granville O. Haller Papers, Suzzallo Library.

12. Quoted in U.S. Congress, House, *Indian Affairs on the Pacific*, 34th Cong., 2d sess., H. Doc. 76, serial 906 (Washington: GPO, 1856–57), 244.

13. William Brooks to unknown, May 28, 1854, William T. H. Brooks Papers, United States Army Military History Institute; Robert G. Athearn, ed., "An Army Officer in the West, 1864–1890," in *The Westerner's Brand Book* (Denver: University of Denver Press, 1950), 72, 73. See also James Fornance to his brother, March 18, 1872, James Fornance Papers, United States Military Academy Library, West Point; Robert Smith LaMotte to his brother, September 11, 1867, [Robert Smith] LaMotte Family Papers, Bancroft Library.

14. Lieutenant Colonel O. L. Hein, *Memories of Long Ago* (New York: G. P. Putnam's Sons, 1925), 75.

15. William Henry Bisbee, *Through Four American Wars* (Boston: Meador Publishing Co., 1931), 164. See also Kane, *Military Life*, 277; John Bourke diary, May 12, 1876, microfilm, Denver Public Library; Randolph Marcy, *Border Reminiscences* (New York: Harper and Brothers, 1872), 334; Glisan, *Journal*, 318; James Fry, *Army Sacrifices; or, Briefs from Official Pigeon-Holes* (New York: D. Van Nostrand, Publisher, 1879), 211.

16. Lieutenant Henry Hodges to Captain George McClellan, June 12, 1856, typescript, George McClellan Papers, Suzzallo Library.

17. Quoted in Charles H. Ambler, ed., "Correspondence of Robert M. T. Hunter," American Historical Association, *Annual Report*, 1916, 2:188–189.

18. Robert M. Utley, ed., *Life in Custer's Cavalry: Diaries and Letters of Albert and Jennie Barnitz, 1867–1868* (New Haven: Yale University Press, 1977), 115; Hugh Lenox Scott, *Some Memories of a Soldier* (New York: Century Co., 1928), 84.

19. Lieut. H. Clay Wood, "The Status of Young Joseph and His Band of Nez Perce Indians," pp. 20, 46, copy at Big Hole National Monument, Wisdom, Montana.

20. Frank Baldwin journal, August 19, 1874, Frank Baldwin Papers, Huntington Library. See also Robert Smith LaMotte to his mother, August 1, 1867, [Robert Smith] LaMotte Family Papers, Bancroft Library; James Parker to Richard Wayne Stites, October 24, 1876, James Parker Papers, United States Military Academy Library.

21. Crook, *His Autobiography*, 16, 158. See also Trobriand in Kane, *Military Life*, 259–260; Ulysses S. Grant, *The Papers of Ulysses S. Grant*, edited by John Y. Simon (Carbondale: Southern Illinois University Press, 1967), 1:296, 310; and Henry B. Carrington, "Religion of the Dakota Indians," Graff Collection, Newberry Library.

22. Margaret Carrington, *Ab-sa-ra-ka: Land of Massacre* (Philadelphia: J. B. Lippincott Co., 1868), 16.

23. Robert Winston Mardock, *The Reformers and the American Indian* (Columbia: University of Missouri Press, 1971), 61, 147.

24. Lieutenant John M. Schofield, *Forty-Six Years in the Army* (New York: Century Co., 1897), 434. Miles is quoted in Virginia W. Johnson, *The Unregimented General: A Biography of Nelson A. Miles* (Boston: Houghton Mifflin Co., 1962), 103.

25. Captain Charles King, *Campaigning With Crook and Stories of Army Life* (New York: Harper and Brothers, 1890), 43.

26. Brigadier General George A. Forsyth, *The Story of the Soldier* (New York: Brampton Society, 1908), 199, 249. Miles is quoted in Johnson, *Unregimented General*, 59. See also Robert M. Utley, "Nelson A. Miles," in *Soldiers West: Biographies from the Military Frontier*, edited by Paul Andrew Hutton (Lincoln: University of Nebraska Press, 1987), 217; Robert G. Carter, *On the Border With Mackenzie; or, Winning West Texas From the Comanches* (New York: Antiquarian Press, 1961), 292; and King, *Campaigning With Crook*, 167.

27. Elizabeth Custer is quoted in Marguerite Merington, ed., *The Custer Story: The Life and Intimate Letters of General George A. Custer and His Wife Elizabeth* (New York: Devin-Adair Co., 1950), 284; Almira Russell Hancock, *Reminiscences of Winfield Scott Hancock* (New York: Charles L. Webster and Co., 1887), 119, 142; see also Abe Laufe, ed., *An Army Doctor's Wife on the Frontier: Letters from Alaska and the Far West, 1874–1878* (Pittsburgh: University of Pittsburgh Press, 1962), 263; and Mrs. Orsemus Boyd, *Cavalry Life in Tent and Field* (New York: J. Selwin Tait, 1894), 315.

28. Edward Steptoe to William Steptoe, January 10, 1842, Edward Steptoe Papers, Suzzallo Library. Steptoe was fighting the Seminoles in Florida at the time he wrote this letter, but he later fought Indians in the Pacific Northwest during the 1850s.

29. Parmenus T. Turnley, *Reminiscences of Parmenus Taylor Turnley, From the Cradle to Three Score and Ten* (Chicago: Donohue and Henneberry, 1892), n.p.; Forsyth, *Story of A Soldier*, 273. For similar comments, see DeWitt Clinton Peters to his father, April 5, 1855, and to his sister, December 20, 1854, and June 1856, DeWitt Clinton Peters Papers, Bancroft Library.

30. Frank Baldwin to unknown, October 10, 1918, Frank Baldwin Papers, Huntington Library; Eugene Carr to Grace Carr, November 26, 1873, March 20, 1874, Eugene A. Carr Papers, United States Army Military History Institute.

31. Edward Steptoe to William Steptoe, January 10, 1842, Edward Steptoe Papers, Suzzallo Library. For similar statements, see Colonel George Sanford as quoted in E. R. Hagemann, ed., *Fighting Rebels and Redskins: Experiences in the Army Life of Colonel George B. Sanford, 1861–1892* (Norman: University of Oklahoma Press, 1969), 17; Alfred Sully as quoted in Langdon Sully, *No Tears for the General: The Life of Alfred Sully, 1821–1879* (Palo Alto, Calif.: American West Publishing Co., 1974), 112; and Granville O. Haller diary, August 7, 1856, Granville O. Haller Papers, Suzzallo Library.

32. See Richard N. Ellis, "The Humanitarian Generals," *Western Historical Quarterly* 3 (April 1972): 172.

33. Dodge, *Our Wild Indians*, 469; for similar comments, see J. Lee Humfreville, *Twenty Years Among Our Hostile Indians* (New York: Hunter and Co., Publishers, 1903), 47; Price, *Across the Continent*, 40; Carter, *On the Border*, 150; Morgan, "Recollections," 128; Walter S. Schuyler is quoted in Crook, *His Autobiography*, 211–212; and Granville O. Haller, "The Indian War of 1855–56 in Washington and Oregon," p. 3, Granville O. Haller Papers, Suzzallo Library.

34. Albert K. Weinberg, *Manifest Destiny: A Study of Nationalist Expansionism in American History* (Chicago: Quadrangle Books, 1963), 1–2; Lewis O. Saum, *The Popular Mood of Pre-Civil War America* (Westport, Conn.: Greenwood Press, 1980), 6.

35. Jack D. Foner, "The United States Soldier Between Two Wars: Army Life and Reforms, 1865–1898" (Ph.D. diss., Columbia University, 1968), 75; James L. Morrison, Jr., "The United States Military Academy, 1833–1866: Years of Progress and Turmoil" (Ph.D. diss., Columbia University, 1971), 137–138. See also Coffman, *Old Army*, 179–180, 390–392.

36. Stow Persons, *American Minds: A History of Ideas* (New York: Henry Holt and Co., 1958), 282. See also Robert F. Berkhofer, Jr., *The White Man's Indian: Images of the American Indian From Columbus to the Present* (New York: Alfred A. Knopf, 1978), 49–55.

37. Persons, *American Minds*, 224; Coffman, *Old Army*, 84.

38. Hazen is quoted in Marvin E. Kroeker, *Great Plains Command: William B. Hazen in the Frontier West* (Norman: University of Oklahoma Press, 1976), 67; Henry B. Carrington, *The Indian Question* (Boston: Charles H. Whiting, Publisher, 1884), 12; Miles, *Serving the Republic*, 164; Forsyth, *Story of the Soldier*, 74.

39. Bisbee, *Through Four American Wars,* 166. See also Parker, *Personal Experiences,* 42; Lieutenant Colonel W. H. Carter, *From Yorktown to Santiago With the Sixth U.S. Cavalry* (Baltimore: Lord Baltimore Press, 1900), 280; Price, *Across the Continent,* 152; and Humfreville, *Twenty Years,* 379.

40. Grace Paulding, "My Army Life," p. 6, William and Grace Paulding Papers, United States Army Military History Institute; Carrington, *Ab-sa-ra-ka,* 16.

41. This poem is included in a scrapbook in the C.E.S. Wood Papers, Huntington Library. For biographical information on C.E.S. Wood, see Edwin R. Bingham, "Oregon's Romantic Rebels: John Reed and Charles Erskine Scott Wood," *Pacific Northwest Quarterly* 50 (July 1959): 77–90; and Erskine Wood, *Life of Charles Erskine Scott Wood* (Portland, Ore.: By the author, 1978).

42. C.E.S. Wood, *The Poet in the Desert* (Portland, Ore.: F. W. Battes, 1915), 103. See also Thomas C. Leonard, "Red, White and the Army Blue: Empathy and Anger in the American West," *American Quarterly* 26 (May 1974): 188–190.

CHAPTER 7. INDIAN WARFARE

1. Lieutenant C.E.S. Wood diary, June 23, 27, 28, July 17, 1877, C.E.S. Wood Papers, Huntington Library, San Marino, California. See also Thomas C. Leonard, "The Reluctant Conquerors: How the Generals Viewed the Indians," *American Heritage* 27 (August 1976): 34–41.

2. Lewis O. Saum, *The Popular Mood of Pre–Civil War America* (Westport, Conn.: Greenwood Press, 1980), 109.

3. Quoted in Edgar I. Stewart, ed., "Letters from the Big Hole," *Montana: The Magazine of Western History* 2 (October 1952): 55–56.

4. Edmund Hardcastle to his aunt, April 10, 1847, typescript, Edmund Hardcastle Papers, United States Military Academy Library, West Point, New York.

5. Robert M. Utley, *Frontiersmen in Blue: The United States Army and the Indian, 1848–1865* (New York, Macmillan Publishing Co., 1967), 31–32; idem, *Frontier Regulars: The United States Army and the Indian, 1866–1891* (New York: Macmillan Publishing Co., 1973), 19–20; and Edward M. Coffman, *The Old Army: A Portrait of the American Army in Peacetime, 1784–1898* (New York: Oxford University Press, 1986), 280–281.

6. DeWitt Clinton Peters to his father, February 3, 1855, DeWitt Clinton Peters Papers, Bancroft Library, Berkeley, California.

7. John G. Bourke diary, May 1, 1876, Denver Public Library; Richard I. Dodge, Powder River Campaign diary, p. 62, typescript, Richard Irving Dodge Papers, Newberry Library, Chicago. Some officers failed to see any glory in Indian warfare; see Robert M. Utley, ed., *Life in Custer's Cavalry: Diaries and Letters of Albert and Jennie Barnitz, 1867–1868* (New Haven: Yale University Press, 1977), 183.

8. Richard I. Dodge, Powder River Campaign diary, p. 76, Newberry Library.

9. Frank Baldwin to Alice Baldwin, August 25, November 4, 1874, Frank D. Baldwin Papers, Huntington Library; Stephen Mills to his mother, May 9, 1882, Stephen C. Mills Papers, United States Army Military History Institute, Carlisle Barracks, Pennsylvania. The information concerning Baldwin's Congressional Medal of Honor is from Francis Heitman, *Historical Register and Dictionary of the United States Army* (Washington: GPO, 1903), 1:186. See also Crook on the Rogue River War in General George Crook, *His Autobiography*, edited by Martin Schmitt (Norman: University of Oklahoma Press, 1960), 43–45. Another officer who stressed the importance of making a good impression on Miles was Henry Lawton. Lawton was chasing Geronimo in Mexico at the time and urged his wife to "be as nice as possible" to Miles to further Lawton's career (Henry Lawton to Mary Lawton, June 22, 1886, Lawton Papers, Library of Congress). When a camp of about thirty Apaches escaped before the army could reach them, Lawton wrote his wife, "I could cry, Mame, if it would do any good, and I know Gen'l Miles will be terribly disappointed and will probably think I have been careless or negligent, and we have worked *so hard* and under such trying circumstances" (Henry Lawton to Mary Lawton, July 7, 1886, Lawton Papers, Library of Congress). Nelson Miles was, of course, interested in his own advancement; see Paul Andrew Hutton, *Phil Sheridan and His Army* (Lincoln: University of Nebraska Press, 1985), 134–135; and Robert M. Utley, "Nelson A. Miles," in Paul Andrew Hutton, ed., *Soldiers West: Biographies from the Military Frontier* (Lincoln: University of Nebraska Press, 1987), 213–227. See also Robert C. Carriker, "Frank D. Baldwin," in Hutton, *Soldiers West*, 228–242.

10. Brigadier General M. R. Morgan, "Recollections of the Spokane Expedition," *Journal of the Military Service Institution of the United States* 42 (May-June 1908): 495.

11. Frances Carrington, *My Army Life and the Fort Phil Kearny Massacre* (Philadelphia: J. B. Lippincott Co., 1911), 98.

12. Teresa Viele, *"Following the Drum": A Glimpse of Frontier Life* (New York: Rudd and Carleton, 1859), 191. Abe Laufe, ed., *An Army Doctor's Wife on the Frontier: Letters from Alaska and the Far West, 1874–1878* (Pittsburgh: University of Pittsburgh Press, 1962), 204, 266.

13. Alice Baldwin to Frank Baldwin, September 18, October 27, 1874, Frank D. Baldwin Papers, Huntington Library; Caroline Frey Winne to Ludlow, October 9, 1879, Caroline Frey Winne Papers, New-York Historical Society Library, New York; and Sarah Ovenshine to Samuel Ovenshine, August 17, 1876, Samuel and Sarah Ovenshine Papers, United States Army Military History Institute.

14. Britton Davis, *The Truth About Geronimo* (New Haven: Yale University Press, 1929), 50, 111.

15. James Fry, *Army Sacrifices; or, Briefs From Official Pigeon-Holes* (New York: D. Van Nostrand, Publishers, 1879), 242, 253.

16. E.O.C. Ord to Molly Ord, May 7, 1856, E.O.C. Ord Papers, Stanford University Library, Palo Alto, California; Gatewood is quoted in Arthur Woodward, ed., *On the Bloody Trail of Geronimo* (Los Angeles: Westernlore Press, 1958), xiii–xiv. See also E.O.C. Ord diary, June 8, 1856, E.O.C. Ord Papers, Bancroft Library.

17. George P. Hammond, ed., *Campaigns in the West, 1856–1861: The Journal and Letters of Colonel John Van Deusen Du Bois* (Tucson: Arizona Pioneers Historical Society, 1949), 30, 29.

18. Laufe, *Army Doctor's Wife*, 289; Caroline Frey Winne to Ludlow, June 29, 1879, Caroline Frey Winne Papers, New-York Historical Society Library; Viele, *Following the Drum*, 123–124. See also Merrill Mattes, ed., *Indians, Infants and Infantry: Andrew and Elizabeth Burt on the Frontier* (Denver: Old West Publishing Co., 1960), 54.

19. Katherine Gibson Fougera, *With Custer's Cavalry* (Caldwell, Idaho: Caxton Printers, 1942), 125; Frances Carrington, *My Army Life*, 45.

20. See Utley, *Frontier Regulars*, 45–46. For more on distinctions that officers made between civilized and savage warfare, see William B. Skelton, "Army Officers' Attitudes Toward Indians, 1830–1860," *Pacific Northwest Quarterly* 63 (July 1976): 121.

21. For some examples, see Captain Charles King, *Campaigning With Crook and Stories of Army Life* (New York: Harper and Brothers, 1890), 38; Lieutenant Lawrence Kip, *Army Life on the Pacific: A Journal of the Expedition Against the Northern Indians, the Tribes of the Coeur d'Alenes, Spokans, and Pelouzes, in the Summer of 1858* (New York: Redfield, 1859), 56; Brigadier General

George A. Forsyth, *The Story of the Soldier* (New York: Brampton Society, 1908), 2:223; and Captain John G. Bourke, *Mackenzie's Last Fight with the Cheyennes: A Winter Campaign in Wyoming and Montana* (Governor's Island, N.Y., 1890), 23, 26–27, reprinted from the *Journal of the Military Service Institution of the United States*.

22. For a sampling of officers' comments on Indian skill in horsemanship, see General George Armstrong Custer, *My Life on the Plains; or, Personal Experiences with Indians* (Norman: University of Oklahoma Press, 1976), 95; Parker, *Personal Experiences*, 11; Brigadier General Richard W. Johnson, *A Soldier's Reminiscences in Peace and War* (Philadelphia: J. B. Lippincott Co., 1886), 142; Brigadier General Oliver O. Howard, *Nez Perce Joseph* (Boston: Lee and Shepard Publishers, 1881), 60–61; Lieutenant Colonel O. L. Hein, *Memories of Long Ago* (New York: G. P. Putnam's Sons, 1925), 88; James W. Steele, *Frontier Army Sketches* (Chicago: Jansen, McClurg and Co., 1883), 94; Major General Grenville M. Dodge, *The Indian Campaign of Winter of 1864–65* (Denver: Colorado Commandery of the Loyal Legion of the United States, 1907), 16; Colonel Richard Irving Dodge, *Our Wild Indians: Thirty-Three Years' Personal Experience Among the Red Men of the Great West* (Hartford, Conn.: A. D. Worthington and Co., 1883), 440–445; and Randolph Marcy, *Border Reminiscences* (New York: Harper and Brothers, 1872), 326.

23. General George Crook, *His Autobiography*, edited by Martin F. Schmitt (Norman: University of Oklahoma Press, 1960), 54; General John Gibbon, "The Pursuit of 'Joseph,'" *American Catholic Quarterly Review* 4 (April 1879): 337. Others who celebrated Indian marksmanship included Howard, *Nez Perce Joseph*, 60–61; Hein, *Memories*, 88; Frederick Benteen, *The Custer Fight: Captain Benteen's Story of the Battle of the Little Big Horn* (Hollywood, Calif.: Privately printed by E. A. Brininstool, 1933), 32–33; Crook, *His Autobiography*, 53–54; Lieutenant Colonel W. H. Carter, *From Yorktown to Santiago With the Sixth U.S. Cavalry* (Baltimore: Lord Baltimore Press, 1900), 208–209; and Grenville Dodge, *Indian Campaign*, 16. Officers did not universally acclaim Indian marksmanship, however. See Nelson Miles, *Personal Recollections and Observations* (Chicago: Werner Co., 1896), 160; idem, *Serving the Republic: Memoirs of the Civil and Military Life of Nelson A. Miles* (New York: Harper and Brothers, 1911), 163; and E.O.C. Ord to Molly Ord, March 26, 1856, E.O.C. Ord Papers, Stanford University Library.

24. Utley, *Life in Custer's Cavalry*, 97, 186; John G. Bourke, *An Apache Campaign in the Sierra Madre* (New York: Charles Scribner's Sons, 1886), 32.

25. Edward J. Steptoe to Colonel, June 2, 1858, in Steptoe's ACP file, 2570 ACP 1884, RG 94, National Archives and Records Service, Washington, D.C.; Frank Baldwin to Alice Baldwin, August 19, 1874, Frank D. Baldwin Papers, Huntington Library. For other comments on this issue, see Richard Dodge, *Our Wild Indians*, 450–451; Edward K. Eckert and Nicholas J. Amato, eds., *Ten Years in the Saddle: The Memoir of William Woods Averell* (San Rafael, Calif.: Presidio Press, 1978), 154; Custer, *My Life*, 170–171; Parker, *Personal Experiences*, 11; Henry Lawton to R. G. Carter, October 15, November 29, 1876, Henry Lawton Papers, Newberry Library; Fry, *Army Sacrifices*, 108; and Hein, *Memories*, 88.

26. Utley, *Frontier Regulars*, 61–72.

27. Coffman, *Old Army*, 278–279. For a summary of army and Indian strengths and weaknesses in combat, see Robert Wooster, *The Military and United States Indian Policy, 1865–1903* (New Haven: Yale University Press, 1988), 13–40.

28. DeWitt Clinton Peters to his father, April 5, 1855, DeWitt Clinton Peters Papers, Bancroft Library. Frederick E. Phelps described equally poor shooting: "Fortunately, the Indians were not as good shots as we were, poor as that was, so we nearly always got the better of them"; Frank D. Reeve, ed., "Frederick E. Phelps: A Soldier's Memories," *New Mexico Historical Review* 25 (April 1950): 111–113. See also Utley, *Frontier Regulars*, 69–72; and Thomas W. Dunlay, *Wolves for the Blue Soldiers: Indian Scouts and Auxiliaries With the United States Army, 1860–1890* (Lincoln: University of Nebraska Press, 1982), 86.

29. Dodge, *Our Wild Indians*, 451.

30. John Bourke diary, July 10, 1876, Denver Public Library; John G. Bourke, "General Crook in the Indian Country," *Century Magazine* 41 (March 1891): 652. For similar comments, see Marvin E. Kroeker, *Great Plains Command: William B. Hazen in the Frontier West* (Norman: University of Oklahoma Press, 1976), 29.

31. Utley, *Frontier Regulars*, 47–48. For William T. Sherman's account of this basic strategy and the army's weaknesses, see Rachel Sherman Thorndike, ed., *The Sherman Letters: Correspondence Between General and Senator Sherman from 1837 to 1891* (New York: Charles Scribner's Sons, 1894), 321–322.

32. Thomas Sweeny to Dodge, August 17, 1855, Thomas William Sweeny Papers, Huntington Library; William H. Beck to Benjamin

Grierson, July 23, 1874, Benjamin Grierson Papers, Newberry Library.

33. Carter, *On the Border With Mackenzie*, 535–536. In a rare example of analogous thinking, Randolph Marcy compared the army's problems with the Plains Indians to those of the French in Algeria, noting the similarity between "the habits of the Arabs and those of the wandering tribes that inhabit our Western prairies." Marcy concluded that the proper strategy involved using mounted infantry and surprise dawn attacks—methods successfully pursued by the Turks against the Arabs. See Marcy, *Thirty Years of Army Life on the Frontier* (New York: Harper and Brothers, 1866), 69. See also W. H. Carter, *From Yorktown to Santiago*, 179–180.

34. Price, *Across the Continent*, 130–131; Grenville Dodge, *Indian Campaign*, 16.

35. Benteen, *Custer Fight*, 33; Fry, *Army Sacrifices*, 110.

36. Richard Dodge, *Our Wild Indians*, 436; Price, *Across the Continent*, 131.

37. Quoted in Laufe, *Army Doctor's Wife*, 312; Miles is quoted in Virginia W. Johnson, *The Unregimented General: A Biography of Nelson A. Miles* (Boston: Houghton Mifflin Co., 1962), 207, 208.

38. Gibbon, "Pursuit of 'Joseph,'" 317, 337. Gibbon also lauded Nez Perce marksmanship in his poem *A Vision of the "Big Hole"* (privately printed by Captain J. W. Jacobs and Captain C. A. Woodruff, no date; copy at Big Hole National Monument, Wisdom, Montana).

39. Bourke, *Apache Campaign*, 2; Miles, *Serving the Republic*, 220.

40. Bourke, *On the Border*, 36, 37, 126; Forsyth, *Thrilling Days*, 80; Davis, *Truth About Geronimo*, 74; Miles, *Serving the Republic*, 225.

41. Luther Bradley to Ione Dewey, June 15, July 1, 1867, Luther P. Bradley Papers, United States Army Military History Institute. See also Robert Smith LaMotte to his mother, May 20, 1867, June 15, August 13, 1868; [Robert Smith] LaMotte Family Papers, Bancroft Library.

42. E.O.C. Ord to Molly Ord, July 4, 1858, E.O.C. Ord Papers, Stanford University Library; Richard Irving Dodge diary, January 11, 1878, Richard Irving Dodge Papers, Newberry Library; Nelson Miles, *Annual Report . . . Department of Arizona, 1888*, pp. 5–6, copy in Graff Collection, Newberry Library; Carter, *On the Border*, 535–536. In another example, Frank Baldwin complained to his wife that he had traveled for seven days on a scout "through the

very worst part of the Indian country but could not get the rascals to fight me. They would keep off in the distance but never could I get within reach of them to get up a good fight which every man of my command was anxious for as much as I was." He added that he was certain he would be victorious if he could bring the Indians to blows. See Frank Baldwin to Alice Baldwin, October 22, 1874, Frank D. Baldwin Papers, Huntington Library.

43. Kane, *Military Life*, 265–266.

44. Granville O. Haller diary, July 16, 1855, Granville O. Haller Papers, Suzzallo Library, University of Washington. See also his August 8, 1856, diary entry. Thomas Dunlay says that the Gatling gun was used rarely in the Indian wars because it could be cumbersome and because many officers did not know how to make the best use of this weapon; *Wolves for the Blue Soldiers*, 73.

45. Anson Mills, *My Story* (Washington, D.C.: By the author, 1918), 111. Sherman's comments are quoted in Utley, *Frontier Regulars*, 410, and in Thomas Leonard, "Red, White and the Army Blue: Empathy and Anger in the American West," *American Quarterly* 26 (May 1974): 187. See also Oliver O. Howard, *My Life and Experiences Among Our Hostile Indians* (New York: De Capo Press, 1972), 166, 173; and Walter S. Schuyler to his father, November 1, 1876, in Crook, *His Autobiography*, 204.

46. Quoted in Leonard, "Red, White and the Army Blue," 187–188.

47. Utley, *Frontier Regulars*, 48.

CHAPTER 8. THE INDIAN SCOUT AS ALLY

1. Leonard Wood diary, July 8, August 15, 1886, ms. copy of diary in Henry Ware Lawton Papers, Library of Congress. For more information on this campaign, see Thomas W. Dunlay, *Wolves for the Blue Soldiers: Indian Scouts and Auxiliaries With the United States Army, 1860–1890* (Lincoln: University of Nebraska Press, 1982), 176–182; Robert Utley, *A Clash of Cultures: Fort Bowie and the Chiricahua Apaches* (Washington, D.C.: GPO, 1977), 43–82; and Paul Andrew Hutton, *Phil Sheridan and His Army* (Lincoln: University of Nebraska Press, 1985), 367.

2. Dunlay, *Wolves for the Blue Soldiers*, 11–24, 43, 55. See also Robert M. Utley, *Frontier Regulars: The United States Army and the Indian, 1866–1891* (New York: Macmillan Publishing Co., 1973), 53–55; Charles Lummis, *General Crook and the Apache Wars* (Flagstaff, Ariz.: Northland Press, 1966).

3. Lieutenant General John M. Schofield, *Forty-Six Years in the*

Army (New York: Century Co., 1897), 488, 489. For a discussion of military attitudes concerning the value of Indian scouts, see Dunlay, *Wolves for the Blue Soldiers*, 59–68. William T. Parker wrote that the "Indian is a natural warrior. He loves war. Thus the whites never had any difficulty in enlisting Indian soldiers or scouts to fight other Indians"; Parker, *Personal Experiences Among Our North American Indians, From 1867 to 1885* (Northampton, Mass., 1913), 38.

4. Lieutenant Colonel W. H. Carter, *From Yorktown to Santiago With the Sixth U.S. Cavalry* (Baltimore: Lord Baltimore Press, 1900), 181.

5. Crook's statements to the scouts are recorded in John G. Bourke, *Mackenzie's Last Fight With the Cheyennes: A Winter Campaign in Wyoming and Montana* (Governor's Island, N.Y., 1890), 9–10. In a recent study, Karen Easton argued that motivations of self-interest, particularly tribal self-interest, played a large role in the scouts' motivations during the Powder River Campaign of 1876; Easton, "Getting Into Uniform: Northern Cheyenne Scouts in the United States Army, 1876–81" (M.A. thesis, University of Wyoming, 1985). DeWitt Clinton Peters recognized the importance of intertribal warfare on the Southern Plains, but he did not see the role whites played in the competition for hunting grounds; Peters to his father, September 24, 1854, DeWitt Clinton Peters Papers, Bancroft Library, Berkeley, California. See also General John Parker Hawkins, *Memoranda Concerning Some Branches of the Hawkins Family and Connections* (Indianapolis, 1913), 86–87; Lieutenant James H. Bradley, "Characteristics, Habits and Customs of Blackfeet Indians," *Contributions to the Historical Society of Montana* 9 (1923): 283; and Dunlay, *Wolves for the Blue Soldiers*, 109–145.

6. Dunlay, *Wolves for the Blue Soldiers*, 108–126.

7. Randolph Marcy, *Adventure on Red River: A Report on the Exploration of the Headwaters of the Red River by Captain Randolph B. Marcy and Captain G. B. McClellan* (Norman: University of Oklahoma Press, 1937), 55–56; idem, *Thirty Years of Army Life on the Frontier* (New York: Harper and Brothers, 1866), 76.

8. August Wolf and J. G. Trimble, "Where the Steptoe Expedition Made Its Last Stand," *Journal of the Military Service Institution of the United States* 42 (May–June 1908): 501.

9. Lieutenant Colonel O. L. Hein, *Memories of Long Ago* (New York: G. P. Putnam's Sons, 1925), 87; George Crook, *Resume of Operations Against Apache Indians, 1882 to 1886* (1886), p. 22, pamphlet copy in Graff Collection, Newberry Library, Chicago.

10. Hutton, *Phil Sheridan*, 363–368; Utley, *Frontier Regulars*, 377–393; Dunley, *Wolves for the Blue Soldiers*, 170–182.

11. Richard I. Dodge diary, November 16, 1876, Richard Irving Dodge Papers, Newberry Library. According to Dunlay, Crook also respected the scouts' opinions on strategy and tactics; Dunlay, *Wolves for the Blue Soldiers*, 95.

12. Hugh Lenox Scott, *Some Memories of a Soldier* (New York: Century Co., 1928), 52. For other positive comments about the scouts' abilities, see August V. Kautz, *Annual Report . . . Department of Arizona, 1875–76*, p. 8, copy in Graff Collection, Newberry Library, Chicago; Arthur Woodward, ed., *On the Bloody Trail of Geronimo* (Los Angeles: Westernlore Press, 1958), 40; John G. Bourke diary, July 13, 1876, microfilm, Denver Public Library; Frank Baldwin to Alice Baldwin, August 1, 1874, Frank D. Baldwin Papers, Huntington Library, San Marino, California; Walter Schuyler to his father, September 29, 1872, Walter Scribner Schuyler Papers, Huntington Library; Wolf and Trimble, "Steptoe Expedition," 501; Bourke, *Mackenzie's Last Fight*, 19, 4; Bourke, "General Crook," 654–655, 657, 659; Thaddeus H. Capron diary, June 14, 1876, Western Heritage Center, University of Wyoming, Laramie, wherein Capron describes the Shoshone allies as a "fine body of Indians" who "will be a great help to us"; William Carey Brown, *The Sheepeater Campaign* (Boise, Idaho: Sys-York, 1926), p. 22, reprinted from the Idaho Historical Society, *Tenth Biennial Report, 1926*; John Fitzgerald, quoted in Abe Laufe, ed., *An Army Doctor's Wife on the Frontier: Letters From Alaska and the Far West, 1874–1878* (Pittsburgh: University of Pittsburgh Press, 1962), 347. In several cases, officers dismissed certain tribes as not useful for scouting. Stephen Mills rejected the Papago as scouts because, he wrote his mother, they were "shiftless, lazy and indifferent. I do not want to travel with them"; Mills to his mother, November 26, 1881, Stephen C. Mills Papers, United States Army Military History Institute, Carlisle Barracks, Pennsylvania. Bourke thought Pima scouts were cowardly and anxious to kill women; Bourke, "General Crook," 657–658.

13. Quoted in Robert M. Utley, ed., *Battlefield and Classroom: Four Decades With the American Indian, 1867–1904* (New Haven: Yale University Press, 1964), 4, 5, 7.

14. Bourke, "General Crook," 657; idem, *An Apache Campaign in the Sierra Madre: An Account of the Expedition in Pursuit of the Hostile Chiricahua Apaches in the Spring of 1883* (New York: Charles Scribner's Sons, 1886), 23.

15. Simon Snyder diary, December 16, 1876, Simon Snyder Pa-

pers, United States Army Military History Institute; Peter J. Powell, *Sweet Medicine: The Continuing Role of the Sacred Arrows, the Sun Dance, and the Sacred Buffalo Hat in Northern Cheyenne History* (Norman: University of Oklahoma Press, 1969), 1:172; Dunlay, *Wolves for the Blue Soldiers*, 203. See also Oliver O. Howard, *My Life and Experiences Among Our Hostile Indians* (New York: De Capo Press, 1972), 366; Bourke diary, June 18, 1876, Denver Public Library; and Eli Lundy Huggins to family, July 25, 1879, Eli Lundy Huggins Papers, Bancroft Library. These officers understood that during a war Anglo-American soldiers could be as capable of such tragic actions as were Indians, but they were more outspoken about Indian atrocities than they were about those committed by regular army troops.

16. Eugene Carr, "Reminiscences of Indian Wars," ms. in Eugene A. Carr Papers, United States Army Military History Institute. Several decades later, Carr, while commanding a company of Indian cavalry, confided to a family member that his Indian company was "not all that the most rose colored fancy would paint them, tho quite *red*." People from neighboring villages complained that the Indian soldiers got drunk and terrorized the towns. Also, he believed that they did not ride as well as the white cavalrymen, sitting sideways on their horses' backs and lolling about. "There is a great blow about the success of this plan of enlisting Indians," he wrote, "but the reverse side is kept quiet." See Eugene Carr to John, November 20, 1891, Eugene Carr Papers, United States Army Military History Institute. See also Scott, *Some Memories*, 169–170. Scott claimed that Indian enlisted men did not work out because there were those in the army who opposed the mustering out of the service of two companies of Anglo-Americans to make room for the Indians. See also Coffman, *Old Army*, 259–260.

17. Dunlay, *Wolves for the Blue Soldiers*, 97–98. Wooden Leg, a Cheyenne, commented in his autobiography that the Northern Cheyennes especially liked Lieutenant Clark because he was adept at sign language. "It appeared he understood Indians better than any white man soldier I ever had seen. I suppose that was why we liked him. . . . [W]e trusted him, so we began to do as he asked." See Thomas Marquis, *Wooden Leg: A Warrior Who Fought Custer* (Lincoln: University of Nebraska Press, 1931), 304.

18. Henry Blanchard Freeman diary, April 9, 1876, Denver Public Library; Edgar I. Stewart, ed., *The March of the Montana Column: A Prelude to the Custer Disaster* (Norman: University of Oklahoma Press, 1961), 105.

19. Bigelow, *On the Bloody Trail*, 98; Lee Clark Mitchell, *Wit-*

nesses to a Vanishing America: The Nineteenth Century Response (Princeton: Princeton University Press, 1981), 215–232. For more on Bourke's relationship with Indian scouts, see Joseph C. Porter, *Paper Medicine Man: John Gregory Bourke and His American West* (Norman: University of Oklahoma Press, 1986).

20. Bourke, *Mackenzie's Last Fight*, 8; Bourke diary, June 14, 1876, and sections of vol. 7 (Bourke recreated this diary after the original was lost), Denver Public Library.

21. Richard I. Dodge diary, November 19, 1876, Richard Irving Dodge Papers, Newberry Library; Frank Baldwin journal, August 19, 1874, Frank D. Baldwin Papers, Huntington Library. See also Eli Lundy Huggins's official report of a scouting mission with Cheyenne scouts dated April 6, 1880, in Eli Lundy Huggins Papers, Bancroft Library.

22. George P. Hammond, ed., *Campaigns in the West, 1856–1861: The Journal and Letters of Colonel John Van Deusen Du Bois* (Tucson: Arizona Pioneers Historical Society, 1949), 11, 21; Stewart, *March of the Montana Column*, 155. Schofield, in contrast to Du Bois, argued in favor of the use of Indian scouts precisely because of their tendency to remain faithful to their war leader. "In only one solitary instance," Schofield maintained, "had the Indian scouts so long employed by the Army ever proved unfaithful, though often employed in hostilities against their own tribes." See Schofield, *Forty-Six Years*, 488. For similar comments on Kiowa scouts, see James Parker to R. Wayne Parker, December 15, 1876, James Parker Papers, United States Military Academy Library.

23. John S. Gray, *Centennial Campaign: The Sioux War of 1876* (Fort Collins, Colo.: Old Army Press, 1976), 74, 76.

24. Stewart, *March of the Montana Column*, 85.

25. Ibid., 52, 71, 51, 72, 43, 48.

26. Ibid., 100, 105, 92–93.

27. Ibid., 97.

28. Ibid., 129.

29. Ibid., 87–88. Crow scouts demonstrated similar interest in recapturing livestock during an encounter with the Sioux in 1880; see Eli Lundy Huggins's official report, dated April 6, 1880, Eli Lundy Huggins Papers, Bancroft Library. In 1886, Henry Lawton expressed frustration with the San Carlos and White Mountain Apaches. The Apaches claimed that they had stolen horses from the Indians they were tracking in Mexico in 1886, but a group of Mexicans stated that the horses were theirs and refused to pay the scouts ten dollars apiece for them. "The whole thing is an annoying

hard thankless work," Lawton wrote. "General Miles wants the scouts to have the horses they capture, and I can't refuse to return to the Mexicans the horses they prove to be theirs and which have been stolen from them. On the other hand, the hope of plunder is the greatest incentive to the scouts and if the horses are taken away, they do not work as well. In fact, I fear they will not work at all." Henry Lawton to Mary, July 22, 1886, Henry Ware Lawton Papers, Library of Congress.

30. Bourke diary, June 14, 1876, Denver Public Library; Bourke, *Mackenzie's Last Fight*, 5; Captain Charles King, *Campaigning With Crook and Stories of Army Life* (New York: Harper and Brothers, 1890), 66; William Carey Brown to his mother, July 9, 1879, William Carey Brown Papers, Norlin Library, University of Colorado, Boulder; Hein, *Memories of Long Ago*, 88.

31. Stephen Mills to his mother, May 9, 1882, Stephen C. Mills Papers, United States Army Military History Institute; Richard Irving Dodge diary, November 19, 1876, Richard Irving Dodge Papers, Newberry Library; King, *Campaigning With Crook*, 66.

32. Bourke, "General Crook," 659.

33. Bourke, *Mackenzie's Last Fight*, 35; Gray, *Centennial Campaign*, 189–190; William Carey Brown to his mother, July 9, 1879, William Carey Brown Papers, Norlin Library.

CONCLUSION

1. Robert M. Utley, *The Contribution of the Frontier to the American Military Tradition*, The Harmon Memorial Lectures in Military History, no. 19 (Colorado Springs: United States Air Force Academy, 1977), 3.

2. See Richard N. Ellis, "The Humanitarian Generals," *Western Historical Quarterly* 3 (April 1972): 169–178.

3. Lee Clark Mitchell, *Witness to a Vanishing America: The Nineteenth Century Response* (Princeton: Princeton University Press, 1981), xvi. See also Jackson Lears, *No Place of Grace: Antimodernism and the Transformation of American Culture, 1880–1920* (New York: Pantheon Books, 1981).

Bibliography

PRIMARY SOURCES

Manuscripts

Bancroft Library, University of California, Berkeley
    Heistand, Mary Rippey. "Scraps from an Army Woman's Diary,"
        typescript, Heistand Papers.
    Huggins, Eli Lundy. Papers.
    LaMotte Family Papers.
    Long, Oscar Fitzalan. Papers.
    Ord, Edward Otho Cresap. Papers.
    Peters, DeWitt Clinton. Papers.
    Schureman, James Wall. Papers.
Big Hole National Monument, Wisdom, Montana
    Wood, Lieut. H. Clay. "The Status of Young Joseph and His Band
        of Nez Perce Indians."
Colorado Historical Society, Denver
    Baldwin, Frank D. Papers.
    Brackett, Albert G., "Fort Bridger." Undated typescript.
    Forsyth, George Alexander. Papers.
    Fort Garland Papers.
    Thornburg, Thomas Tipton. Papers.
Denver Public Library
    Bourke, John G. Diaries, microfilm. The original diaries are de-
        posited in the United States Military Academy Library, West
        Point, New York.
    Freeman, Henry Blanchard. Papers.
    Norton, Henry. Papers.
    Patterson, Robert M. Papers.
    Trask, Samuel H. Papers.
Huntington Library, San Marino, California
    Baldwin, Frank D. Papers.
    Fort Dalles Papers.

Schuyler, Walter Scribner. Papers.

Stanley, David Sloane. "Diary of an Expedition . . . from Fort Smith, Arkansas, . . . to San Diego, 1853–1854."

Sweeny, Thomas William. Papers.

Vogdes, Ada Adams. Journal.

Wood, C.E.S. Papers.

Kansas State Historical Society, Topeka

Baird, George. Papers.

Library of Congress, Washington, D.C.

Carlton, Caleb Henry. Papers.

Hatch, John Porter. Papers.

Heintzelman, Samuel Peter. Papers.

Lawton, Henry Ware. Papers.

Scott, Hugh Lennox. Papers.

National Archives and Records Administration, Washington, D.C.

Record Group 94, Records of the Adjutant General's Office, 1780–1917.

Newberry Library, Chicago

Edward E. Ayer Collection

Augur, C. C. Papers.

Frederick Benteen–Theodore Goldin Correspondence.

Grierson, Benjamin. Papers.

McCormick, Major L. S. "Wounded Knee and the Drexel Mission Fight." Typescript.

Woodward, C. A. "Journal of an Expedition to Wichita Mountains from June 1 to July 13, 1863." In Benjamin Grierson Papers.

Everett D. Graff Collection

Dodge, Richard Irving. Papers.

Lawton, Henry. Papers.

Templeton, George M. Diary.

New-York Historical Society Library, New York

Winne, Caroline Frey. Papers.

Norlin Library, University of Colorado, Boulder

Brown, William Carey. Papers.

Hough, Alfred Lacey. Papers.

San Juan Island National Historic Site, Friday Harbor, San Juan Island, Washington

Allen, Colonel Harvey Abner, and Mary Allen. Papers. Typescript.

Stanford University Library, Palo Alto, California

Ord, E.O.C. Papers.

Suzzallo Library, University of Washington, Seattle

Haller, Granville O. Papers.

Kautz, August V. Diary. Microfilm.
McClellan, George. Papers.
Steptoe, Edward. Papers.
United States Army Military History Institute, Carlisle Barracks, Pennsylvania
    Bradley, Luther P. Papers.
    Brooks, William T. H. Papers.
    Brown, William Carey. Papers.
    Carr, Eugene A. Papers.
    George Crook—L.W.V. Kennon Papers.
    Fuller, Ezra. Papers
    Gibson, Joseph R. Papers.
    Godfrey, E. S. Papers.
    Haustead-Maus Family Papers.
    Henry, Guy V. Papers.
    Kautz, August V. Papers.
    Lenihan, Michael Joseph. Papers.
    Mackenzie, Ranald S. Papers.
    Mills, Stephen C. Papers.
    Nolan, Nicholas. Papers.
    Order of the Indian Wars Collection.
    Ovenshine, Samuel and Sarah. Papers.
    Paulding, William and Grace. Papers.
    Sladen, Joseph, to Mrs. Alice Crane, October 26, 1896.
    Snyder, Simon. Papers.
    Steele, Matthew Forney. Papers.
    Turner, John Wesley. Papers.
    Whitside, Samuel. Papers.
    Young, S.B.M. Papers.
United States Military Academy Library, West Point, New York
    Bigelow, John. Papers.
    Fornance, James. Papers.
    Hardcastle, Edmund. Papers.
    Heartt, Frank Edmunds. Papers.
    Heistand, Henry O. S. Papers.
    Noyes, Charles. Papers.
    Parker, James. Papers.
    Tilman, Samuel E. Papers.
    Vogdes, Ada Adams. Papers.
University of Wyoming, Western Heritage Center, Laramie
    Capron, Thaddeus H. Papers.
Wyoming Archives, Museums, and Historical Department, Cheyenne

Carter, William Harding. Papers.
Stansbury, Howard. Papers.

Government Documents

U.S. Congress. House. *Correspondence Between the Late Secretary of War and General Wool.* 35th Cong., 1st sess., H. Doc. 88. Washington, D.C.: GPO, 1857–58.

———. *Indian Affairs on the Pacific.* 34th Cong., 2nd sess., H. Doc. 76. Washington: GPO, 1856–57.

———. *Indian Hostilities in Oregon and Washington.* 34th Cong., 1st sess., H. Doc. 93. Washington: GPO, 1855–56.

———. *Indian War in Oregon and Washington Territories.* 35th Cong., 1st sess., H. Doc. 38. Washington: GPO, 1857–58.

———. *Inspection by Generals Rusling and Hazen.* 39th Cong., 2nd sess., H. Doc. 45. Washington: GPO, 1866–67.

———. *Military Road from Fort Benton to Fort Walla Walla.* 35th Cong., 2nd sess., H. Doc. 44. Washington: GPO, 1860–61.

———. *Topographical Memoir of the Department of the Pacific.* 35th Cong., 2nd sess., H. Doc. 114. Washington: GPO, 1858–59.

U.S. Congress. Senate. *Indian Operations on the Plains.* 50th Cong., 1st sess., S. Doc. 33. Washington: GPO, 1888.

———. *Report of the Secretary of War.* 34th Cong., 1st sess., S. Doc. 66. Washington: GPO, 1855–56.

———. *Report of the Secretary of War: Topographical Memoir of Colonel Wright's Campaign.* 35th Cong., 2nd sess., S. Doc. 32. Washington: GPO, 1858–59.

Published Letters, Diaries, and Reminiscences

Adams, Donald K., ed. "The Journal of Ada A. Vogdes." *Montana: The Magazine of Western History* 13 (Summer 1963): 2–17.

Ambler, Charles H., ed. "Correspondence of Robert M. T. Hunter." American Historical Association, *Annual Report*, 1916. Vol. 2.

Anderson, Harry H., ed. "An Army Wife Among the Sioux: The Experiences of Mrs. Cyrus S. Roberts at Cheyenne River Agency, Dakota Territory, 1872–73." *The Westerners Brand Book* 20 (December 1963): 73–75, 79–80.

Armes, Colonel George A. *Ups and Downs of an Army Officer.* Washington, D.C., 1900.

Armstrong, Major A. N. *Oregon: Comprising a Brief History and Full Description of the Territories of Oregon and Washington.* Chicago: Chas. Scott and Co., 1857.

Athearn, Robert G., ed. "An Army Officer in the West, 1864–1890."

In *The Westerners Brand Book*, 61–76. Denver: University of Denver Press, 1950.

Baldwin, Alice Blackwood. *Memoirs of Major General Frank D. Baldwin*. Los Angeles: Wetzel Publishing Co., 1929.

Bandel, Eugene. *Frontier Life in the Army*. Edited by Ralph E. Bieber. Glendale, Calif.: Arthur C. Clark Co., 1932.

Bates, Colonel Charles Francis. *Custer's Indian Battles*. Bronxville, N.Y., 1936.

Beall, Lieutenant Colonel John B. *In Barrack and Field: Poems and Sketches of Army Life*. Nashville: Smith and Lamar, 1906.

Benteen, Frederick. *The Custer Fight: Captain Benteen's Story of the Battle of the Little Big Horn*. Hollywood, Calif.: Privately printed by E. A. Brininstool, 1933.

Beyer, W. F., and O. F. Keydel, eds. *Deeds of Valor*. Vol. 2. Detroit: Perrien-Keydel Co., 1907.

Biddle, Ellen McGowan. *Reminiscences of a Soldier's Wife*. Philadelphia: J. B. Lippincott Co., 1907.

Bieber, Ralph P., ed. *Marching With the Army of the West, 1846– 1848*. Glendale, Calif. Arthur H. Clark Co., 1936.

Bisbee, William Henry. *Through Four American Wars*. Boston: Meador Publishing Co., 1931.

Bourke, John G. *An Apache Campaign in the Sierra Madre: An Account of the Expedition in Pursuit of the Hostile Chiricahua Apaches in the Spring of 1883*. New York: Charles Scribner's Sons, 1886.

———. "General Crook in the Indian Country." *Century Magazine* 41 (March 1891): 643–660.

———. "The Laws of Spain in their Application to the American Indians." *American Anthropologist* 7 (April 1894): 193–201.

———. *Mackenzie's Last Fight with the Cheyennes: A Winter Campaign in Wyoming and Montana*. Governor's Island, N.Y., 1890.

———. *On the Border With Crook*. New York: Charles Scribner's Sons, 1891.

———. *The Snake-Dance of the Moquis of Arizona*. New York: Charles Scribner's Sons, 1884.

Boyd, Mrs. Orsemus. *Cavalry Life in Tent and Field*. New York: J. Selwin Tait, 1894.

Boyles, William Henry. *Personal Observations on the Conduct of the Modoc War*. Edited by Richard H. Dillon. Los Angeles: Dawson's Book Shop, n.d.

Brackett, Albert G. *History of the United States Cavalry*. New York: Harper and Brothers Publishers, 1865.

Bradley, Lieutenant James H. "Characteristics, Habits and Customs of the Blackfeet Indians." *Contributions to the Historical Society of Montana* 9 (1923): 255–287.

——. "History of the Sioux." *Contributions to the Historical Society of Montana* 9 (1923): 29–140.

——. "The Sioux Campaign of 1876 Under the Command of General John Gibbon." *Contributions to the Historical Society of Montana* 2 (1896): 140–228.

Brown, Colonel W. C. *The Sheepeater Campaign.* Boise, Idaho: Sys-York, 1926.

Bryan, Roger B. *An Average American Army Officer: An Autobiography.* San Diego, Calif.: Buck-Molina Co., 1914.

Byrne, Bernard J. *A Frontier Army Surgeon: Life in Colorado in the Eighties.* New York: Exposition Press, 1962.

Capron, Cynthia J. "The Indian Border War of 1876." *Journal of the Illinois State Historical Society* 13 (January 1921): 476–503.

Carriker, Robert C., and Eleanor R. Carriker, eds. *An Army Wife on the Frontier: The Memoirs of Alice Blackwood Baldwin, 1867–1877.* Salt Lake City: Tanner Trust Fund, 1975.

Carrington, Frances C. *My Army Life and the Fort Phil Kearny Massacre.* Philadelphia: J. B. Lippincott Co., 1911.

Carrington, Henry B. *The Indian Question.* Boston: Charles H. Whiting, Publisher, 1884.

Carrington, Margaret. *Ab-sa-ra-ka: Land of Massacre.* Philadelphia: J. B. Lippincott Co., 1868.

Carroll, John M., ed. *The Two Battles of the Little Big Horn.* New York: Liveright, 1974.

Carter, Captain Robert G. *On the Border With Mackenzie; or, Winning West Texas From the Comanches.* New York: Antiquarian Press, 1961.

——. *The Sergeant's Story: Winning the West from the Indians and the Bad Men in 1870 to 1876.* New York: Frederick H. Hitchcock, Publisher, 1926.

Carter, Lieutenant Colonel W. H. *From Yorktown to Santiago With the Sixth U.S. Cavalry.* Baltimore: Lord Baltimore Press, 1900.

——. *Horses, Saddles and Bridles.* Baltimore: Lord Baltimore Press, 1906.

Clark, W. P. *The Indian Sign Language.* Philadelphia: L. R. Hamerslyand Co., 1885.

Clifford, Josephine. *"Another Juanita" and Other Stories.* Buffalo: Charles Wells Moulton, 1893.

——. *Overland Tales.* Philadelphia: Claxton, Remsen and Haffelfinger, 1877.

Cochran, Mrs. M. A. *Posie; or, From Reveille to Retreat, An Army Story.* Cincinnati: Tobert Clarke Co., 1896.

Cooke, Philip St. George. *Scenes and Adventures in the Army; or, Romance of Military Life.* Philadelphia: Lindsay and Blakiston, 1859.

Corbusier, William T. *Verde to San Carlos: Recollections of a Famous Army Surgeon and His Observant Family on the Western Frontier, 1869–1886.* Tucson: Dale Stuart King, Publisher, 1968.

Cox, Rev. John E. *Five Years in the United States Army.* Owensville, Ind.: General Baptist Publishing House, 1892.

Cramer, Jesse Grant, ed. *Letters of Ulysses S. Grant to His Father and His Youngest Sister, 1857–1878.* New York and London: G. P. Putnam's Sons, 1912.

Cremony, John C. *Life Among the Apaches.* San Francisco: A. Roman and Co., 1868.

Crook, General George. *His Autobiography.* Edited by Martin F. Schmitt. Norman: University of Oklahoma Press, 1960.

Crook, George. *Resume of Operations Against Apache Indians, 1882 to 1886* (1886). Pamphlet copy in Graff Collection, Newberry Library, Chicago.

Custer, Elizabeth B. *"Boots and Saddles"; or, Life in Dakota With General Custer.* Norman: University of Oklahoma Press, 1961.

———. *Following the Guidon: Into the Indian Wars With General Custer and the Seventh Cavalry.* Norman: University of Oklahoma Press, 1966.

———. *Tenting on the Plains; or, General Custer in Kansas and Texas.* Norman: University of Oklahoma Press, 1971.

Custer, George Armstrong. *My Life on the Plains; or, Personal Experiences with Indians.* Norman: University of Oklahoma Press, 1976.

Daly, H. W. "The Geronimo Campaign." *Arizona Historical Review* 3 (July 1930): 26–44.

Davis, Britton. *The Truth About Geronimo.* New Haven: Yale University Press, 1929.

Doane, Lieutenant Gustavus Cheyney. *Battle Drums and Geysers: The Life and Journals of Lt. Gustavus Cheyney Doane, Soldier and Explorer of the Yellowstone and Snake River Regions.* Edited by Orrin H. Bonney and Lorraine Bonney. Chicago: Swallow Press, 1970.

Dodge, Major General Grenville M. *The Indian Campaign of Winter of 1864–65.* Denver: Colorado Commandery of the Loyal Legion of the United States, 1907.

Dodge, Colonel Richard Irving. *Our Wild Indians: Thirty-Three*

Years' Personal Experience Among the Red Men of the Great West. Hartford, Conn.: A. D. Worthington and Co., 1883.

Eckert, Edward K., and Nicholas J. Amato, eds. *Ten Years in the Saddle: The Memoir of William Woods Averell.* San Rafael, Calif.: Presidio Press, 1978.

English, Mary Katherine Jackson. "Army Girl: Experiences on the Frontier." *The Westerners Brand Book* 3 (1949).

Flipper, Henry O. *Negro Frontiersman: The Western Memoirs of Henry O. Flipper, First Negro Graduate of West Point.* El Paso: Texas Western College Press, 1963.

Forsyth, Brigadier General George A. *The Story of the Soldier.* New York: Brampton Society, 1908.

———. *Thrilling Days in Army Life.* New York and London: Harper and Brothers, 1900.

Fougera, Katherine Gibson. *With Custer's Cavalry.* Caldwell, Idaho: Caxton Printers, 1942.

Fry, James. *Army Sacrifices; or, Briefs from Official Pigeon-Holes.* New York: D. Van Nostrand, 1879.

Gatewood, Charles B. "Lieutenant Charles B. Gatewood and the Surrender of Geronimo." *Proceedings of the Order of the Indian Wars,* 1929.

———. "The Surrender of Geronimo." *Arizona Historical Review* 4 (April 1931): 29–49.

Gibbon, General John. "The Pursuit of 'Joseph.'" *American Catholic Quarterly Review* 4 (April 1879): 317–344.

———. *A Vision of the "Big Hole"* (privately printed by Captain J. W. Jacobs and Captain C. A. Woodruff, n. d.). Copy available at Big Hole National Monument, Wisdom, Montana.

Glisan, Rodney. *Journal of Army Life.* San Francisco: A. L. Bancroft and Co., 1874.

Godfrey, Lieutenant Edward Settle. *The Field Diary of Lt. Edward Settle Godfrey . . . in the Sioux Encounter at the Battle of the Little Big Horn.* Edited by Edgar I. Stewart. Portland, Ore.: Champoeg Press, 1957.

———. "Some Reminiscences." *Cavalry Journal* 36 (July 1927): 417–425; 37 (October 1928): 481–500.

Grant, Ulysses S. *General Grant's Letters to a Friend, 1861–1880.* Edited by James Grant Wilson. New York and Boston: T. Y. Crowell, 1897.

———. *The Papers of Ulysses S. Grant.* Edited by John Y. Simons. Vol. 1. Carbondale: Southern Illinois University Press, 1967.

———. *Personal Memoirs of U.S. Grant.* Vol. 1. New York: Charles L. Webster and Co., 1885.

Greely, Major General A. W. *Reminiscences of Adventure and Service: A Record of Sixty-Five Years.* New York: Charles Scribner's Sons, 1927.

Hafen, LeRoy R., and Ann W. Hafen, eds. *Powder River Campaigns and Sawyers Expedition of 1865: A Documentary Account Comprising Official Reports, Diaries, Contemporary Newspaper Accounts, and Personal Narratives.* Glendale, Calif.: Arthur H. Clark Co., 1961.

Hagemann, E. R., ed. *Fighting Rebels and Redskins: Experiences in the Army Life of Colonel George B. Sanford, 1861–1892.* Norman: University of Oklahoma Press, 1969.

Hamilton, Henry S. *Reminiscences of a Veteran.* Concord, N. H.: Republican Press Association, 1897.

Hammond, George P., ed. *Campaigns in the West, 1856–1861: The Journal and Letters of Colonel John Van Deusen Du Bois.* Tucson: Arizona Pioneers Historical Society, 1949.

Hancock, Almira Russell. *Reminiscences of Winfield Scott Hancock.* New York: Charles L. Webster and Co., 1887.

Hawkins, General John Parker. *Memoranda Concerning Some Branches of the Hawkins Family and Connections.* Indianapolis, Ind., 1913.

Hein, Lieutenant Colonel O. L. *Memories of Long Ago.* New York: G. P. Putnam's Sons, 1925.

Hitchcock, Ethan Allen. *Fifty Years in Camp and Field.* New York: G. P. Putnam's Sons, 1909.

Holmes, Kenneth L., ed. "A Military Wife on the Santa Fe Trail." In Kenneth L. Holmes, ed., *Covered Wagon Women: Diaries and Letters From the Western Trails, 1840–1890,* 2:15–43. Glendale, Calif.: Arthur H. Clark Co., 1983.

Howard, Major General Oliver O. *Famous Indian Chiefs I Have Known.* New York: Century Co., 1908.

———. "How Indians Fight." *Seattle Post-Intelligencer,* January 6, 1891.

———. *My Life and Experiences Among Our Hostile Indians.* New York: De Capo Press, 1972.

———. *Nez Perce Joseph.* Boston: Lee and Shepard, Publishers, 1881.

Huggins, Captain E. L. *Winona: A Dakota Legend and Other Poems.* New York: G. P. Putnam's Sons, 1890.

Humfreville, J. Lee. *Twenty Years Among Our Hostile Indians.* New York: Hunter and Co., 1903.

Jocelyn, Stephen Perry. *Mostly Alkali.* Caldwell, Idaho: Caxton Printers, 1953.

Johnson, Brigadier General Richard W. *A Soldier's Reminiscences in Peace and War.* Philadelphia: J. B. Lippincott Co., 1886.

Judd, A. N. *Campaigning Against the Sioux.* New York: Sol Lewis, 1973.

Kane, Lucille M., ed. *Military Life in Dakota.* St. Paul: Alvord Memorial Commission, 1951.

Kautz, August V. *Annual Report . . . Department of Arizona, 1875–76.* Copy in Graff Collection, Newberry Library, Chicago.

Keim, De B. Randolph. *Sheridan's Troopers on the Borders: A Winter Campaign on the Plains.* Philadelphia: Claxton, Remsen and Huffelfinger, 1870 .

Kelver, Gerald O., ed. *Fifteen Years on the Western Frontier, 1866–1881.* Fort Collins, Colo.: Robinson Press, 1975.

Keyes, Erasmus Darwin. *Fifty Years' Observation of Men and Events, Civil and Military.* New York: Charles Scribner's Sons, 1884.

———. *From West Point to California.* Oakland, Calif.: Biobooks, 1950.

Kimball, Maria Brace. *My Eighty Years.* Boston: Privately printed, 1936.

———. *A Soldier-Doctor of Our Army: James P. Kimball.* Boston: Houghton Mifflin Co., 1917.

King, Charles. *An Apache Princess: A Tale of the Indian Frontier.* New York: Hobart Co., 1903.

———. *Campaigning With Crook and Stories of Army Life.* New York: Harper and Brothers, 1890.

King, Richard C., ed. *Marion T. Brown: Letters from Fort Sill, 1886–1887.* Austin: Encino Press, 1970.

Kip, Lieutenant Lawrence. *Army Life on the Pacific: A Journal of the Expedition Against the Northern Indians, the Tribes of the Coeur d'Alenes, Spokans, and Pelouzes, in the Summer of 1858.* New York: Redfield, 1859.

———. "The Indian Council at Walla Walla." In F. G. Young, ed., *Sources of the History of Oregon,* 1:4–28. Eugene, Ore.: Star Job Office, 1897.

Kress, Brigadier General John. *Autobiography.* N.p., 1929.

Lane, Jack C., ed. *Chasing Geronimo: The Journal of Leonard Wood, May-September, 1886.* Albuquerque: University of New Mexico Press, 1970.

Lane, Lydia Spencer. *I Married a Soldier; or, Old Days in the Old Army.* Albuquerque: Horn and Wallace Publishers, 1964.

Laufe, Abe, ed. *An Army Doctor's Wife on the Frontier: Letters from*

Alaska and the Far West, 1874–1878. Pittsburgh: University of Pittsburgh Press, 1962.

Luce, Edward S., ed. "The Diary and Letters of Dr. James M. De-Wolf, Acting Assistant Surgeon, U.S. Army; His Record of the Sioux Expedition of 1876 as Kept Until His Death." *North Dakota History* 25 (April–July 1958): 33–81.

McCall, Major General George A. *Letters From the Frontiers, Written During a Period of Thirty Years' Service in the Army of the United States.* Philadelphia: J. B. Lippincott Co., 1868.

McClernand, Lieutenant Edward J. *With the Indian and the Buffalo in Montana, 1870–1878.* Glendale, Calif.: Arthur H. Clark Co., 1969.

McConnell, H. H. *Five Years a Cavalryman; or, Sketches of Regular Army Life on the Texas Frontier, Twenty Odd Years Ago.* Jacksboro, Tex.: J. N. Rogers and Co., 1889.

McCrackin, Josephine Clifford. *The Woman Who Lost Him and Tales of the Frontier Army.* Pasadena, Calif.: George Wharton James, 1913.

McKay, R. H. *Little Pills: An Army Story, Being Some Experiences of a United States Army Medical Officer on the Frontier Nearly a Half Century Ago.* Pittsburg, Kan.: Pittsburg Headlight, 1918.

Marcy, Randolph B. *Adventure on the Red River: Report on the Exploration of the Headwaters of the Red River by Captain Randolph B. Marcy and Captain G. B. McClellan.* Edited by Grant Foreman. Norman: University of Oklahoma Press, 1937.

———. *Border Reminiscences.* New York: Harper and Brothers, 1872.

———. *Thirty Years of Army Life on the Frontier.* New York: Harper and Brothers, 1866.

Mattes, Merrill J., ed. *Indians, Infants and Infantry: Andrew and Elizabeth Burt on the Frontier.* Denver: Old West Publishing Co., 1960.

Mattison, Ray, ed. "An Army Wife on the Upper Missouri: The Diary of Sarah E. Canfield, 1866–1868." *North Dakota History* 20 (October 1953): 191–220.

———. "Diary of Surgeon Washington Matthews, Fort Rice, D.T." *North Dakota History* 21 (January–April 1954): 5–72.

Maury, General Dabney H. *Recollections of a Virginian in the Mexican, Indian and Civil Wars.* New York: Charles Scribner's Sons, 1894.

Merington, Marguerite, ed. *The Custer Story: The Life and Inti-

mate Letters of General George A. Custer and His Wife Eliza-beth. New York: Devin-Adair Co., 1950.

Michie, Peter S. *The Life and Letters of Emory Upton.* New York: D. Appleton and Co., 1885.

Miles, Nelson A. *Personal Recollections and Observations.* Chicago: Werner Co., 1896.

————. *Serving the Republic: Memoirs of the Civil and Military Life of Nelson A. Miles.* New York: Harper and Brothers Publishers, 1911.

Mills, Anson. *My Story.* Washington, D.C.: By the author, 1918.

Morgan, Brigadier General M. R. "Recollections of the Spokane Expedition." *Journal of the Military Service Institution of the United States* 42 (May–June 1908): 489–496.

Mullan, Lieutenant John. *Journal from Fort Dalles, O.T. to Fort Wallah Wallah, W.T. July 1858.* Historical Reprints, no. 18. Missoula: State University of Montana.

Myres, Sandra L., ed. *Cavalry Wife: The Diary of Eveline M. Alexander, 1866–1867.* College Station: Texas A & M University Press, 1977.

————. "Evy Alexander: The Colonel's Lady at McDowell." *Montana: The Magazine of Western History* 24 (Summer 1974): 26–38.

O'Brien, Emily Boynton. "Army Life at Fort Sedgwick, Colorado." *Colorado Magazine* 7 (September 1929): 173–178.

Overfield, Loyd J., ed. *The Little Big Horn 1876: The Official Communications, Documents and Reports With Rosters of the Officers and Troops of the Campaign.* Glendale, Calif.: Arthur H. Clark Co., 1971.

Owen, Major John. *The Journals and Letters of Major John Owen.* Edited by Seymour Dunbar. Vols. 1 and 2. New York: Edward Eberstadt, 1927.

Parker, General James. *The Old Army: Memories, 1872–1918.* Philadelphia: Dorrance and Co., 1929.

Parker, William Thornton. *Annals of Old Fort Cummings, New Mexico, 1867–68.* Fort Davis, Tex.: Frontier Book Co., Publisher, 1968.

————. *Personal Experiences Among Our North American Indians, From 1867 to 1885.* Northampton, Mass., 1913.

Parsons, John E., ed. "The Northern Cheyenne at Fort Fetterman: Colonel Woodward Describes Some Experiences of 1871." *Montana: The Magazine of Western History* 9 (Spring 1959): 16–27.

Price, George. *Across the Continent With the Fifth Cavalry.* New York: Antiquarian Press, 1959.

Reeve, Frank D., ed. "Frederick E. Phelps: A Soldier's Memories." *New Mexico Historical Review* 25 (January–October 1950): 37–56, 109–135, 187–221, 305–327.

Roberts, Gary L. "Condition of the Tribes, 1865: The Report of General McCook." *Montana: The Magazine of Western History* 24 (January 1974): 14–25.

Rodenbough, Theodore F. *From Everglade to Cañon with the Second Dragoons*. New York: D. Van Nostrand, 1875.

Rodenbough, Theodore F., and William Haskin, eds. *The Army of the United States: Historical Sketches of Staff and Line, With Portraits of Generals-in-Chief*. New York: Maynard, Merrill and Co., 1896.

Roe, Frances M. A. *Army Letters From an Officer's Wife*. New York: D. Appleton and Co., 1909.

Rusling, General James F. *Across America; or, The Great West and the Pacific Coast*. New York: Sheldon and Co., 1874.

Sargent, Alice Applegate. *Following the Flag: Diary of a Soldier's Wife*. Kansas City, Mo.: E. B. Barnett, Publisher, n.d.

Schofield, Lieutenant General John M. *Forty-Six Years in the Army*. New York: Century Co., 1897.

Scott, Hugh Lenox. *Some Memories of a Soldier*. New York: Century Co., 1928.

Sedgwick, Major-General John. *Correspondence of John Sedgwick, Major-General*. Vol. 2. New York: Carl Stoeckel, 1903.

Sheridan, General Philip H. *Personal Memoirs*. Vols. 1 and 2. New York: Charles L. Webster and Co., 1888.

Sherman, William T. *Reports of Inspection Made in the Summer of 1877 by Generals P. H. Sheridan and W. T. Sherman of Country North of the Union Pacific Railroad*. Washington, D.C.: GPO, 1878.

Steele, James W. *Frontier Army Sketches*. Chicago: Jansen, McClurg and Co., 1883.

Stewart, Edgar I., ed. "Letters from the Big Hole." *Montana: The Magazine of Western History* 2 (October 1952): 53–56.

————, ed. *The March of the Montana Column: A Prelude to the Custer Disaster*. Norman: University of Oklahoma Press, 1961.

Summerhayes, Martha. *Vanished Arizona: Recollections of the Army Life of a New England Woman*. Tucson: Arizona Silhouettes, 1960.

Thorndike, Rachel Sherman, ed. *The Sherman Letters: Correspondence Between General and Senator Sherman from 1837 to 1891*. New York: Charles Scribner's Sons, 1894.

Turnley, Parmenus T. *Reminiscences of Parmenus Taylor Turnley, From the Cradle to Three Score and Ten.* Chicago: Donohue and Henneberry, 1892.

Utley, Robert M., ed. *Battlefield and Classroom: Four Decades With the American Indian, 1867–1904.* New Haven: Yale University Press, 1964.

———, ed. *Life in Custer's Cavalry: Diaries and Letters of Albert and Jennie Barnitz, 1867–1868.* New Haven: Yale University Press, 1977.

Viele, Teresa. *"Following the Drum": A Glimpse of Frontier Life.* New York: Rudd and Carleton, 1859.

Walker, Captain J. G., and Major O. L. Shepherd. *The Navajo Reconnaissance: A Military Exploration of the Navajo Country in 1859.* Edited by L. R. Bailey. Los Angeles: Westernlore Press, 1964.

Waters, William E. *Life Among the Mormons, and a March to Their Zion.* New York: Moorhead, Simpson and Bond, 1868.

Winder, Captain C. S. "Captain C. S. Winder's Account of a Battle With the Indians." *Maryland Historical Magazine* 35 (March 1940): 56–59.

Wolf, August, and J. G. Trimble. "Where the Steptoe Expedition Made Its Last Stand." *Journal of the Military Service Institution of the United States* 42 (May–June 1908): 498–501.

Wood, C.E.S. "Chief Joseph, the Nez Perce." *Century Magazine* 28 (May–October 1884): 132–148.

———. "Famous Indians: Portraits of Some Indian Chiefs." *Century Magazine* 46 (May–October 1893): 436–445.

———. *The Poet in the Desert.* Portland, Ore.: F. W. Battes, 1915.

———. "Private Journal, 1878." *Oregon Historical Quarterly* 70 (June 1969): 139–170.

Woodward, Arthur, ed. *Journal of Lt. Thomas W. Sweeny, 1849–1853.* Los Angeles: Westernlore Press, 1956.

———. *On the Bloody Trail of Geronimo.* Los Angeles: Westernlore Press, 1958.

Zogbaum, Rufus Fairchild. *Horse, Foot and Dragoons: Sketches of Army Life at Home and Abroad.* New York: Harper and Brothers, 1888.

SECONDARY SOURCES

Theses and Dissertations

Andrews, Richard Allen. "Years of Frustration: William T. Sherman, the Army and Reform, 1869–1883." Ph.D. diss., Northwestern University, 1968.

Dillard, Walter Scott. "The United States Military Academy, 1865–1900: The Uncertain Years." Ph.D. diss., University of Washington, 1972.

Easton, Karen. "Getting Into Uniform: Northern Cheyenne Scouts in the United States Army, 1876–81." M.A. thesis, University of Wyoming, 1985.

Foner, Jack D. "The United States Soldier Between Two Wars: Army Life and Reforms, 1865–1898." Ph.D. diss., Columbia University, 1968.

Gherman, Dawn Lander. "From Parlour to Tepee: The White Squaw on the American Frontier." Ph.D. diss., University of Massachusetts, 1975.

Morrison, James L., Jr. "The United States Military Academy, 1833–1866: Years of Progress and Turmoil." Ph.D. diss., Columbia University, 1971.

Articles, Pamphlets, and Books

Agonito, Joseph. "The Art of Plains Indian Warfare." *Order of the Indian Wars Journal* 1 (Winter 1980): 1–21.

Albers, Patricia, and Beatrice Medicine, eds. *The Hidden Half: Studies of Plains Indian Women.* Washington, D.C.: University Press of America, 1983.

Bailey, Lynn R. *The Long Walk.* Los Angeles: Westernlore Press, 1964.

Beal, Merrill D. *"I Will Fight No More Forever": Chief Joseph and the Nez Perce War.* Seattle: University of Washington Press, 1963.

Berkhofer, Robert F., Jr. *Salvation and the Savage: An Analysis of Protestant Missions and the American Indian Response, 1787–1862.* Lexington: University of Kentucky Press, 1965.

———. *The White Man's Indian: Images of the American Indian From Columbus to the Present.* New York: Alfred A. Knopf, 1978.

Bernstein, Alison. "Outgrowing Pocahontas: Toward a New History of American Indian Women." *Minority Notes* 2 (Spring/Summer 1981): 3–8.

Bingham, Edwin R. "Oregon's Romantic Rebels: John Reed and Charles Erskine Scott Wood." *Pacific Northwest Quarterly* 50 (July 1959): 77–90.

Bledsoe, Anthony Jennings. *Indian Wars of the Northwest.* Oakland, Calif.: Biobooks, 1956.

Briggs, Marion F., and Sarah D. McAnulty. *The Ghost Dance Tragedy at Wounded Knee: A Visual Presentation.* Washington, D.C.: Smithsonian Institution, 1977.

Brininstool, E. A. *Troopers With Custer: Historic Incidents of the*

Battle of the Little Big Horn. Harrisburg, Pa.: Stackpole Co., 1952.

Brown, Jennifer S. H. *Strangers in Blood: Fur Trade Company Families in Indian Country.* Vancouver: University of British Columbia Press, 1980.

Burlingame, Merrill G. "The Andrew Jackson Hunter Family–Mary Hunter Doane." *Montana: The Magazine of Western History* 1 (January 1951): 5–13.

Burns, Robert Ignatius. *The Jesuits and the Indian Wars of the Northwest.* New Haven: Yale University Press, 1966.

Butler, Anne. *Daughters of Joy, Sisters of Misery: Prostitutes in the American West, 1865–90.* Urbana: University of Illinois Press, 1985.

————. "Military Myopia: Prostitution on the Frontier." *Prologue* 13 (Winter 1981): 233–250.

Coffman, Edward M. *The Old Army: A Portrait of the American Army in Peacetime, 1784–1898.* New York: Oxford University Press, 1986.

Cooling, B. Franklin. "Military History: A Blending of Old and New," *OAH Newsletter,* February 1984, 14–15.

Cullum, George W. *Biographical Register of the Officers and Graduates of the U.S. Military Academy at West Point, N.Y., From Its Establishment in 1802 to 1890.* Boston: Houghton, Mifflin and Co., 1891.

————. *Supplement.* Vol. 4. Cambridge, Mass.: Riverside Press, 1901.

Cunliffe, Marcus. *Soldiers and Civilians: The Martial Spirit in America, 1775–1865.* Boston: Little, Brown and Co., 1968.

Deibert, Ralph C. *A History of the Third United States Cavalry.* Harrisburg, Pa.: Telegraph Press, 1933.

Dippie, Brian W. *The Vanishing American: White Attitudes and U.S. Indian Policy.* Middletown, Conn.: Wesleyan University Press, 1982.

Downey, Fairfax. *The Indian-Fighting Army.* New York: Charles Scribner's Sons, 1941.

Downey, Fairfax, and Jacques Noel Jacobsen, Jr. *The Red/Bluecoats: The Indian Scouts of the U.S. Army.* Fort Collins, Colo.: Old Army Press, 1973.

Drinnon, Richard. *Facing West: The Metaphysics of Indian-Hating and Empire Building.* Minneapolis: University of Minnesota Press, 1980.

Dunlay, Thomas W. *Wolves for the Blue Soldiers: Indian Scouts and Auxiliaries With the United States Army, 1860–1890.* Lincoln: University of Nebraska Press, 1982.

Ellis, Richard N. *General Pope and U.S. Indian Policy.* Albuquerque: University of New Mexico Press, 1970.

————. "The Humanitarian Generals." *Western Historical Quarterly* 3 (April 1972): 169–178.

————. "The Political Role of the Military on the Frontier." In James P. Tate, ed., *The American Military on the Frontier: Proceedings of the 7th Military History Symposium, United States Air Force Academy.* Washington, D.C.: Office of Air Force History, 1978.

Faragher, John Mack. *Women and Men on the Overland Trail.* New Haven: Yale University Press, 1979.

Forman, Sidney. *West Point: A History of the United States Military Academy.* New York: Columbia University Press, 1950.

Gibson, Arrell Morgan. *The American Indian: Prehistory to the Present.* Lexington, Mass.: D. C. Heath and Co., 1980.

Glassley, Ray Hoard. *Pacific Northwest Indian Wars.* Portland, Ore.: Binfords and Mort, 1953.

Gray, John S. *Centennial Campaign: The Sioux War of 1876.* Fort Collins, Colo.: Old Army Press, 1976.

Green, Rayna. "The Pocahontas Perplex: The Image of Indian Women in American Culture." *Massachusetts Review* 26 (Autumn 1975): 698–714.

Guie, H. Dean. *Bugles in the Valley: Garnett's Fort Simcoe.* Yakima, Wash.: Republic Press, 1956.

Hammer, Kenneth. *Custer in '76: Walter Camp's Notes on the Custer Fight.* Provo, Utah: Brigham Young University, 1976.

Haskell, Thomas L. *The Emergence of Professional Social Science: The American Social Science Association and the Nineteenth-Century Crisis of Authority.* Urbana: University of Illinois Press, 1977.

Heitman, Francis. *Historical Register and Dictionary of the United States Army.* Vols. 1 and 2. Washington, D.C.: GPO, 1903.

Hunt, Aurora. *The Army of the Pacific, 1860–1866.* Glendale, Calif.: Arthur H. Clark Co., 1951.

Hutton, Paul Andrew. "From Little Bighorn to Little Big Man: The Changing Image of a Western Hero." *Western Historical Quarterly* 7 (January 1976): 19–45.

————. *Phil Sheridan and His Army.* Lincoln: University of Nebraska Press, 1985.

————, ed. *Soldiers West: Biographies from the Military Frontier.* Lincoln: University of Nebraska Press, 1987.

Jeffrey, Julie Roy. *Frontier Women: The Trans-Mississippi West, 1840–1880.* New York: Hill and Wang, 1979.

Johnson, Virginia W. *The Unregimented General: A Biography of Nelson A. Miles.* Boston: Houghton Mifflin Co., 1962.

Josephy, Alvin M. *Indian Heritage of America.* New York: Alfred A. Knopf, 1968.

Keegan, John. *The Face of Battle.* New York: Viking Press, 1976.

Kemble, Robert C. *The Image of the Army Officer in America: Background for Current Views.* Westport, Conn.: Greenwood Press, 1973.

Knight, Oliver. *Life and Manners in the Frontier Army.* Norman: University of Oklahoma Press, 1978.

Koury, Captain Michael J. *Diaries of the Little Big Horn.* Bellevue, Nebr.: Old Army Press, 1968.

Kroeker, Marvin E. *Great Plains Command: William B. Hazen in the Frontier West.* Norman: University of Oklahoma Press, 1976.

Lears, Jackson. *No Place of Grace: Antimodernism and the Transformation of American Culture, 1880–1920.* New York: Pantheon Books, 1981.

Leckie, William H., and Shirley A. Leckie. *Unlikely Warriors: General Benjamin H. Grierson and His Family.* Norman: University of Oklahoma Press, 1984.

Leonard, Thomas C. *Above the Battle: War-Making in America From Appomattox to Versailles.* New York: Oxford University Press, 1978.

————. "Red, White and the Army Blue: Empathy and Anger in the American West." *American Quarterly* 26 (May 1974): 176–190.

————. "The Reluctant Conquerors: How the Generals Viewed the Indians." *American Heritage* 27 (August 1976): 34–41.

Lummis, Charles. *General Crook and the Apache Wars.* Flagstaff, Ariz.: Northland Press, 1966.

Manring, B. F. *Conquest of the Coeur d'Alenes, Spokans & Palouses.* Spokane: John W. Graham and Co., 1912.

Mardock, Robert Winston. *The Reformers and the American Indian.* Columbia: University of Missouri Press, 1971.

Marquis, Thomas. *Wooden Leg: A Warrior Who Fought Custer.* Lincoln: University of Nebraska Press, 1931.

Mattison, Ray H. "The Army Post on the Northern Plains, 1865–1885." *Nebraska History* 35 (March 1954): 17–43.

Miles, Susan. *Fort Concho in 1877.* San Angelo, Tex.: Bradley Co., 1972.

Miller, Christopher L. *Prophetic Worlds: Indians and Whites on the Columbia Plateau.* New Brunswick, N.J.: Rutgers University Press, 1985.

Mitchell, Lee Clark. *Witnesses to a Vanishing America: The*

Nineteenth Century Response. Princeton: Princeton University Press, 1981.

Morton, Desmond. "Comparison of U.S./Canadian Military Experience on the Frontier." In James P. Tate, ed., *The American Military on the Frontier: Proceedings of the 7th Military History Symposium, United States Air Force Academy.* Washington, D.C.: Office of Air Force History, 1978.

Myres, Sandra L. "Romance and Reality on the American Frontier: Views of Army Wives." *Western Historical Quarterly* 13 (October 1982): 409–427.

––––––. *Westering Women and the Frontier Experience, 1800–1915.* Albuquerque: University of New Mexico Press, 1982.

Pearce, Roy Harvey. *Savagism and Civilization: A Study of the Indian and the American Mind.* Baltimore: Johns Hopkins Press, 1967.

Persons, Stow. *American Minds: A History of Ideas.* New York: Henry Holt and Co., 1958.

Porter, Joseph C. *Paper Medicine Man: John Gregory Bourke and His American West.* Norman: University of Oklahoma Press, 1986.

Powell, Peter J. *Sweet Medicine: The Continuing Role of the Sacred Arrows, the Sun Dance, and the Sacred Buffalo Hat in Northern Cheyenne History.* 2 vols. Norman: University of Oklahoma Press, 1969.

Powers, Marla N. *Oglala Women: Myth, Ritual and Reality.* Chicago: University of Chicago Press, 1986.

Price, Byron. "The Utopian Experiment: The U.S. Army and the Indian: 1890–1897." *By Valor and Arms* 3 (1977): 15–35.

Prucha, Francis Paul. *American Indian Policy in Crisis: Christian Reformers and the Indian, 1865–1900.* Norman: University of Oklahoma Press, 1976.

––––––. *The Great Father: The United States Government and the American Indians.* Lincoln: University of Nebraska Press, 1984.

––––––. *The Sword of the Republic: The United States Army on the Frontier, 1783–1846.* New York: Macmillan, 1969.

––––––, comp. *A Bibliographical Guide to the History of Indian-White Relations in the United States.* Chicago: University of Chicago Press, 1977.

––––––, comp. *Indian-White Relations in the United States: A Bibliography of Works Published, 1975–1980.* Lincoln: University of Nebraska Press, 1982.

Rampp, Larry C., and Donald L. Rampp. *The Civil War in the Indian Territory.* Austin, Tex.: Presidial Press, 1975.

Richards, Kent. "Isaac I. Stevens and Federal Military Power in Washington Territory." *Pacific Northwest Quarterly* 63 (July 1972): 81–86.

Riley, Glenda. *Women and Indians on the Frontier, 1825–1915*. Albuquerque: University of New Mexico Press, 1984.

Rister, Carl Coke. *Border Command: General Phil Sheridan in the West*. Norman: University of Oklahoma Press, 1944.

Saum, Lewis O. *The Fur Trader and the Indian*. Seattle: University of Washington Press, 1965.

——. *The Popular Mood of Pre–Civil War America*. Westport, Conn.: Greenwood Press, 1980.

Schlissel, Lillian. *Women's Diaries of the Westward Journey*. New York: Schocken Books, 1982.

Sheehan, Bernard. *Savagism and Civility: Indians and Englishmen in Colonial Virginia*. Cambridge: Cambridge University Press, 1980.

——. *Seeds of Extinction: Jeffersonian Philanthropy and the American Indian*. New York: W. W. Norton and Co., 1973.

Simonin, Louis L. *The Rocky Mountain West in 1867*. Translated by Wilson O. Clough. Lincoln: University of Nebraska Press, 1966.

Skelton, William B. "Army Officers' Attitudes Toward Indians, 1830–1860." *Pacific Northwest Quarterly* 67 (July 1976): 113–124.

Slotkin, Richard. *The Fatal Environment: The Myth of the Frontier in the Age of Industrialization, 1800–1890*. New York: Atheneum, 1985.

——. *Regeneration Through Violence: The Mythology of the American Frontier*. Middletown, Conn.: Wesleyan University Press, 1973.

Smith, Sherry L. "Beyond Princess and Squaw: Army Officers' Perceptions of Indian Women." In Susan Armitage and Elizabeth Jameson, eds., *The Women's West*, 63–75. Norman: University of Oklahoma Press, 1987.

——. "Officers' Wives, Indians and the Indian Wars." *Order of the Indian Wars Journal* 1 (Winter 1980): 35–46.

——. "Private Conscience versus Public Duty: Army Officers' Reflections on the Indian Wars." In David Tebaldi, ed., *Reflecting on Values: The Unity and Diversity of the Humanities*, 71–80. Laramie, Wyoming: Wyoming Council for the Humanities, 1983.

——. *Sagebrush Soldier: Private William Earl Smith's View of the Sioux War of 1876*. Norman: University of Oklahoma, 1989.

——. "A Window on Themselves: Perceptions of Indians by Military Officers and Their Wives." *New Mexico Historical Review*

64 (October 1989): 447–461.

Stallard, Patricia Y. *Glittering Misery: Dependents of the Indian Fighting Army.* Fort Collins, Colo.: Old Army Press, 1978.

Stedman, William. *Shadows of the Indian: Stereotypes in American Culture.* Norman: University of Oklahoma Press, 1982.

Sully, Langdon. *No Tears for the General: The Life of Alfred Sully, 1821–1879.* Palo Alto, Calif.: American West Publishing Co., 1974.

Tate, James P., ed. *The American Military on the Frontier: Proceedings of the 7th Military History Symposium, United States Air Force Academy.* Washington, D.C.: Office of Air Force History, 1978.

Turner, Frederick W. *Beyond Geography: The Western Spirit Against the Wilderness.* New York: Viking Press, 1980.

Utley, Robert M. *A Clash of Cultures: Fort Bowie and the Chiricahua Apaches.* Washington, D.C.: GPO, 1977.

———. *The Contribution of the Frontier to the American Military Tradition.* The Harmon Memorial Lectures in Military History, no. 19. Colorado Springs: United States Air Force Academy, 1977.

———. *Frontier Regulars: The United States Army and the Indian, 1866–1891.* New York: Macmillan Publishing Co., 1973.

———. *Frontiersmen in Blue: The United States Army and the Indian, 1848–1865.* New York: Macmillan Publishing Co., 1967.

———. *The Indian Frontier of the American West, 1846–1890.* Albuquerque: University of New Mexico Press, 1984.

———. *The Last Days of the Sioux Nation.* New Haven: Yale University Press, 1963.

Van Kirk, Sylvia. *Many Tender Ties: Women in Fur-Trade Society, 1670–1870.* Norman: University of Oklahoma Press, 1983.

Webb, Walter Prescott. *The Great Plains.* New York: Grosset and Dunlap, 1931.

Weinberg, Albert K. *Manifest Destiny: A Study of Nationalist Expansionism in American History.* Chicago: Quadrangle Books, 1963.

Werner, Fred H. *The Dull Knife Battle.* Greeley, Colo.: By the author, 1981.

Whitman, S. E. *The Troopers: An Informal History of the Plains Cavalry, 1865–1890.* New York: Hastings House Publishers, 1962.

Wood, Erskine. *Life of Charles Erskine Scott Wood.* Portland, Ore.: By the author, 1978.

Wooster, Robert. *The Military and United States Indian Policy, 1865–1903.* New Haven: Yale University Press, 1988.

Index

Acculturation: Indian resistance to, 116; military's role in, xvii, 8, 127; officers' views on, xiv, 106, 108–12, 210n.29. *See also* Reservation system

Adoption. *See* Indian children

Agents. *See* Indian agents

Ah-tlan-tiz-pa (Navajo), 88–89

Alexander, Eveline, 34

Allen, Harvey Abner, 77

Allen, Mary (Mrs. Harvey Abner Allen), 77

Allen, Maud, 77

Allotment policy, 109, 110–11, 112, 211n.36

Alvord, Henry E., 105

Anglo-American culture: compared to Indian, 21–27, 58; influence on Indian cultures, 40–41, 84–85, 108; officers' views on, 134, 136; perceptions of Indians in, 183–84; views on military in, 8–9, 189n.16; whites' criticism of, 38

Apache Princess, An, 86–87

Apaches: Bourke's views on, 28, 36, 37, 152, 157, 180; Crook's views on, 109, 111, 168–69; Sladen's views on, 36, 47, 51; sympathy for, 145, 146; as warriors, 155, 156–57; women and children, 65, 66, 67, 69, 71, 74, 85–86, 201n.5, 206n.49;

mentioned, 34, 35, 41, 45, 218n.9. *See also* Apache-Mohaves; Chiricahua; Scouts, Apache

Apache-Mohaves, 71, 78, 205n.41

Arapahoes, 57, 83–84, 89, 99, 123, 158

Army, United States: as enforcer of Indian policy, xiv, 8, 92; promotion in, 4, 141, 186n.6; public opinion of, 9–10, 128–29; recruitment by, 152; use of scouts by, 164–65

Assimilation, 21, 35, 107, 108–9, 110, 171, 211n.32

Assiniboines, 40

Averell, William Woods, 42–43, 44, 60, 88–89, 197n.29

Aztecs, 164

Baker, Eugene, 68

Baldwin, Alice, 17, 76, 144–45, 195n.13

Baldwin, Frank: on duty of soldiers, 130–31; on Indian agents and traders, 94, 124, 150; on Indian warfare, 142–43, 174, 222n.42

Banning Committee, 80

Bannocks, 47

Bannock War, 72, 145, 179

Barnitz, Albert, 39, 83–84, 123

Barnitz, Jennie, 17

Bates, Alfred E., 92, 109
Battles: of the Adobe Walls, 174;
    of Big Hole Basin, 155; of Four
    Lakes, 143; of the Little Big
    Horn, 11, 15, 40, 127, 144, 147,
    154, 177; of the Slim Buttes,
    73; of the Washita, 39, 68, 75,
    82, 86, 127, 128, 147; of
    Wounded Knee, xvii, 68,
    204n.33
Beaver (Comanche), 84
Beck, William H., 153
Beecher, Henry Ward, 49, 50,
    199n.38
Benteen, Frederick, 82–83, 86,
    154
Berkhofer, Robert, xviii, 12
Biddle, Ellen, 45, 57, 76
Big Bear (Sioux), 28
Bigelow, John, 111–12, 173, 208
Big Tree (Kiowa), 31, 105
Bisbee, William Henry, 122, 135
Blackfoot, 41–42, 129, 200n.1,
    202n.20
Blakely, Neil, 86–87
Board of Indian Commissioners,
    96, 104
Bonneville, Benjamin, 146
Bosque Redondo Reservation, 35
Bourke, John: on allotment,
    211n.36; on Apaches, 28, 36,
    37, 71, 157–78; on Hopis, 28,
    36, 37, 60; on Indian agents,
    94–95; on Indian warfare, 118,
    142, 152, 163; interest of, in
    Indian cultures, 23, 55, 173–74;
    on Papagos, 41; on scouts, 171,
    179, 180, 225n.12; mentioned,
    73, 90
Boyd, Mrs. Orsemus, 77–78
Brackett, Albert, 55, 59, 60, 64
Bradley, Ione, 46
Bradley, James H., 39, 140, 175,
    180–81, 199n.1, 202n.20

Bradley, Luther, 53, 83, 158–59,
    209n.16
Brooks, William, 120–21
Brown, William Carey, 179, 180
Brunot, Felix, 104
Buffalo, 117–18, 119
Burt, Elizabeth, 50, 62

Camps: Cooke, 18; Grant, 131;
    Independence, 102; Supply, 46;
    Verde, 69; Wichita, 103
Canby, E. S., 213n.8
Canfield, Sarah, 18, 46, 205n.38
Capron, Thaddeus H., 225n.12
Captives, 105, 146; Indian
    women as, 76, 81, 82, 85, 86, 87
Captivity narratives, 18, 39, 56
Carlisle Indian School, 108–9
Carr, Eugene, 131, 172, 226n.16
Carrington, Frances, 76, 144,
    147
Carrington, Henry B., 100, 106,
    134, 144
Carrington, Margaret, 125–26,
    135, 209n.16
Carter, Robert G., 31, 68, 117–18,
    153, 159
Carter, W. H., 1, 10, 165
Charley (Cocopah), 45–46
Charlie (Apache), 45
Chatto (Chiricahua Apache
    chief), 169
Cherokees, 30, 31, 44, 86, 110
Cheyenne: Custer's campaigns
    against, 127, 154; Fetterman's
    engagement with, 96, 100; at
    Medicine Lodge council, 123;
    officers' and wives' views of,
    39, 40, 46, 57, 197n.24; in
    warfare, 153–54, 155; women
    and children, 57, 62, 75, 76, 78,
    82, 83, 89; mentioned, 99, 105,
    142, 158, 174, 176
Chickasaw, 30

Chie (Chiricahua Apache),
198n.34
Childbirth, 58, 63, 64–66,
202n.20
Children. *See* Indian children
Chiricahua Apaches: officers'
views on, 58, 94, 132, 169,
195n.15; women, 70, 81. *See
also* Scouts, Chiricahua Apache
Choctaw, 30
Christianity, 8, 56, 106, 107,
192n.7; among Nez Perce, 31–
32, 33, 115
Citizenship, 109, 111, 171
Civilization and savagery,
officers' views on, 20–27, 69,
133, 182, 184
Civil War, xiv, 3, 4, 7, 9, 10, 11
Clark, Ben, 40, 83
Clark, William Philo, 172,
226n.17
Cleveland, Grover, 169
Coastal tribes (California and
Pacific Northwest), 37
Cochise (Chiricahua Apache), 36,
47, 50, 51, 69, 70, 198n.34;
sister of, 69
Cocopahs, 45–46, 102
Code of ethics, officers', 6, 37, 67,
87, 97, 188n.10. *See also*
Professionalism
Coffman, Edward M., 9
Colby, L. W., 204n.33
Columbia Plateau, tribes of, 160
Colville Indian Reservation,
206n.61
Comanches: horsemanship of,
59, 149; warfare against, 105;
women, 56, 59, 84, 85;
mentioned, 104, 119, 144
Congress, United States, 8, 9, 80,
141, 165
Congressional Medal of Honor,
68, 143

Cooper, James Fenimore: and
noble savage image, 19, 22, 45,
56–57, 89, 183, 191n.2;
rejection of, 12, 16–17, 129
Corbusier, Fanny, 50, 62–63
Counting coup, 159
Crazy Horse (Sioux), 53, 172
Creeks, 30
Crook, George: on Apaches, 109,
111, 132, 158; on Indian
character, 24, 193n.14, 213n.8;
on Indian warfare, 125, 126;
relationship with scouts, 170;
relationship with Sheridan,
169–70; on scouts, 166,
169–70, 171, 225n.11; on
segregation of Indians, 211n.32;
sympathy for Indians, 113, 132;
on treatment of Indians, 106;
mentioned, xvi, 142, 150, 168,
179, 184
Crow Belly (Gros Ventre), 43–44
Crows, 32, 40, 76, 83, 125, 174,
175–78
Cultural relativism, 174
Custer, Elizabeth: on captivity,
18; in defense of husband, 128–
29; on Indian women, 57, 62,
75–76, 204n.36; use of brevet
rank by, 187n.6; mentioned,
83, 147
Custer, George Armstrong:
brevet rank of, 187n.6; defeat
of, 11, 40, 127, 144, 152, 175,
177, 180; defense of, 127, 128–
29; on Indian character, 15–16;
relationship with Mo-nah-see-
tah, 76, 82–83, 86, 89;
romantic views on Indians, 19,
38; mentioned, 3, 75. *See also*
Battle of the Little Big Horn

Darwinism. *See* Social
Darwinism

Davis, Britton, 58, 69, 85–86, 145, 158
Dawes, H. L., 108
Delawares, 61
Detribalization, 109, 110
Diablo, Chief, 46
Dinges, Bruce, 210n.21
Dippie, Brian W., 12
Dodge, Grenville, 154
Dodge, Richard Irving: on the Cheyenne, 197n.24; on Crook, 170; on Indian agents, 95–96; on Indian character, 15, 20, 22, 29, 110, 154–55; on Indian wars and warfare, 132, 142, 152, 159; on Indian women, 59, 61; on Nez Perce, 31; on Pawnee scouts, 179; on Plains Indians, 192n.8; on Sheridan, 206n.61; on squaw men, 86; mentioned, 62, 174
Dreamer Cult, 33, 115–16
Du Bois, John Van Deusen, 35, 69, 85, 146, 175, 197n.29, 227n.22
Dull Knife (Cheyenne), 142
Dunlay, Thomas, 164, 223n.44, 225n.11

Eastern reformers, 9, 12, 68, 106, 111, 127–28, 129, 184
Easton, Karen, 224
Eliot, William Greenleaf, 113
Enlisted men, xvi, xvii, 4, 9, 80, 100, 151–52, 155
Expansionism. *See* Manifest Destiny
Extermination, 92, 106, 112, 113, 144

Farmers and farming, 8, 33–34, 35, 126, 161. *See also* Allotment policy
Federal Indian policy. *See* Indian policy

Fetterman, William, 32, 96; 1866 engagement with Sioux and Cheyenne, 96, 100, 125, 147
Fifth Cavalry, 172
First Dragoons, 86
Fitzgerald, Emily, 46, 144, 147
Fitzgerald, John, 71, 72–73, 155
Five Civilized Tribes, 30
Forsyth, George A., 128, 130, 134–35, 158, 195n.15
Forts: Abraham Lincoln, 15, 40; Apache, 17, 46, 195n.15; Arbuckle, 66; Berthold, 46, 205n.38; Bowie, 47, 69; Bridger, 160; Buford, 80; C. F. Smith, 32, 158, 209n.16; D. A. Russell, 1; Fauntleroy, 80; F. D. Pease, 175; Fetterman, 29; Garland, 34; Hayes, 82; Keough, 76; Lapwai, 144; Laramie, 28, 29, 76, 100; Leavenworth, 40, 99; Lyon, 57; McDowell, 69; Massachusetts, 5; Phil Kearny, 32, 83, 96, 125, 144; Pierre, 153; Randall, 80; Rice, 15; Riley, 17; Shaw, 155; Sill, 5, 31, 75, 84, 104, 105; Sitka, 77; Stevenson, 43, 80; Totten, 15; Vancouver, 159; Walla Walla, 83, 143; Wingate, 17, 46, 118, 195n.13
Frances (Rogue River Indian), 89
"Friends of the Indians." *See* Eastern reformers
Fry, James, 154
Fur traders and trading, 79

Garland, Gen., 121
Garnett, Robert Seldon, 122–23
Gatewood, Charles, 48, 146, 164
Gatling gun, 160, 223n.44
Genocide. *See* Extermination
Geronimo (Chiricahua Apache), 198n.35; surrender of, 48, 146,

164, 169; mentioned, 50, 51, 163, 218n.9
Gibbon, John, 71, 94, 150, 155–56, 173, 175–76, 177, 222n.38
Gibson, Capt., 65, 67
Gibson, Katherine, 65, 147
Gila River Expedition, 69, 85, 146, 175, 197n.29
Glisan, Rodney, 11, 45, 110, 118–19
Government agents. *See* Indian agents
Grant, Ulysses S., 43, 89, 92, 93, 97, 103
Grierson, Benjamin H., 31, 99, 103–6, 107, 110–11, 210n.21, 212n.4
Gros Ventres, 40, 43
Grummond, George, 147
Guerrilla warfare. *See* Warfare, Indian tactics

Haller, Granville O., 37, 98, 114–15, 160, 196n.16
Hancock, Almira, 78, 129
Hancock, Winfield Scott, 78
Hardcastle, Edmund, 140–41
Hazen, William B., 104, 134, 183
Hein, O. L., 121, 168
Heistand, Henry, 201nn.12, 13
Hidatsas, 86
Hitchcock, Ethan Allen, xiv, 113–14
Hodges, Henry, 122
Hopis, 28, 36, 60, 118, 173–74
Horsemanship, 59–60, 149–50, 158, 220n.22
Hough, Alfred Lacey, 121
Howard, Oliver O.: on Chief Joseph, 48; on Cooper's influence, 191n.2; on Indian character, 24; on miscegenation, 86; on the Sioux, 39; on tribal factions,

33, 115–17, 194n.9; mentioned, 47, 124, 212n.4
Huggins, E. L., 25–26
Humanitarians. *See* Eastern reformers
Humfreville, J. Lee, 20, 22
Hunter, Robert M. T., 122
Hutton, Paul A., 83, 170

Immigrants, 4
Indian affairs, 8, 92, 93, 96, 97, 121–22, 148, 182. *See also* Indian agents; Indian Department
Indian agents, 92, 207n.3; officers' criticism of, 94–96, 102, 122, 124, 126, 127; mentioned, 86, 103
Indian character: compared to American, 24–25, 26; generalizations about, xviii, 11, 19–20, 29–30; officers' and wives' views on, 55, 98, 99, 101, 175, 176, 181, 184, 193n.14; romantic views of, 16, 19, 26, 37, 44–45, 149, 199n.36; sympathetic views of, 183, 184; views on courage and loyalty in, 154–55, 172–73; views on savagery in, 192n.11; whites' influence on, 22, 23, 24, 27
Indian children, 62, 69, 71–73, 75, 76–78, 86, 204n.33, 205n.41
Indian Commissioners, Board of, 96, 104
Indian cultures: compared to American, 21–27, 67; extinction of, 106, 111; officers interested in, 13, 23, 55, 172, 173–74; officers' lack of knowledge of, 10, 12, 13, 41, 162, 166, 172, 173, 179; whites'

influence on, 40–41, 86, 96, 107, 108

Indian Department, 119–20, 124. *See also* Indian affairs; Indian agents

Indian men: officers' and wives' relations with, 28–29, 42–48, 78; officers' and wives' relations with leaders, 48, 50–51, 75; officers' views of, 161–62, 197n.29, 199n.1

Indian policy: army as enforcer of, xiv, xviii, 2, 8, 91, 92; consultation of Indians on, 111, 114; Indian resistance to, xvii, 100–101, 111, 115; local control of, 208n.8; officers' views on, 91, 92–112, 121–29, 136, 184; use of force in, 209nn.14, 16. *See also* Acculturation; Assimilation; Allotment; Indian affairs; Reservation system

Indian princess image, 56, 57, 85, 86–88

Indian Problem, the, xviii, 2, 9, 91, 110

Indian Ring, 93–94

Indian Sign Language, The, 172

Indian wars: atrocities in, 146, 226n.15; blame of whites for, 11, 113, 114, 115, 117–26, 213n.9; ethical views on, 13, 129–30, 131–38, 182; officers' justification of role in, 127–38, 184, 212nn.4, 6; tribal factionalism and, 115, 116, 117, 212n.4; veterans of, 4, 189n.17. *See also* Warfare

Indian women: Anglo-American women compared to, 55, 58–60, 64; exploitation of, and by, 80–82, 84, 85–86; health of,

64–65; officers' and wives' views on, 55, 57, 64–65, 69, 75, 89–90, 204n.36; relations with officers, 58, 79–80, 82–88; relations with wives, 66–67, 75–78; rights of, 61–62, 201n.12; romantic views of, 56–60, 86, 89; slave image of, 57, 60, 62, 63; in warfare, 67–69, 71–72, 81. *See also* Indian princess image; Squaw image

Interior Department, 8, 92, 94, 121–22

Intermarriage. *See* Marriage

Iroquois, 128

Isolation of frontier life, 7–9

Is-sa-keep (Comanche), 84, 85

Jackson, Helen Hunt, 12

Jeffords, Thomas J., 47

Johnson, Richard, 57

Joseph, Chief, 50, 156, 199n.36; Howard's views on, 48, 115, 116; physical appearance of, 40, 46; Woods's relationship with, 48, 136

Kanaskat (Klickitats), 52–53

Kautz, August V., 107–8

Kemble, Robert C., 6, 7

Keogh, Myles, 82, 86

Keyes, Erasmus Darwin, 30–31, 44, 52

King, Charles, 2, 39, 73, 86–87, 128, 179, 180

Kiowas, 31, 66–67, 75, 101, 104, 105, 117, 119

Kip, Lawrence, 32, 37, 51–52

Klickitats, 52

Knight, Alice Margaret, 204n.33

Kress, John, 194n.8

Lane, Lydia, 18, 65

Lapwai, Nez Perce reservation at, 116

Lawton, Henry, 198n.35, 218n.9, 227n.29

Lawton, Henry, 198n.35, 218n.9, 227n.29
Lemly, Henry, 73
Loco (White Mountain Apache), 179
Long Walk, the, 35

McCall, George, 34, 35
McClellan, George, 122
McConnell, H. H., 11
McCook, Alexander, 92
Mackenzie, Ranald, 105, 142, 170
Mahan, Dennis Hart, 10
Mandans, 40
Manifest Destiny, 132, 133
Marcy, Randolph, 84, 85, 107; on Indian women, 59–60, 61, 62; on Indian warfare, 222n.33; on scouts, 168
Mardock, Robert, 127
Marguerite (Sioux orphan), 204n.33
Marksmanship, 150, 151, 155–56, 158, 220n.23, 221n.28, 222n.38
Marriage, 58, 60, 61–62, 79, 80, 86, 201n.13
Martin, Alice, 46
Mathews, Washington, 86
Maus, Anna, 51, 77
Medicine Lodge, 1867 Council of, 39, 83, 123
Meeker, Nathan, 95
Merchants, 120, 121, 126, 161
Mescalero Apache Agency, 107
Mescalero Apaches, 111
Miles, Nelson: on Apaches, 157, 158, 195n.15; on army's abilities, 159; on Chief Joseph, 199n.36; defense of army's role, 127, 128, 134; on Indian policy, 109–10, 184; on Nez Perce, 33, 155; romantic views on Indians, 19, 24–25, 26, 38–39;

on Sitting Bull, 50; use of scouts by, 163, 169, 171–72; mentioned, 135, 142, 145, 218n.9, 228n.29
Mills, Anson, 48, 73, 74, 160–61
Mills, Nannie, 48, 73
Mills, Stephen, 143, 179, 225n.12
Miners, 114, 120, 124, 126, 161
Miscegenation. *See* Marriage
Mitchell, Lee Clark, 38, 173–74, 185
Modocs, 146, 213n.8
Modoc War, 213n.8
Mohaves, 102
Mo-nah-see-tah (Cheyenne), 57, 76, 82–83
Monos, 44
Montana Column, 175, 177–78
Moquis. *See* Hopis
Morgan, Lewis Henry, 19, 133
Moros, 136–37
My Life on the Plains, 15

Na-Chise. *See* Natchez
Nantaje (scout), 180
Natchez (Apache), 51, 70
Naturalism, 6, 134, 136
Natzie (fictional Apache), 86–87
Navajos: army's views on, 34–35; wives' views on, 46, 76, 195n.13; women, 60, 76, 80, 88; mentioned, 42–44, 118–21, 197n.29
Navajo War, 35, 44, 88
Nevada Paiutes, 63
Nez Perce: admiration and sympathy for, 31–33, 123–24, 147, 155–56; factions among, 115–17; horsemanship and marksmanship of, 149, 150, 155; negative view of, 194n.8; Scott's views on, 40; mentioned, 46, 48, 71, 139. *See also* Scouts, Nez Perce

Nez Perce War, 140, 144, 150, 170, 177
Noble savage image, 16–17, 21–22, 25–27, 56, 149, 183
Noche (Chiricahua Apache), 169
Nodt, Nicholas, 80–82
North, Frank, 179

Officers: backgrounds of, 3–6, 133; diversity of views of, 182–83; education of, xiv, 10–12; examination of views of, xiii–xix; heroic image of, xiii, 3; moderating views of, 184–85; as observers of Indian cultures, 10–14, 37, 41, 111, 173–74; public image of, 2–3, 6; self-image of, 2, 6, 7–8, 12 37–38, 129, 145, 184; views on failure in warfare, 143; West Pointers, xiv, 3, 4, 5, 11, 12, 187n.4
Officers' wives. *See* Wives
Ogarita (Indian orphan), 73, 74, 204n.33
Oglala Sioux, 171–72
Old Tom (undisclosed tribe), 45
Ord, E.O.C., 83, 146, 151, 159, 213n.9
Orphans, Indian, 72–74, 78
O'Shaughnessy, Cpl., 53
"Outing" plan, 109
Overshine, Sarah, 145
Owhi (Yakima), 52, 143

Paiutes, 50
Papago. *See* Tohono O'odham
Parker, James, 5, 84, 119, 201n.12
Parker, William T., 29, 64–65, 99, 139, 224, 189n.17, 202n.20
Pasqual, Chief (San Joaquin), 44
Paulding, Grace, 135
Peace Commission, 213n.8
Peace Policy, 92, 93, 94, 97, 103, 104, 105, 128
Pearce, Roy Harvey, xix, 18

Pequots, 128
Persons, Stow, 133, 134
Peters, DeWitt Clinton, 5, 141, 151, 203n.27, 224n.5
Phelps, Frederick E., 221n.28
Philanthropists. *See* Eastern reformers
Phillips, Wendell, 127
Piegans, 68, 129
Pike's County Men, 119
Plains Indians: admiration of, 30, 38, 39, 59; romantic views of, 19, 20, 25, 149, 192n.8; warfare against, 72, 153, 222n.33; mentioned, 31, 37, 75, 92, 159
Pocahontas, 56, 86, 191n.2
"Poet in the Desert," 137
Polygamy. *See* Marriage
Poncas, 65, 67, 132
Pope, John, xvi, 183, 211n.36
Powder River Expedition, 142, 166, 170, 174, 180, 224n.5
Pratt, Richard, 66–67, 107, 108–9, 171
Price, George, 153
Primitivism, 17, 26
Professionalism, xiv, xvi, 6–7, 96–97, 100, 130, 136. *See also* Code of ethics
Promotions. *See* Army, United States
Prucha, Paul, xviii
Pueblo Indians, 33–34, 35, 55, 60, 61, 146
Pueblo Revolt of 1680, 34
Puget Sound Indians, 37, 194n.9

Qualchin (Yakima), 52

Railroads, 161, 162
Randall, Jake, 174
Ranks. *See* Army, United States, promotion in
Recruitment. *See* Army, United States

Red Cloud (Sioux), 28–29, 48, 50
Red Leaf (Sioux), 28
Red River War, 105
Rees, 40
Reformers. *See* Eastern reformers
Remington, Frederic, 10
Reservation system:
    acculturation role of, 8, 92–93,
    107–8; officers' views on, 85,
    107–9; resistance to, 93, 116;
    mentioned, xvii
Rockwell, Charles, 179
Roe, Frances, 46
Rogue River Indians, 89, 100–
    101, 213n.9
Rogue River War, 119, 146
Romeo (Mexican interpreter), 82
Rucker, D. H., 86
Rusling, James F., 40–41, 56

Salt Creek Massacre, 117
Sam (Mono), 44
San Carlos Reservation, 94, 163
San Joaquins, 44
Santiago (Yuma), 197n.29
Santo Domingo Indians, 55, 90
Satank (Kiowa), 101, 105
Satanta (Kiowa), 31, 105, 199n.36
Saum, Lewis O., 132
Savagery. *See* Civilization and
    savagery
Schofield, John, 11, 127, 165, 168,
    227n.22
Schoolcraft, Henry, 19
Schuyler, Walter, S., 69–70, 98–99
Schuyler, William, 102
Scott, Hugh, 20, 40, 123, 170,
    209n.14, 226n.16
Scouts: abilities of, 168–69, 170–
    71; Apache, 157, 173, 179;
    army's use of, 162, 164–65;
    Caddo, 171; Cayuse, 179, 180;
    Chiricahua Apache, 164, 169;
    communication problems
    with, 174–75, 176; Crow, 171–

72, 173, 175–78, 180, 227n.29;
    Delaware, 168, 174; Indian
    enlisted troops as, 226n.16;
    motivation and loyalty of, 164,
    165–66, 175–76, 224nn.3, 5;
    Nez Perce, 168; Northern
    Cheyenne, 170, 172; officers'
    relations with, 163–64, 172–
    73, 175, 179–81, 227n.19;
    opposition to use of, 169, 172–
    73, 176; Pawnee, 172, 179–80;
    Pima, 225n.12; Pueblo, 146;
    San Carlos Apache, 163,
    227n.29; Shoshone, 174, 180,
    225n.12; support for use of,
    168–69, 225n.11, 227n.22;
    Umatilla, 72; views of, on
    army, 173, 176, 177, 178, 180–
    81; White Mountain Apache,
    163, 179, 227n.29; Wichita,
    171; Yuma-Apache, 167;
    mentioned, 8, 83, 159
Sedgwick, John, 120
Seminoles, 30, 113, 215n.28
Seventh Cavalry, 15, 82, 150
Severalty. *See* Allotment policy
Shahaptian (Nez Perce), 116
Sharp Nose (Arapahoe), 174
Shawnee, 61
Sheridan, Philip: on Indian
    savagery, 118; relationship
    with Cheyenne, 40;
    relationships with Indian
    women, 89, 206n.61; on scouts,
    169; on use of force, 99–100,
    100–101, 103, 105, 204n.29;
    mentioned, xvi, 5, 34, 128
Sherman, William T.: on agents,
    97, 207n.3; on officers' public
    image, 2; on role of railroad,
    161; on use of force, 101,
    204n.29; mentioned, xvi, 99,
    103, 105
Shoshones, 49, 50, 59, 160–61,
    174

Sierra Nevada Indians, 119
Simonin, Louis Laurent, 1, 14
Sioux: campaigns against, 40, 96,
142, 154, 175; Crows' relations
with, 125, 176, 177–78,
227n.29; officers' views on, 32,
39, 50, 53, 158; use of force
against, 100; warfare abilities
and tactics, 153–54, 155, 158–
59, 160; wives' views of, 28, 46,
48, 77, 145; mentioned, 99,
144, 180
Sitting Bull (Hunkpapa Sioux),
50–51, 171
Sitting Bull (Oglala Sioux), 171
Skelton, William B., 26
Sladen, Joseph, 36, 47, 51, 59–60,
69, 198n.34
Smith, John, 86
Smohalla (Nez Perce), 116
Social Darwinism, xiv, 6, 109,
133–35, 136, 183
Spaulding, Eliza, 32
Spaulding, Henry, 32
Speculators, 120–21
Spotted Tail, 48, 50
Squaw image, 55, 56, 57, 62, 68,
86
Steele, James, 34, 56–57, 60–61,
98
Steptoe, Edward J., 130, 131, 136,
150, 168, 215n.28
Stevens, Isaac, 122–23
Summerhayes, Martha, 17, 34; on
Apaches, 66, 201n.5, 206n.49;
on Indian men, 45–46, 50
Sweeny, Thomas W., 88, 102, 153,
197n.29

Tall Bull (Sioux), 172
Taos Pueblo, 34
Tatum, Lawrie, 103–4, 105
Templeton, George, 32, 183
Tenth Cavalry, 103
Tesuque Pueblo, 34

Thomas, L., 120
Thompson, Lewis, 72
Tohono O'odham, 41, 225n.12
Toos-clay-zay (Chiricahua
Apache), 70
Total war, 72, 204n.29
Training, military, 10–11, 19–20,
151–152
Treaty rights and violations, 10,
123, 124
Tribal factionalism, 33, 116, 117
Trimble, J. G., 168
Trobriand, Philippe Regis de: on
assimilation, 21; on Indian
childbirth and marriage, 61–62,
64–65; on Sioux warfare, 160;
on specific Indians, 43–44, 50;
on tribal factionalism, 117;
mentioned, 24, 202n.20
Turnley, Parmenus T., 9, 77
Turnley, Mrs. Parmenus T., 77

Umatillas, 72
United States Army. *See* Army,
United States
Utes, 56, 59, 95, 121, 141, 151,
203n.27
Utley, Robert M., 3, 93, 152–53,
182

Van Kirk, Sylvia, 79
Venereal disease, 80
Verde Reservation, 98
Veterans of Indian wars, 189n.17
Viele, Teresa, 144, 147
Vogdes, Ada Adams, 28, 48
Volunteer militias, xvi, 3, 7, 9, 10,
11, 126

Walla Walla conference, 122
Wallowa Valley, 116, 124
War Department, 8, 92, 93, 96,
97, 122, 128
Warfare: army's abilities in, 158,
162, 221n.27; army's

superiority in, 158, 159, 160–61, 162; army's weapons in, 160–61, 223n.44; career advancement through, 14, 143; goals in, 148; Indian abilities in, 148, 149–51, 154, 155, 158, 161–62, 221n.27; Indian tactics, 147, 153–54, 223n.42; Indians' weapons in, 150–51; intertribal, 224n.5; Marcy's strategy, 222n.33; role of tribal factions in, 117; training in, 10–11; tribal warfare traditions, 159–60; troop dispersal in, 152–53, 162, 221n.31; views on battle conduct and response, 139–42; views on Indians during, 143–45; West Point training in, 10, 11; women in, 67–69. *See also* Indian wars

Warm Springs Apaches, 58, 143, 195n.15

Washakie (Shoshone), 49, 50, 199n.38

Washita, battle of the. *See* Battles

Wauk (Arapaho), 57

Weapons. *See* Warfare

Weinberg, Albert K., 132

West Point: education at, xv, 10, 11, 133; pro-Southern image, 187n.4; mentioned, 1, 5, 24, 106. *See also* Officers, West Pointers

White Bird (Nez Perce), 115

Winne, Caroline Frey, 145, 147, 199n.38

Winnemuca (Paiute), 50

"Winona: A Dakota Legend," 25–26

Winter campaigning, 72

Wives: backgrounds of, 4–5; diversity of views of, 182–83; examination of views of, xiii–xix; fear of Indians by, 191n.3; Indians' reactions to, 205n.38; moderating views of, 185; as observers of Indian culture, 13–14, 41–44; social status of, 63–64

Women. *See* Indian women; Wives

Wood, C.E.S., 48, 136–37, 139, 146

Wood, Erskine, 48

Wood, H. Clay, 124

Wood, Leonard, 136, 163–64

Wooden Leg (Cheyenne), 226n.17

Woodruff, C. A., 140

Woodward, C. A., 56

Wool, John, 120, 121

Wooster, Robert, 204n.29

Wounded Knee. *See* Battles

Wren, Angela, 87

Wren, Robert, 86

Wright, George, 52

Yakimas, 52, 114, 122, 143

Yakima War, 114–15

Yanktonais Sioux, 40

Young, S.B.M., 73, 74, 204n.33

Young Joseph, 124

Yumas, 41, 88, 102

Zunis, 118

ABOUT THE AUTHOR

Sherry L. Smith is an assistant professor of history at the University of Texas, El Paso. Holder of a doctorate in history from the University of Washington, Smith is also the author of *Sagebrush Soldier: Private William Earl Smith's View of the Sioux War of 1876*. Her research interests include Anglo-American images of Indian people and the role of women in the West.